Innovation–Development Detours for Latecomers

Many developing countries still face difficulties in initiating and sustaining economic development. Such difficulties have been exacerbated by the COVID-19 pandemic, resulting in an increasing divergence between rich and poor countries. For developing countries, one crucial question is whether to follow the trajectories of present-day rich countries or seek out different, new trajectories. Although this is a fundamental question, scholars offering mainstream prescriptions have not sufficiently explored it. Drawing on extensive empirical studies of firms and industries around the world, *Innovation–Development Detours for Latecomers* proposes an effective alternative to prevailing development thinking. It presents a rich menu of development pathways, including a new role for Schumpeterian states whereby they do not follow the paths of technological development already taken by advanced countries. Rather, they can skip certain stages and even create their own detours, thereby leapfrogging advanced countries in both manufacturing and service sectors. This title is also available as Open Access on Cambridge Core.

KEUN LEE is Distinguished Professor at Seoul National University, Fellow of the Canadian Institute for Advanced Research (CIFAR), an editor for *Research Policy*, a regular writer for Project Syndicate, and the winner of the 2014 Schumpeter Prize and the 2019 Kapp Prize. He served as an economic advisor to the President of Korea, as the President of the International Schumpeter Society, and was a member of the UN Committee for Development Policy (CDP) and the World Economic Forum (Global Future Council).

T0382459

Innovation–Development Detours for Latecomers

Managing Global-Local Interfaces in the De-Globalization Era

KEUN LEE

Seoul National University

Shaftesbury Road, Cambridge CB2 8EA, United Kingdom

One Liberty Plaza, 20th Floor, New York, NY 10006, USA

477 Williamstown Road, Port Melbourne, VIC 3207, Australia

314–321, 3rd Floor, Plot 3, Splendor Forum, Jasola District Centre, New Delhi – 110025, India

103 Penang Road, #05–06/07, Visioncrest Commercial, Singapore 238467

Cambridge University Press is part of Cambridge University Press & Assessment, a department of the University of Cambridge.

We share the University's mission to contribute to society through the pursuit of education, learning and research at the highest international levels of excellence.

www.cambridge.org
Information on this title: www.cambridge.org/9781009456258

DOI: 10.1017/9781009456234

First published 2024

A catalogue record for this publication is available from the British Library

Library of Congress Cataloging-in-Publication Data
Names: Lee, Keun, 1960– author.
Title: Innovation–development detours for latecomers : managing global-local interfaces in the de-globalization era / Keun Lee, Seoul National University.
Description: Cambridge, United Kingdom ; New York, NY : Cambridge University Press, 2024. | Includes bibliographical references and index.
Identifiers: LCCN 2023040232 (print) | LCCN 2023040233 (ebook) | ISBN 9781009456258 (hardback) | ISBN 9781009456234 (ebook)
Subjects: LCSH: Economic development – Developing countries. | Technological innovations – Economic aspects – Developing countries.
Classification: LCC HC59.7 .L351628 2024 (print) | LCC HC59.7 (ebook) | DDC 338.9009172/4–dc23/eng/20230912
LC record available at https://lccn.loc.gov/2023040232
LC ebook record available at https://lccn.loc.gov/2023040233

ISBN 978-1-009-45625-8 Hardback
ISBN 978-1-009-45626-5 Paperback

Contents

List of Figures   *page* viii
List of Tables   ix
Preface   xi
List of Abbreviations   xvii

1   Introduction   1
    1.1   De-Globalization and the Need for New Thinking   1
    1.2   Innovation–Development Detours   4
    1.3   Further Elaboration of Key Themes   14
    1.4   Innovation–Development Detour in South Korea   20
    1.5   The Roles of Government in Development Detours   22
    1.6   Key Messages and Contributions of the Book   23

2   National Innovation Systems and Alternative
    Pathways for Latecomers   25
    2.1   Introduction   25
    2.2   Catching up, Forging ahead, and Falling behind
          of Nations   28
    2.3   Varieties of NIS and their Linkages to Economic Growth 31
    2.4   Contrasting Pathways of the Two Imbalanced NIS:
          Catching-up versus Trapped   42
    2.5   The Balanced System and the Indian Pathway   48
    2.6   A Pathway Out of the Trap: Resource-based
          Development in Chile and Malaysia   55
    2.7   Summary and Concluding Remarks   59

3   From Global–Local Interfaces to Local Value Added,
    Knowledge, and Ownership   64
    3.1   Introduction   64

3.2 Global–Local Interfaces and Industrial Policy in Chile
and Malaysia   67

3.3 Global–Local Interfaces and Industrial Policy in
Auto Sectors in Asia   76

3.4 Global–Local Interfaces in Innovation Systems
of Taipei, Penang, and Shenzhen   90

3.5 Summary and Concluding Remarks   103

4 Coevolution of Firms with Sectoral, Regional,
and National Systems   106

4.1 Introduction   106

4.2 Catching Up by Similar or Different Technologies   109

4.3 Local vs. Foreign Firms in their Coevolution
with Surrounding Institutions in China   118

4.4 Core Firm Leading the Growth of a Region:
TSMC in Hsinchu   126

4.5 Firm-level Convergence Matching the Macro-level
Convergence: Korean Firms   135

4.6 Summary and Concluding Remarks   141

5 Innovation–Development Detour in South Korea   145

5.1 Introduction   145

5.2 A Very Brief History of Korea   147

5.3 The Myth of the "Korean Model"   151

5.4 Korea's First Detour: Big Businesses First,
SMEs Later   170

5.5 Korea's Second Detour: From Short- to Long-cycle
Specialization   188

5.6 The Korean Model as a Detour to Manage
the Global–Local Interfaces   200

5.7 Summary and Concluding Remarks   205

6 The Roles of Government in Development Detours   207

6.1 Introduction   207

6.2   A Detour in the Role of Government: The Inverted
      U-Shape or "Less, More, and Less"   210
6.3   The Role of Government in Global–Local Interfaces   215
6.4   The Role of Government in the Detour from
      Big Businesses to SMEs   227
6.5   The Role of Government in the Detour from
      Short- to Long-cycle Technologies   240
6.6   Summary and Concluding Remarks   243

7   Summary and Concluding Remarks   246
7.1   The Three Themes of the Book   246
7.2   Korea's Innovation–Development Detours and
      the Role of Government   249
7.3   Contributions, Limitations, and the Future   251

References   254
Index   279

Figures

1.1   Innovation–development detour   *page* 10

2.1   Per capita income as percentage of that of the
United States: Mexico, Brazil, Chile, Argentina,
South Africa, and Mauritius   29

2.2   Per capita income as percentage of that of the
United States: Korea, Taiwan, China, Hong Kong,
Singapore, Malaysia, and Thailand   30

2.3A   Dynamic changes of NIS variables: relative
cycle time of technologies   45

2.3B   Dynamic changes of NIS variables: technological
diversification   45

2.3C   Dynamic changes of NIS variables: knowledge
localization   46

2.3D   Dynamic changes of NIS variables: decentralization
of innovations   46

2.4   Relative distribution of patents by six categories:
A: India and B: South Korea   53

2.5   Two alternative pathways of catching up:
balanced and imbalanced   61

3.1   Local ownership of innovation: Taipei, Shenzhen,
and Penang   98

4.1   Productivity catch-up by interaction of firm
ownership and surrounding institutions   125

5.1   Trend of economic concentration in South Korea   178

5.2   Trend of relative (normalized) cycle time in
selected economies   196

Tables

2.1	Values of the five NIS variables in the sample economies, average 2008–2015	*page* 34
2.2	Comparison of NIS by selected groups	37
4.1	Catching up by similar or different technologies: comparison between a latecomer (L) vs. incumbent (I)	117
4.2	Comparison of the core firms and the regions without the core firms, 2000–2002 and 2016–2018	132
4.3	Trends of innovation variables of the Korean firms over the three periods	139
5.1	Number of supplier companies of each chaebol company: Chaebols' affiliate suppliers and non-affiliate suppliers by size	184
5.2	List of top ten firms in Korea by market values	185
5.3	Top ten classes and number of patents registered by South Korea, 2000–2003 and 2013–2017	197
6.1	Platform companies' year of establishment and stock market listing: The United States, China, and South Korea	237
6.2	Cumulative numbers of unicorns created by country, 2012–2021	238

Preface

When I was born, in 1960, my home country of South Korea (hereafter often just Korea) was one of the poorest in the world. Its per capita gross domestic product (GDP) was lower than that of Nigeria and near that of Ghana. This is not surprising, as Korea shared many similar initial conditions with typical African countries. Korea had been subjected to foreign colonial rule for over four decades and had gone through a three-year civil war. The country was also suffering from food shortages and had been relying on food aid from the United States since the end of World War II despite more than 85% of South Korean GDP coming from agriculture.

Over the course of my life, I have directly witnessed Korea's rapid economic catch-up. In the 1960s, Koreans were extremely poor. I wore rubber shoes as a child and ate just one piece of cornbread, provided as a part of US food aid, each day for lunch during elementary school. To provide my siblings and me with better educations, my parents decided to move from a small southern city to the capital city of Seoul in 1968. Indeed, my family was a part of the mass urban migration wave in South Korea. While I was attending high school in the late 1970s, my father bought a used car despite my mother's concerns that we couldn't afford it. I entered university as a first-year student in 1979; this was also the year that former dictator-modernizer President Park Chung-Hee was shot and killed suddenly by a member of his inner circle. A resulting emergency military decree closed all colleges for over a year in response to pro-democracy demonstrations. However, around 1980, South Korea's per capita GDP in purchasing power parity (PPP) terms reached 20% of the US level, which corresponds with the lower bound of an upper middle-income country. Fifteen years after that, it reached 40% of the US level, enabling South Korea to join the Organisation for Economic

Co-operation and Development (OECD) as a high-income economy. In the 2020s, South Korea's per capita GDP in PPP terms surpassed that of Japan and reached over 70% of that of the United States.

My life experiences in South Korea over the past sixty years have also provided me with insights into the meaning of economic development for latecomers. I have always felt that what I have witnessed in Korea does not correspond with what is taught about development by conventional economics. Economic development in any country is a long, winding journey; any controlled experiment lasting just a couple of months is too short and narrow to reflect the uncertainty and variability of economic development. In this book, I have attempted to conceptualize the Korean experience and compare stylized facts with the experiences of other developing countries. South Korea pursued an export-oriented growth strategy. Its success provides a counterexample to so-called dependency theory, which asserts that if a country opens its markets to global forces, it will never develop because all of its surplus will be exploited and sent abroad. This dismal prediction of "development of underdevelopment" was popular in Korea, as well as in Latin America, where it originated, when I was in college during the 1970s and 1980s. Moreover, South Korea's success also went against the tenets of the so-called Washington Consensus, as its process of opening up and liberalization did not happen all at once but rather very gradually, with the government continuing to protect domestic markets and remaining involved in industrial policy. South Korea's success was an exception, in that many countries before had opened up but had failed to achieve as successful a catch-up as South Korea. Indeed, many countries suffered from the liberalization trap and became stuck in the middle-income trap, unable to advance beyond the middle-income stage and close the gap with the United States.

Neither a closed nor an open economy guarantees rapid catch-up. Opening an economy is necessary for local economies and entities to benefit from foreign capital and learn from foreign companies, eventually generating domestically owned sources of innovation and developing capabilities beyond foreign direct investment (FDI)-linked companies. Managing such global–local interfaces is one of the key challenges that decides the long-term fate of an emerging economy; it is also one of the first key themes dealt with in this book. That is, in this book's discussion of the development detour, I demonstrate that latecomer economies should generate a critical mass of domestically owned companies by opening their economies and obtaining knowledge and technologies from foreign firms before globalizing their own firms during the final stage of development. This book also addresses the experiences of many countries beyond South Korea to provide robust empirical evidence demonstrating that opening should be managed by public policies so as to provide local firms with opportunities to build up their own capabilities.

The second detour involves the coevolution of firms with surrounding institutions and innovation systems. This second detour first generates growth-leading big businesses and then, at a later stage, small- and medium-sized enterprises (SMEs) and startups. Detouring from big businesses to SMEs is needed, because having thousands of SMEs does not enable a middle-income economy to overcome entry barriers and break into high-end segments and sectors. Once a country possesses a necessary mass of innovative big businesses, these businesses will become flagship companies that contract with SME suppliers as part of their supplier network while also generating spinoffs and viable startups. It can take decades to build up a sound institutional or investment climate that can nurture startups. It takes less time, however, to concentrate resources and competencies among a few firms so that they may grow into leading flagship companies. South Korea and Taiwan became high-income economies not by having thousands of SMEs but rather by growing a few large firms, such as Samsung and Taiwan Semiconductor Manufacturing Company (TSMC), which incorporated many small suppliers into their networks.

The third detour involves governmental intervention. Although this detour ends with the government playing a minimal role during the final stage of development, I make the provocative assertion that the role of government should not decrease in a linear fashion over the course of development but rather should increase at the upper middle-income stage, with the scope of government intervention forming an inverted U-shaped curve. Specialization according to a country's comparative advantages at the low-income stage does not necessitate considerable direct government intervention. However, for a country to enter high value-added sectors and catch up with leading countries in global markets, governments may need to undertake more direct forms of intervention, such as pursuing public–private joint research and development (R&D) initiatives. Such interventions become necessary because firms at this stage face increased difficulties in terms of entry barriers and intellectual property disputes. Technology transfers become more difficult the closer a country gets to frontier technologies, and more high-end sectors in the global market tend to be oligopolistic or monopolistic in nature and heavily dominated by incumbents.

South Korea is an exemplary case of a country that took a detour to development. Indeed, during its rapid catch-up period, which lasted until the mid-1990s, South Korea pursued a selective opening and promoted big businesses rather than SMEs, nurturing domestic value added rather than simply joining global value chains (GVCs). South Korea maintained a relatively closed posture and protected its markets; however, it is now one of the most open markets in the world and the only country that holds free-trade agreements (FTAs) with the United States, the European Union (EU), China, and India.

In summary, the overarching argument of this book is that there exist multiple pathways that latecomers can take to achieve catch-up and close the income gap with incumbent countries. For latecomer countries, one crucial question is whether to follow the trajectories of present-day rich countries or to seek out different and new trajectories (Lee 2019). Although this is a fundamental question, scholars offering mainstream prescriptions have not sufficiently explored it. Instead, they have suggested that latecomers should follow the trajectories of forerunners or, at the least, attempt to emulate them as soon as possible. The linear perspective also asserts that latecomers should follow the path of structural transformation taken by the current mature economies, focusing first on the primary sector, then manufacturing, and finally services. Another line of scholarship within the linear view bases its policy suggestions on the concept of economic complexity, suggesting – without consideration for entry barriers – that latecomers should attempt to move into product spaces dominated by advanced economies. This book proposes an effective alternative to prevailing development thinking by focusing on nonlinearity and the multiplicity in pathways for the economic development of latecomers. It explores the possibility that latecomer economic catch-up is possible not only by relying on manufacturing sectors but also on IT services, as in the case of India, or resource-based sectors, as in the cases of Chile (wine, salmon, fruits, and wood products) and Malaysia (palm oil, rubber products, and petroleum products).

Given that innovation is considered to be both a bottleneck for continued growth beyond the middle-income stage and the solution to the middle-income trap, this book explores economic development detours pursued by latecomers that rely on the power of innovation. Therefore, the title of this book employs the term "innovation–development detours." It seeks to offer new insights regarding detours to economic growth that have become more viable in the age of de-globalization, with a focus on global–local interfaces, nonmanufacturing industries, and the coevolution of firms and surrounding systems.

Regarding the book's theoretical framework, I apply a Schumpeterian approach, adopting the framework of innovation systems, which have been theorized at the national, sectoral, regional, and firm levels. Thus, I am greatly indebted to intellectual pioneers in this field, including Richard Nelson and Bengt-Åke Lundvall, who jointly developed the intellectual network of Globelics and the Catch-Up Project.

The manuscript has also benefitted from academic interaction with, and learning from, many scholars, including Eduardo Albuquerque, Antonio Andreoni, Daniel Benoliel, Mehmet Bilgin, Philip Boeing, Ron Boschma, Dan Breznitz, Jose Cassiolato, Ha-Joon Chang, Jin Chen, Javier Diez, Joao Ferraz, Manuel Gonzalo, Mike Gregory, Alenka Guzman, Bronwyn Hall, Bert Hofman, Patarapong Intarakumnerd, KJ Joseph, Erika Kraemer-Mbula, Hyeogug Kwon, William Lazonick, Sebastien Lechevalier, Jeong-dong Lee, Justin Lin, Franco Malerba, William Maloney, Sunil Mani, John Mathews, Mariana Mazzucato, Dirk Meissner, Celestin Monga, Jose Ocampo, Arkebe Oqubay, Donghyun Park, Sangwook Park, Eva Paus, Carlota Perez, Tiago Porto, Annalisa Primi, Slavo Radosevic, Dani Rodrik, Clement Ruiz, Jang-sup Shin, Lakhwinder Singh, Jaeyong Song, Barbara Stallings, Marina Szapiro, Elizabeth Thurbon, Fiona Tregenna, Marco Vivarelli, Nicholas Vonortas, Wing Woo, Xiaobo Wu, and Henry Yeung. I must also thank the scholars who engaged with my ideas and provided feedback. Specifically, several (sub) sections of some chapters of the book rely on earlier articles copublished with fellow colleagues, including Qu Di, Buru Im, Si Hyung Joo, Jinhee Kim, Amir Lebdioui, Hyuntai Lee, Jongho Lee, Juneyoung Lee, Zhuqing Mao, Chul Oh, Carlo Pietrobelli, and Chan-yuan Wong. I also must thank Max Balhorn for editing the manuscript, as well as Raeyoon Kang, Joonyup Kim, and Damhee Shin for their research assistance.

The research that made this book possible was completed with financial support from the Laboratory Program for Korean Studies through the Ministry of Education of the Republic of Korea and the Korean Studies Promotion Service of the Academy of Korean Studies (AKS-2018LAB-1250001). In addition, I must thank the CIFAR for its financial support and its Innovation, Equity, and Prosperity Program, as well as the Korea Marine Transport Company and Auroral World. Finally. My thanks also go out to the team at Cambridge University Press, and Phil Good in particular, for their continued help during every stage of publication.

Abbreviations

AC	Absorptive capacity
AMC	Advance market commitment
ASEAN	Association of Southeast Asian Nations
BGs	Business groups
BOP	Balance of payments
CBUs	Completely built units
CEO	Chief executive officer
CEPAL	Comisión Económica para América Latina y el Caribe
CES	Consumer Electronics Show
CKD	Complete knock-down
CMO	Contract manufacturing organization
CORFO	Corporación de Fomento de la Producción
CTT	Cycle time of technologies
DRAM	Dynamic random access memory
DVAFXSH	Domestic value added embodied in foreign exports as a share of the gross exports of a foreign country
EEs	Emerging economies
E&E	Electrical and electronic
EU	European Union
FAW	First Automotive Works
FCh	Fundación Chile
FDI	Foreign direct investment
FELDA	Federal Land Development Agency
FIZ	Free industrial zone
FOE	Foreign-owned enterprise
FTA	Free trade agreement
FVA	Foreign value added
GDP	Gross domestic product

GM	General Motors
GNP	Gross national product
GPAC	Guangzhou Peugeot Automobile Company
GVC	Global value chain
HaS	Hub-and-spoke
HHI	Herfindahl–Hirschman Index
HICOM	Heavy Industries Corporation of Malysia Berhad
HKEX	Hong Kong Exchanges and Clearing
HSIP	Hsinchu Science and Industrial Park
IMF	International Monetary Fund
IPO	Initial public offering
IPR	Intellectual property rights
ITRI	Industrial Technology Research Institute
JVs	Joint ventures
KOSDAQ	Korean Securities Dealers Automated Quotations
KSE	Korea Stock Exchange
LCRs	Local content requirements
M&A	Merger and acquisition
MICs	Middle-income countries
MIT	Middle-income trap
MNCs	Multinational corporations
MPOB	Malaysian Palm Oil Board
MRB	Malaysian Rubber Board
NBS	National Bureau of Statistics
NERI	National Economic Research Institute
NIS	National Innovation System
NYSE	New York Stock Exchange
OBM	Original brand manufacturer
ODM	Original design manufacturer
OECD	Organisation for Economic Co-operation and Development
OEM	Original equipment manufacturer
PDA	Petroleum Development Act
PDC	Penang Development Centre

POLE	Privately owned local enterprise
PORIM	Palm Oil Research Institute of Malaysia
PORLA	Palm Oil Registration and Licensing Authority
PPP	Purchasing power parity
PSC	Production-sharing contract
PSDC	Penang Skill Development Centre
RCA	Revealed comparative advantage
R&D	Research and development
RIS	Regional innovation system
SAIC	Shanghai Auto Industry Corporation
SEAT	Spanish Touring Automobiles Company
SEC	Securities & Exchange Commission
SEZ	Special economic zone
SME	Small- and medium-sized enterprise
SMIC	Semiconductor Manufacturing International Corporation (Shanghai)
SOE	State-owned enterprise
TDX	Time-Division Exchange (public–private R&D consortium)
TFP	Total factor productivity
TIPS	Technology incubator programs for startups
TSMC	Taiwan Semiconductor Manufacturing Company
UMC	United Microelectronics Corporation
UNDP	United Nations Development Programme
UNESCO	United Nations Educational, Scientific and Cultural Organization
USAMG	US Army Military Government
USPTO	United States Patent and Trademark Office
VoC	Varieties of capitalism
WTO	World Trade Organization

I Introduction

I.I DE-GLOBALIZATION AND THE NEED FOR NEW THINKING

Once the dominant paradigm, globalization has faced a series of setbacks. The first was the 2008–2009 global financial crisis, which was the first red flag indicating a crisis of finance-led globalization. This was followed in 2016 by the first referendum on Brexit and public support for Great Britain exiting the European Union (EU). The second setback was the beginning of trade de-globalization triggered by struggles over hegemonic dominance between the United States and China following Trump's election in 2017 and his imposition of tariffs on Chinese exports to the United States. The third setback was the de-globalization of manufacturing (and value chains) caused by the COVID-19 pandemic that began in early 2020. The pandemic revealed the vulnerabilities of global value chains (GVCs), which are fragmented globally and rely on production operations in multiple countries. The most recent setback has been the 2022 Russian invasion of Ukraine, which disrupted the global supply of agricultural products, oil and other minerals, as well as foreign exchange settlement systems, such as SWIFT. Consequently, the paradigm of free trade and production has been thrust into a state of uncertainty, and countries are rebalancing GVC efficiency and resiliency by pursuing new modes of production and value chains while reconsolidating alliances with key allies (Stiglitz, 2022) In general, the trend has been toward more in-sourcing than out-sourcing and promoting domestic production over foreign imports. This sudden and radical change in the environment of global capitalism has left emerging countries struggling to find a solution.

Once a strong promoter of globalization and free trade, the United States has now switched to protectionism and alliance-based economic coalitions. China, in contrast, continues to advocate free trade and multilateralism while also employing strategic interventions to promote specific industries. For emerging economies, this new global environment seems to have disavowed the "one-size-fits-all" model for economic growth that is associated with international integration and the so-called Washington Consensus. This shift away from the conventional economic paradigm can also be interpreted in terms of the so-called "globalization paradox" raised by Rodrik (2011), which highlights the trilemma of being unable to simultaneously pursue economic globalization, national sovereignty, and democracy. Therefore, given the constraints facing globalization, countries have become freed from this trilemma and are seeking to focus on national autonomy. Each economy and government is free to operate according to the new premise that markets and governments are not adversarial but rather complementary, and that economic prosperity can be achieved through diverse institutional arrangements (Rodrik, 2011, xviii). Each country has suddenly been given the freedom to pursue its own economic policies, including protecting domestic industries as a form of industrial or innovation policy.

Some have predicted that there will be a return to globalization. However, the world is currently split into two blocs of similar economic sizes, with the US-led bloc on one side and the China-led bloc on the other with their respective GVCs. This bifurcation of the world economy will likely continue to act as a structural force keeping the world decoupled for some time (Lee, 2021a). The next several decades will continue to be influenced by the two opposing forces of integration and disintegration. Regardless of the direction in which the pendulum swings, the role of the state is expected to increase either to counterbalance the costs of past globalization or to respond to the challenge of de-globalization. In this context, the role of the state may go beyond the regulatory or welfare state to include preemptive investments and interventions not only at the pre- and postproduction stages but also at the production stage (Rodrik & Stantcheva, 2021). Currently, we are witnessing the reinforcement of developmental states conducting industrial policies (Johnson, 1982), as well as progress toward entrepreneurial states conducting mission-oriented innovation policies (Mazzucato, 2011).

Regardless of the roles they assume, governments around the world are placing additional emphasis on keeping manufacturing value chains within their own territory, and agriculture and other primary industries are also gaining importance. Simultaneously, manufacturing, agriculture, and other industries have been undergoing digitalization, a trend that has been further reinforced by the COVID-19 pandemic and value-chain disruptions. From an emerging or latecomer economy perspective, this global paradigm shift points to the need to identify a new model of economic development and strike a balance within various global–local interfaces while giving more weight to domestically owned and controlled firms as well as resource and value chains. Therefore, this book focuses on the following three points.

First, there are several alternative development pathways for latecomers who currently either do not have to or cannot follow the standard paths of forerunners. Even before the advent of de-globalization, many emerging economies were having difficulty generating growth beyond the middle-income stage or obtaining high-income status. Whereas market opening and international integration have been the typical prescriptions for growth, such approaches have largely failed in the Global South. Meanwhile, success stories of economic catch-up in East Asia indicate that opening should be more strategically managed and combined with policy interventions.

Second, although developing and emerging economies have to be open to global forces and knowledge by inviting foreign direct investment (FDI) and multinational corporations (MNCs), latecomers should strategically manage global–local interfaces to promote domestically owned firms that can eventually generate value added and domestic jobs. Otherwise, latecomers will remain stuck in low value-added sectors or value segments with no hope of transitioning into high-end value segments. This is because technology transfers and market access become more difficult as a country gets closer to the frontier. Additionally, foreign capital is constantly on the move and seeking to enter low-wage territories to secure higher margins.

Third, although the prevailing view is that no country has obtained high-income status without nurturing a sizable manufacturing sector, obtaining high-income status and sustaining a robust economic catch-up drive requires generating a certain number of domestically embedded big businesses that command some export power in world markets regardless of the sector. This is because breaking through the barriers to entering medium and high-end manufacturing requires the consolidation of available resources and competencies within big businesses. This is also because non-manufacturing industries and some agricultural and resource-based industries are becoming more knowledge-oriented and could emerge as sources of export-based profit in global markets.

I will elaborate on these three arguments in my explanation of the innovation–development detours framework that follows.

I.2 INNOVATION–DEVELOPMENT DETOURS

I.2.I *Problems with the Linear View: The More, the Better?*

Many developing countries continue to face difficulty initiating and sustaining economic development, and this situation has been exacerbated by the COVID-19 pandemic, resulting in a larger divergence between rich and poor countries. One important economic development question for latecomer countries is whether they should follow the similar trajectories of present-day rich countries or follow a different path (Lee, 2019).

While it would appear to be a fundamental question, economists studying latecomer development have not explored this question adequately and have simply indicated that latecomers should follow the trajectories of forerunners. For example, the policy prescriptions of the Washington Consensus advocate for an immediate and comprehensive liberalization of trade and investment and privatization of state-owned enterprises, given that all rich countries are liberalized economic systems with few publicly owned enterprises. Although this term – Washington Consensus – is now seldom used, even by the World Bank, no workable alternative has been identified.

There is another stream within the development literature that includes the structural transformation school. Scholars in this group tend to offer linear prescriptions and advocate that latecomers should follow a similar path to that of mature economies, meaning they should begin with primary sectors and subsequently develop their manufacturing and service sectors. According to this perspective, latecomers should first achieve an economic structure in which manufacturing constitutes a significant share of the economy. Another example of the linear view would be those who base their policy suggestions on the concept of economic complexity, which holds that latecomers should attempt to enter the same product spaces as advanced economies. This approach, however, does not consider entry barriers to some product spaces.

The early studies on the technological development of latecomers, such as those by Lall (2000) and Hobday (1995a, 1995b), have observed that latecomers have tried to catch up with advanced countries by assimilating and adapting the incumbents' obsolete technology. However, in a previous co-authored paper (Lee & Lim, 2001), a colleague and I asserted that latecomers have not always followed advanced countries' path of technological development; rather, they sometimes skip certain stages or even create their own paths that differ from those of the forerunners. In a previous book (Lee, 2019), I suggested an explicit nonlinear alternative centered around the concept of detours and leapfrogging that is responsive to the catch-up paradox of "You cannot catch up if you just keep catching up." Indeed, once a country reaches the middle-income stage, several barriers to entering high-end sectors and industries emerge that justify the need for latecomers to attempt detours and leapfrogging (Lee, 2019; Saviotti & Pyka, 2011). These barriers include restrictions on intellectual property rights, counteractive or protectionist measures by incumbent countries, and the limitation of latecomers' policy spaces by the World Trade Organization (WTO).

This book attempts to propose an effective alternative to mainstream development thinking by focusing on nonlinearity and multiplicity in pathways for economic development by latecomers, especially those in the middle-income stage. Given that innovation is considered to be both a bottleneck for continued growth beyond the middle-income stage and the solution for the middle-income trap (MIT) (Lee, 2013c; World Bank, 2010), this book explores detour paths of economic development pursued by latecomers that rely on the power of innovation, and therefore the title of this book employs the term "innovation–development detours." Detours are necessitated by the presence of the various barriers latecomers face in their efforts to use innovation to aid development. In my previous work (Lee, 2019), I suggested three specific detours as solutions to the obstacles latecomers face when attempting to enhance their innovation capabilities.

The first detour involves adopting imitative innovation under a loose IPR (intellectual property rights) regime in the form of utility models (or petty patents) and trademarks instead of promoting and strengthening regular patent rights. The second detour is directly opposed to the linear view of GVCs (Baldwin, 2016), which argues that the more participation in GVCs, the better, and rather promotes a GVC-related detour whereby an economy initially learns by participating in GVCs but later reduces its reliance on these chains by building increased domestic value chains and entering high-end segments. Without such a detour, latecomers will remain stuck in low value-added sectors, which is a symptom of the MIT. The third detour involves specializing first in short-cycle technology sectors and products (e.g., IT) and later in long-cycle sectors and segments (e.g., pharmaceuticals). Long-cycle technologies are highly profitable and desirable but also enable existing knowledge to be utilized for a long period of time, thus acting as an entry barrier against latecomers. Therefore, latecomers are advised to first target short-cycle technologies – where entry barriers are low, but growth prospects are high – because high innovation frequency often disrupts the dominance of the incumbent.

This book seeks to offer new insights regarding detours to economic growth that have become more viable in the age of deglobalization, with a focus on non-manufacturing industries, global–local interfaces, and the coevolution of firms and surrounding systems. Regarding the book's theoretical framework, it applies a Schumpeterian approach, with a focus on the concept of innovation systems, which have been theorized at the national, sectoral, regional, and firm levels (Lundvall, 1992; Nelson, 1993). This book explores the following three issues, which have been relatively neglected in the existing literature: (1) the possibility of multiple linear and non-linear pathways for latecomers to upgrade their innovation systems; (2) the importance of strategically managing global–local interfaces and, by extension, the necessity of domestic ownership and knowledge for long-term growth; and (3) the coevolution of firms, in particular domestically owned firms, with several tiers of innovation systems, including national innovation systems (NIS), sectoral innovation systems, regional innovation systems, and even corporate innovation systems (Granstrand, 2000).

1.2.2 Multiple Pathways and Detours

First, this book applies the innovation systems perspective to the context of latecomer economies and focuses on the possibility of latecomers following multiple nonlinear pathways. The term "non-linear" implies that latecomers will not necessarily follow the same paths as advanced economies and may not increase the key variables of innovation systems in a linear fashion. This book also intervenes in the longstanding debate on balanced versus imbalanced economic development paths and compares the utility of balanced versus imbalanced NIS for latecomers attempting to achieve sustained economic catch-up. The book also discusses the "trapped NIS" responsible for the catch-up failure that leads to countries becoming caught in the MIT (Lee, Lee, & Lee, 2021).

Various NIS have been measured and analyzed in diverse ways. In a previous paper (Lee, Lee, & Lee, 2021), colleagues and I adopted a definition from Lundvall of NIS as the "elements and relationships which interact in the production, diffusion and use of new and economically useful knowledge" (Lundvall, 1992). This approach uses the five key variables of knowledge localization, diversity of knowledge portfolio, decentralization of innovators, the cycle time of technologies (CTT), and knowledge combinations (originality). National innovation systems in mature and advanced economies tend to be well balanced, scoring high values for all five variables. Their innovations tend to be strongly based on local knowledge (high knowledge localization) and dispersed over a large number of firms (decentralization) and sectors (technological diversification). They also often specialize in long CTT-based sectors where entry barriers and profitability are high. Therefore, a balanced, catch-up NIS pathway for latecomers may focus on improving in a linear and balanced manner five indices of NIS, such as in the cases of Spain, Ireland, and most recently, Russia and India. Contrastingly, imbalanced catch-up NIS pathways may refer to cases in East Asia. That is, in some East Asian countries, a handful of big businesses rather than a large number of small- and medium-sized enterprises (SMEs) have led specialization in short rather than long CTT while attaining a level of technological diversity and knowledge localization commensurate with advanced economies.

This understanding of the imbalanced catch-up NIS pathway is consistent with the concept of nonlinearity in the sense that latecomers do not follow the path of forerunners (or adopt long CTT and decentralized NIS) but rather forge their own paths and seek out their own niches. Such nonlinearity can be rationalized in terms of the existence of entry barriers in long-CTT sectors and the need for latecomers to concentrate their resources within a few big businesses that successfully enter low barrier-to-entry (short-CTT) sectors and technologies (Lee, 2013c; Han & Lee, 2022). In short-CTT sectors, "creative destruction" (Schumpeter, 1942) occurs more frequently, and therefore, the knowledge base of existing technologies is more quickly destroyed or made obsolete.[1] In this sense, short CTT-based sectors have lower barriers to entry because existing technologies owned by incumbents either become quickly outdated or are frequently disrupted. In contrast, the trapped NIS pathway is discussed in terms of its "too early" specialization in long-CTT technologies without achieving substantial commercial success from innovation and failing to sustain economic growth while being stuck in the MIT.

Late latecomers facing higher entry barriers to high-end sectors and technologies may seek diverse entry points in knowledge-intensive IT services or resource-based sectors rather than hard manufacturing by adopting a detour or leapfrogging strategy. Such possibilities are also consistent with the idea of the multiplicity and nonlinearity of development paths. Figure 1.1 summarizes the above discussion on innovation–development detours, which is further explored in Chapter 2. The top of Figure 1.1 features a box of multiple pathways, including imbalanced (short cycle) and balanced (medium cycle) catch-up pathways as well as the imbalanced, trapped pathway. The same box also lists services and resource-based sectors that are alternatives to manufacturing-based catch-up. The potential of these alternative trajectories will be discussed in Chapter 2 with reference to the examples of Chile and Malaysia (resource-based development) and India (IT service-based development).

Given that all economies around the world, both developing and developed, have undergone several decades of opening up and globalization, competing successfully in international markets is a crucial factor that determines the fortunes of economies. Due to the

---

[1] Schumpeter (1942, p. 73) explains creative destruction as follows, "The opening of new markets, ... the organizational development ... illustrate the same process of industrial mutation – I may use that biological term – that incessantly revolutionizes the economic structure from within, incessantly destroying the old one, incessantly creating a new one. This process of Creative Destruction is the essential fact about capitalism."

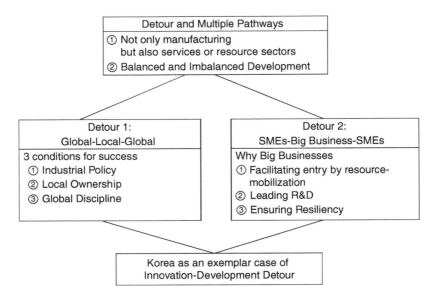

Detour and Multiple Pathways
① Not only manufacturing
but also services or resource sectors
② Balanced and Imbalanced Development

Detour 1:
Global-Local-Global
3 conditions for success
① Industrial Policy
② Local Ownership
③ Global Discipline

Detour 2:
SMEs-Big Business-SMEs
Why Big Businesses
① Facilitating entry by resource-
mobilization
② Leading R&D
③ Ensuring Resiliency

Korea as an exemplar case of
Innovation-Development Detour

FIGURE I.I Innovation–development detour

lack of stable sources of export earnings and convertible currencies, export competition is vital for latecomer economies to be able to earn dollars to pay for imported capital goods. However, the innovation system literature has been somewhat sluggish in exploring the international dimension of innovation systems and articulating such concepts as global innovation systems (Binz & Truffer, 2017) in discussions over building technological capabilities.

To address this gap in the literature, this book argues that managing successfully global–local interfaces is a key condition for building up technological capabilities. This is represented by the box on the left marked as "Detour 1: Global–Local–Global" in the middle tier of Figure 1.1. The first term, "global," indicates that all latecomer economies have been open to global knowledge and know-how in the form of inviting FDI for development. However, they have experienced difficulty leveraging FDI to enhance domestic capabilities in production and innovation. When this dimension of the global–local interface is poorly managed, latecomers often fall into the liberalization trap where local capabilities fail to grow, and MNCs become dominant to command market power in local economies (Bresser-Pereira et al., 2020; Rodrik 2006). Billmeier and Nannicini (2013) report many cases of trade liberalization leading to decline or stagnation of economic growth in emerging economies in Latin America or Africa.[2] The worst consequence of this trap is premature de-industrialization and falling into an MIT.

Domestic ownership becomes important during the middle-income stage or later because FDI firms tend to become increasingly reluctant to transfer or sell technology and are prepared to move to other production sites with lower wages. Therefore, the focus should shift from the global to the local, as noted in the box for Detour 1. The success of Taiwan's catch-up was also supported by the growth of domestic firms (Amsden & Chu, 2003). Moreover, the spillover effect of FDI does not occur if the host country does not focus on the linkages between FDI and the domestic economy (Chang & Andreoni, 2020; Fu et al., 2011; Marin & Bell, 2006). These observations are consistent with the so-called "in–out–in again" hypothesis (Lee et al., 2018). That is, it is not sufficient for latecomers to integrate themselves into GVCs by inviting FDI or MNCs at an early stage of development; they must also enhance domestically owned production and innovation capabilities, thereby increasing domestic value added and reducing the backward linkages to GVCs (the share of foreign value added in gross exports). During the final stage, latecomers must utilize their enhanced local capabilities to engage with more GVCs. Therefore, the box for Detour 1 is titled "Global–Local–Global."

The key message of the box for Detour 1 is that successful catching-up requires meeting the following three conditions: the enactment of public initiatives, including industrial policy, the emergence of domestic ownership, and discipline by world markets.

---

[2] Chile is such a case in Latin America, and African cases include Cameroon, Gambia, Kenya, Niger, South Africa, and Zambia, as well as Ivory Coast.

The importance of domestic ownership and knowledge is discussed in Chapter 3, where I apply the GVC framework to several cases, including three IT sectors in Asia (Kim & Lee., 2022), auto sectors in Thailand, Malaysia, China, and South Korea (Lee, Qu & Mao, 2021), and several resource sectors in Chile and Malaysia (Lebdioui et al., 2021). The above studies on IT clusters, auto sectors, and resource sectors are based on separate regional, sectoral, and national innovation systems perspectives; however, in this study, they will be reinterpreted with a new focus on global–local interfaces.

Next, the box titled "Detour 2: SMEs–Big Businesses–SMEs" indicates that although latecomer economies tend to have only SMEs at the initial stage, it is critical to generate and establish big businesses during the catch-up stage. During the final stage, SMEs will emerge and grow, interacting with and following big businesses. It is also necessary for a latecomer to generate more big businesses than is normally expected from an economy of its size as a prerequisite for achieving growth beyond the middle-income stage. My colleagues and I proved this in a previous econometric study (Lee et al., 2013) that used the data of countries at upper-middle and high-income stages, with Korea as the prime example. In addition to big business-friendly Korea, SME-friendly Taiwan was also able to generate eight Global Fortune 500 firms by 2010. This is a considerable feat, considering that the economy had just two or fewer such firms in the 1990s. In contrast, Turkey, South Africa, and Thailand have had either one or no such firms since the 1990s up until now. Interestingly, a study by Beck et al. (2005) funded by the World Bank failed to identify a robust causal link between SME growth and economic growth. Indeed, it only found a positive correlation, which implies that SMEs are not a trigger for growth but rather a result of economic growth.

The importance of big businesses for driving economic growth via large-scale R&D (research and development) has been observed in the United States and Germany during the nineteenth and early twentieth centuries. Whereas young Schumpeter emphasized the role of entrepreneurship primarily in the form of startups and SMEs,[3] the older Schumpeter (1942) recognized the importance of big businesses (pp. 71–72). One prevailing view in the development literature is that no countries have successfully achieved a high-income economy without generating a relatively sizable manufacturing sector. In particular, this argument has been made by scholars who emphasize structural transformation, such as Szirmai and Verspagen (2015). Somewhat breaking with this approach, this book argues that no successful catch-up has ever occurred without generating a certain number of big businesses, which are needed not only to overcome latecomer disadvantages regarding entry barriers at the middle-income stage but also to secure a certain degree of resiliency against crises. This leading role of big businesses is consistent with the nonlinear pattern of increasing rather than decreasing the degree of the concentration of innovation during the catching-up stage in latecomer economies.

Of course, it is important not to apply binary thinking to SMEs and big businesses. That is, the key is not to achieve a large number of startups and SMEs but rather to have them grow quickly into big businesses. If a country is able to generate a certain number of big businesses, it means that a country has been able to grow its SMEs into big businesses either by maintaining a market-friendly economy or engaging in public intervention and promotion. The United States may have succeeded without market intervention; however, latecomer countries, such as Korea, often experience a higher degree of market failure, especially in capital markets, and therefore often require public intervention. When big businesses do emerge in a country, they tend to serve as umbrellas for supplier SMEs while generating many spinoffs. In this sense, the generation of startups and

---

[3] Schumpeter (1911/1934) discussed the role of entrepreneurs in economic development. His shift in emphasis from entrepreneurship to large businesses was later developed into concepts like Schumpeter Mark I and Mark II, which differentiate between two different types of sectors. The Mark I sector is composed of small firms and has high entry rates for new firms; the Mark II sector is composed of large firms and has high industrial concentration (Malerba & Orsenigo, 1996).

their growth into big businesses depend on the effective coevolution of firms with surrounding institutions and innovation ecosystems.

Thus, Chapter 4 focuses on the issue of coevolution and discusses how firms, in particular privately owned domestic firms, grow faster than foreign-owned firms by exploiting surrounding institutions. This chapter also addresses how the rise of a single core firm can change surrounding regions' innovation systems. Additionally, as indicated in the box for Detour 2, big businesses are important in terms of their role in overcoming entry barriers by mobilizing resources and competencies, carrying out the R&D necessary for entering high-end sectors, ensuring resiliency against external disruptions, and serving as an umbrella for SMEs. These four roles will be elaborated further in Chapter 5 (Innovation–Development Detour in South Korea).

In summary, in this emerging era of de-globalization, exploring innovation–development detours according to the aspects outlined above is particularly relevant. This is a nontechnical book that draws upon new and existing empirical evidence from my own research and that of other scholars.

1.3   FURTHER ELABORATION OF KEY THEMES

1.3.1   The Possibility of Non-Manufacturing-Based Development

In Chapter 2, I first provide an overview of the history of economic growth in diverse economies. Next, I group economies into several clusters according to the diversity of NIS, followed by a discussion of multiple pathways for emerging economies. Then, I discuss the potential of non-manufacturing-based development as a solution to the MIT. More specifically, Chapter 2 discusses Chile and Malaysia as examples of resource-based development and India as an example of IT service-based development.

The per capita incomes of Chile and Malaysia have recently exceeded 40% of that of the United States; this is despite the fact that both countries used to belong to the group of imbalanced and trapped countries. Chapter 2 demonstrates that both Chile and Malaysia have sustained their economic growth not because of manufacturing but rather because of the success of several leading resource-based sectors – petroleum, rubber, and palm oil in Malaysia and salmon, fruit, wine, and wood-based products in Chile (Lebdioui et al., 2021). To determine which sectors are responsible for growth beyond the MIT, I compare the contributions of different sectors to export performance, including their share of national exports, trade balance, and revealed comparative advantage over time. I focus on export performance because, in the Global South, it is a more important binding factor for economic growth than trade openness measured by the trade-to-GDP ratio (Ramanayake & Lee, 2015). Developing countries must earn hard currency via exports to purchase the imported capital goods that are required for investments and sustained economic growth. Without strong exports, developing countries cannot free themselves from the balance of payment deficit problem, which is a chronic problem in the Global South. Furthermore, I present evidence demonstrating that a progressive downstream value addition has taken place in the exports of these sectors in Malaysia and Chile.

These examples of successful catch-up through specialization in resource-based sectors support this book's argument that latecomers should identify low barrier-to-entry sectors within the international division of labor. For many resource-rich emerging economies, such resource-based sectors represent low barrier-to-entry sectors. Achieving growth by relying on domestically available resources makes more sense in the post-pandemic era when countries are seeking a more resilient model of development that is less constrained by the risks of GVC disruption.

Chapter 2 discusses the case of India, which also belongs to the group of balanced and gradual catching-up economies. India is not yet a high-income economy. However, considering its increasingly faster rate of economic growth and balanced (between short and long CTT) industrial structure, it will likely soon emerge as a fast catching-up economy. India is also quite different from other trapped economies on account of its high level of technological diversification. I also discuss India's patent portfolio to show that whereas India previously pursued imbalanced specialization into two long-cycle technologies (drugs and chemicals), since the 2000s its economy has become more balanced as a result of increased strength in IT services. The share of the patents from computer and communication technologies rose from less than 15% of total US patents registered by India in the early 2000s to over 60% by the mid-2010s. In this way, India has become a more balanced, medium-cycle, tech-based NIS, and, at the same time, it has steadily increased its level of technological diversification.

1.3.2 From the Global–Local Interfaces to Domestic Ownership and Knowledge

Chapter 3 argues that successful catch-up by latecomers is possible only when they strategically manage the global–local interface to promote domestically owned firms, which serve as the basis for additional domestic value added and jobs. Specifically, the following three conditions are prerequisites for success: (1) the enactment of public initiatives, including industrial policy, (2) the emergence of domestic ownership, and (3) discipline by world markets. To elaborate on these three conditions, I draw on three examples: three regions specializing in the same IT sector in Asia (Kim & Lee, 2022), auto sectors in four countries (Lee, Qu, & Mao, 2021), and several resource sectors in Chile and Malaysia (Lebdioui et al., 2021).

The first case study examines the short CTT-based IT sector in Taipei, Shenzhen, and Penang. I contrast their different paths to development, such as fast catch-up in Shenzhen and slow catch-up in Penang. These deviant pathways are explained with reference to the various patterns of firm ownership in each region. For example, I compare the emergence of strong domestic firm ownership in Shenzhen with the persistent dominance by MNCs in Penang.

Second, using the example of various auto sectors in Asia, the book argues that domestic ownership and knowledge should be subject to global market discipline. For instance, the auto industry in Malaysia, which is led by Proton, used to be mostly domestically owned and tightly regulated; however, it was not export-oriented and lacked global market discipline. Consequently, it failed to be competitive in markets. In contrast, the auto sector in Thailand achieved mixed success that has been limited in terms of domestic value added due to a lack of domestic ownership. In the end, success depends on whether domestically owned enterprises grow to become successful exporters in global markets.

Third, I discuss how the emergence and growth of several resource sectors in Chile (wine, fruit, and wood products) and Malaysia (palm oil, rubber, and petroleum products) into leading export engines enabled the success of economic catch-up beyond the middle-income stage in both countries. I also show that their emergence and growth did not occur spontaneously but rather as a result of policy interventions by the government. These examples also illustrate that successful catch-up by latecomers can be not based on manufacturing but on resource-based sectors; indeed, for both countries, resource-based sectors drove economic growth beyond the middle-income stage. After South Korea and Taiwan, Chile and Malaysia may be the first economies to successfully escape the MIT.

1.3.3   The Coevolution of Firms with Sectoral, Regional, and National Systems

In contrast to the majority of studies, which tend to study a single innovative system in isolation, this book explores the interactions between various innovative systems. More specifically, this book focuses on the interactions between corporate innovation systems and sectoral, regional, and national innovation systems. In Chapter 4, I study these interactions to outline the importance of firms, in particular big businesses, as the ultimate drivers of economic catch-up in the latecomer context. Thus, the focus is on how the growth of (domestic) firms drives the development of sectors, regions, and nations.

The overarching theme of this book is alternative pathways for latecomers for catch-up development, and one way of exploring this theme at the firm level is to ask whether latecomers use *similar* or *different* technologies from incumbent firms to catch up and forge ahead. Using similar technologies implies that latecomers simply attempt to imitate forerunners, whereas using different technologies indicates that latecomers pursue new technologies and take different technological paths from incumbents. Accordingly, Chapter 4 explores the paths of latecomer firms striving to catch up with incumbent firms. Specifically, Section 1.2 of Chapter 4 addresses the question of whether latecomer firms can catch up with and eventually overtake incumbent firms by merely imitating incumbents or whether they must go beyond imitation by initiating their own technological innovations that differ from those of incumbents. I seek answers to these questions by examining three cases of latecomer firms overtaking incumbent firms – that is, Samsung overtaking Sony, Hyundai Motors overtaking Mitsubishi Motors, and Huawei overtaking Ericsson.[4]

Section 1.3 of Chapter 4 deals with the coevolution of firms and surrounding institutions in the context of post-reform China, where firms with diverse ownership have emerged and formed an ideal setting for examining the interactions between firm ownership and institutions. This section also explores the specificities of the post-reform Chinese experience, such as privately owned enterprises (POEs) catching up with foreign-owned enterprises (FOEs) and state-owned enterprises (SOEs) via POEs' more effective exploitation of the surrounding institutional development, as I discussed in a co-authored paper, Lee and Lee (2022). Although the initial productivity of POEs was lower than that of FOEs when institutional development was low, POEs eventually caught up with FOEs because institutions have improved over time and have been more effectively

---

[4] We draw on the quantitative analyses of Joo and Lee (2010), Oh and Joo (2015), and Joo et al. (2016), which have analyzed each pair of a latecomer vs. an incumbent.

utilized by POEs than FOEs. The implication is that although private firms cannot prosper without sound institutions, institutional development may be useless without the existence of domestically owned private firms (rather than FOEs) that can benefit from this institutional development.

Next, I analyze the region of Hsinchu in Taiwan to show that the region's long-term trajectory has been strongly influenced by the rise of leading big businesses, such as Taiwan Semiconductor Manufacturing Company (TSMC), in Hsinchu City (Wong & Lee, 2021). Hsinchu used to be characterized as a Marshallian industrial district with an equal distribution of differently sized firms and diverse sectors. However, with the growth of the core firm TSMC, the region has steadily come to resemble a hub-and-spoke industrial district with increasing centralization in the distribution of firms and innovations.

Finally, the match between the micro and macro dimensions of innovation will be discussed with reference to the changes in the corporate innovation systems of Korean firms. Korean firms used to behave like typical catching-up firms (e.g., firms that prioritize growth over profitability, borrow and invest heavily, and specialize in short-cycle technologies); however, Korean firms have undergone radical changes in their behavioral patterns, which shows that their behaviors are converging with those of mature firms in advanced economies such as the United States (Im & Lee, 2021). They now prioritize profitability and dividend payments over sales growth and re-investment; they are also moving into long CTT-based sectors, such as bio-medicals. This shift from catching up to convergence at the firm level mirrors the macro-level convergence of South Korea with respect to Anglo-American economic systems in terms of the slowing down of employment and growth and rising inequality. Such changes in firms have been driven by the post-1997 crisis reforms imposed by the International Monetary Fund (IMF) as a condition for receiving emergency loans, which forced Korean firms to adopt corporate governance measures typical of shareholder capitalism in the United States and the United Kingdom.

1.4   INNOVATION–DEVELOPMENT DETOUR IN SOUTH KOREA

Chapter 5, which is the longest of the book, is dedicated to South Korea. The long-term evolution of the Korean economy is used to illustrate the three themes discussed above. Beginning as a low-income country in 1960, South Korea underwent a remarkable economic ascent and emerged as a high-income status country by the mid-1990s. The South Korean economy is an exemplary case of taking a nonlinear development detour, in that during its catching-up period, which lasted until the 1990s, it pursued selective opening, promoted big businesses over SMEs, and prioritized domestic value added over simply joining GVCs. South Korea's market used to be mostly closed and protected; however, it is now one of the most open markets in the world. Indeed, it is the only country in the world to have free-trade agreements with the United States, the EU, China, and India. Thus, from the South Korean example, we can generate a paradoxical, nonlinear view of development that says, "To be open, you must be closed for a while."

Yet, the Korean journey also involved some turbulence. Korea experienced a major crisis in 1997 and came close to another crisis during the global economic turmoil of 2008–2009. Whereas the former crisis was linked to excessive indebtedness and investment by big businesses, the latter was a global financial crisis that began in the United States, which led to capital flight from South Korea back to Wall Street and the substantial depreciation of the Korean currency. It is interesting to note that South Korea recovered remarkably quickly from both crises, raising questions over the sources of such resiliency that extend beyond the sources of growth during the earlier period at the MIT range. In pursuit of an answer to this question, this chapter redefines the Korean model of catch-up development.

Scholars have put forth many theories to explain South Korea's miraculous catch-up. Therefore, this chapter first begins by providing an evaluation of existing views and myths regarding the factors affecting South Korea's miraculous growth and resiliency, such as the role of initial conditions, markets versus government intervention, inclusive versus exclusive institutions, and import substitution versus export promotion. Based on my evaluation of the various myths and misunderstandings of the Korean model, I elaborate and redefine the Korean model as an exemplary case of an "innovation–development detour," focusing on elements that have been seldom mentioned in the literature.

The first element is the role of domestically owned big businesses and their capacity building for export orientation. The second element is smart specialization in low barrier-to-entry, short-CTT sectors during the upper middle-income stage. By combining these two factors, I define the Korean model as "short CTT-sector specialization led by domestically owned and export-oriented big businesses." In this way, the Korean pathway is redefined as an exemplary case of detouring from short-CTT to long-CTT sectors and from big business dominance to SME emergence. This constitutes a detour because advanced economies tend to be dominant in long-CTT or high barrier-to-entry sectors, with sources of growth dispersed among both SMEs and big businesses. This detour reflects the actual path of Korea, in that the dominance of big businesses has now been checked by the rise of SMEs and startups. Beginning in the 2000s, during the post-catch-up stage, this caused the reversal of the existing pattern of the centralization of innovation.

Given that decentralization and diversification are typical attributes of advanced economies in the West, South Korea's long-term detour can also be considered the process of the Korean model converging with the Anglo-American model (Lee & Shin, 2021). However, it is crucial to note that such convergence was only possible for South Korea by taking a detour that took the country in the opposite direction of the current trajectory of advanced economies. Moreover, when discussing Korea's detour, it is important to note that the Korean economy used to be protected by high tariffs and asymmetric support for domestic companies. South Korea now, however, is a mostly open economy. Therefore, it has also detoured from a closed to an open economy. This convergence via divergence (or detour) constitutes the so-called "catch-up paradox" (Lee, 2019, p. xxi), which can be expressed through the following statements: "You cannot catch up if you just keep catching up." "To be open, you have to be closed for a while." And, "A detour can be faster than a straight road."

Additionally, I discuss the Korean experience to show that most successful catching-up experiences have included strategically navigating the global–local interface in order to promote the emergence of domestically owned big businesses. I also emphasize that no successful catch-up has ever occurred without generating a certain number of big businesses.

1.5   THE ROLES OF GOVERNMENT IN DEVELOPMENT DETOURS

Chapter 6 will be devoted to discussing the role of government in innovation–development detours and related policy implications. Here, the main issue is whether the ideas of detour and nonlinearity are applicable to the roles of the government. Thus, this chapter will discuss the provocative assertion that the role of government should not decrease in a linear fashion over the stage of development but rather may need to increase at the upper-middle-income stage, with the scope of the government intervention forming an inverted U-shaped curve. The theory of comparative advantages holds that during the low-income stage, economic growth does not necessitate direct government intervention in the affairs of firms. However, for a country at the upper-middle-income stage to enter high value-added sectors and catch up with leading countries, governments may need to undertake more direct forms of intervention, such as pursuing public–private R&D initiatives. Such interventions become necessary because firms at this stage face increased difficulty in terms of entry barriers and IPR disputes. Moreover, technology transfer becomes more difficult the closer a country gets to frontier technologies, and high-end sectors in the global market tend to be oligopolistic or monopolistic in nature, with a strong dominance by incumbents. Thus, this chapter will elaborate on two modes of government involvement – that is, slow and fast modes of catching up – for overcoming the challenge of strategically managing the global–local interface.

Specifically, in overcoming the challenge of strategically managing the global–local interface, the two modes of government involvement are possible, which can be called a slower vs. faster mode of catching up. In a slow but steady mode of catching up, the main focus of public intervention is on re-skilling and up-skilling local labor forces so that FDI or MNCs may not move to other locations but stay in the same localities to engage in high-value activities hiring local labor forces. The other, faster catching-up mode is close to what has happened in Shenzhen city or the auto sector in China, in which asymmetric intervention is mobilized to foster locally owned firms and their R&D activities, as opposed to foreign-owned firms.

Chapter 6 also discusses the issue of how to first generate big businesses as an engine for growth beyond the middle-income stage and then SMEs and startups at a later stage of development. Managing the coevolution of large and small firms is a serious challenge for latecomers, given its high degree of market failures including the thinness and smallness of markets.

1.6 KEY MESSAGES AND CONTRIBUTIONS OF THE BOOK

This book explores the coevolution of firms, sectors, regions, and national economies in the Global South and explains their economic performance as a dynamic outcome of interactions between the multiple levels of innovation systems. The key arguments are as follows. First, multiple pathways for economic catch-up by latecomers are possible, and latecomers do not necessarily follow the trajectories of the incumbent advanced economies in a linear manner in their efforts to overcome entry barriers and other challenges at the middle-income stage. Second, most successful catch-up experiences have included strategically navigating global–local interfaces to promote the emergence of domestically owned big businesses and bring about a phase of increasing concentration rather than decentralization. Third, the creation of growth poles – whether they be firms, sectors, or regions – has been enabled by effective interactions between the diverse dimensions of innovation systems, including active policy interventions by national and subnational governments.

Based on these findings, this book counters prevailing views on economic development and offers a unique contribution to the literature on economic catch-up. Whereas the traditional linear view of development has taken a "more is better" approach, this book advocates that latecomers should pursue detours or leapfrogging, which conforms with a "less is better" approach. Instead of the conventional prioritization of manufacturing, this book proposes prioritizing domestic ownership and knowledge in specific sectors and regions and asserts that no country has successfully developed a high-income economy without generating a certain number of globally recognized big businesses. Instead of placing priority on free markets as the Washington Consensus does, this book argues that economic catch-up is only possible with active and planned government interventions, which are needed to overcome latecomers' disadvantages regarding barriers to entry at the middle-income stage.

2 National Innovation Systems and Alternative Pathways for Latecomers

2.1 INTRODUCTION

The MIT is a situation where a middle-income economy faces decelerated growth and consequently fails to join the ranks of high-income economies. The MIT has become the subject of an increasing volume of research,[1] and many countries currently have become stagnated at the middle-income stage. A study by the World Bank jointly done with the Development Research Center of the State Council of China (World Bank 2012, p. 12), found that 101 middle-income economies have joined the ranks of the high-income economies since 1960. Among these, the ten economies of Greece, Portugal, Spain, Ireland, Hong Kong, Israel, Japan, Mauritius, Puerto Rico, and Singapore used to be upper-middle-income economies, that is, with income levels of 20–40% of US per capita income. Korea and Taiwan were low- and lower-middle-income economies respectively, and Equatorial Guinea was an oil-exporting country.

This chapter first focuses on these economies to identify alternative pathways to grow beyond the middle-income stage as well as pathways to escape the MIT. The World Bank (2010) has suggested that middle-income economies tend to fall into the MIT because they become caught between low-wage manufacturers and high-wage innovators. In fact, innovation capability has increasingly been recognized as a key prerequisite for middle-income economies to achieve and sustain economic growth.[2] However, the search for

---

[1] This phenomenon of the MIT was first mentioned in Gill et al. (2007) and has become the subject of an increasing volume of research. For example, see World Bank (2010); World Bank (2012); Eichengreen et al. (2013); and Lee (2013c).

[2] See such works as Lavopa and Szirmai (2018); Eichengreen et al. (2012); Lee (2013c); and Cirera and Maloney (2017).

growth pathways beyond the middle-income stage does not have to be confined to manufacturing. There are alternatives, such as resource-based development, as witnessed in Chile and Malaysia, which will be explored in this chapter.

This chapter approaches these issues from a Schumpeterian perspective, utilizing the concept of NIS, which is a key theoretical framework of Schumpeterian economics. Lundvall (1992) defined NIS as composed of "elements and relationships which interact in the production, diffusion, and use of new, and economically useful, knowledge." The Schumpeterian thesis suggests that the effectiveness of a country's NIS determines its innovation performance and, by extension, its economic performance.[3] This chapter discusses the alternative pathways for sustaining growth beyond the middle-income stage by classifying the NIS of thirty-two economies around the world into several types. It then confirms the linkages of each NIS type with economic growth.

The chapter will demonstrate that there are two varieties of successful catching-up economies. The first group includes the four economies of Ireland, Spain, Hong Kong, and Singapore from the above-mentioned thirteen economies, as well as the economies of India and Russia. The second group comprises the economies of Korea, Taiwan, and China. In this sense, a central question in this chapter is whether multiple types of NIS exist and whether they represent different pathways of growth beyond the middle-income stage that can enable countries to achieve catch-up with advanced economies in terms of per capita income. If NIS associated with successful catching up can be identified, then it can be compared with the NIS of countries stuck in the MIT, which is characterized by stagnant per capita income (20–40% that of the United States) for long periods of time (World Bank 2012, p. 12). Thus, the NIS of stagnating countries is referred to as the "trapped NIS." The discussion

---

[3] Such a view is also endorsed by international organizations such as the Organisation for Economic Co-operation and Development (OECD) (1997).

of various NIS types also connects this study to the broader literature on varieties of capitalism (VoC) by providing some comparisons of NIS types and types of capitalism.[4]

The literature tends to measure NIS by using multiple variables to capture various aspects of an economy, ranging from techno-economic to political-institutional dimensions, IT-related infrastructure, and even openness and financial systems. In comparison, this chapter presents research I conducted with colleagues (Lee, Lee, & Lee, 2021) and uses a narrowly focused measure of NIS that conforms closely with Lundvall's original definition, which highlights NIS's capacity to generate, diffuse, and use knowledge. Therefore, this study uses a single dataset comprising patents filed in the United States. The advantage of using such a dataset is that the data sources are homogeneous, and, therefore, the variables can be easily and consistently collected and measured for different countries over a long period of time.[5] We measured NIS using the following five variables: knowledge localization (diffusion), technological diversification, decentralization of innovators, originality of knowledge, and CTT. In an earlier study (Lee & Lee, 2019), colleagues and I developed a composite NIS index using these five variables and demonstrated that it is a sufficiently comprehensive predictor of economic growth and more robust than, or equally robust as, the index of economic complexity.[6]

The chapter is organized as follows. Section 2.2 discusses the catching up, forging ahead, and falling behind of various economies around the world to derive a hypothesis regarding the grouping of NIS types. Section 2.3 presents the results of cluster analyses of the

---

[4] The literature on VoC initiated by Soskice and Hall (2001) classifies economies around the world in terms of several key institutions and identifies three representative types of capitalism: liberal market economies, coordinated market economies, and mixed market economies.

[5] Using and relying on patent data can be justified by the fact that the focus of analysis is only on those countries at the middle- or higher-income stage, which tend to file a certain number of patents.

[6] Colleagues and I (Lee & Lee, 2019) showed that adding or omitting one or two components does not affect the explanatory power of NIS in analyzing economic growth. The index of economic complexity is suggested by Hausmann et al. (2014).

varieties of NIS around the world and economic growth analysis, thus verifying the linkage between NIS types and economic growth. Section 2.4 discusses the dynamic transition from the middle-income to the high-income stage by comparing catch-up NIS with trapped NIS. Section 2.5 discusses the path of catching up with a balanced NIS, with particular attention paid to India. Section 2.6 discusses another alternative path of catch-up that relies not on manufacturing but on resource-based sectors, with Chile and Malaysia presented as examples. Section 2.7 concludes the study by summarizing the main results and discussing the broader implications of the findings.

2.2   CATCHING UP, FORGING AHEAD, AND FALLING BEHIND OF NATIONS

The initial focus of this chapter is the group of economies that have successfully transitioned to become high-income economies, particularly the thirteen economies identified by the World Bank as having sustained growth beyond the middle-income stage (World Bank 2012, p. 12).[7] These economies can be compared with other countries, particularly those stuck in the MIT, as well as high-income economies. I discuss the economic growth of some of these economies in terms of the long-term trends of their per capita GDP relative to that of the United States.

First, Figure 2.1 examines economies that are relatively large and at the upper middle-income stage yet suspected to be in the MIT, namely, Brazil, Argentina, Mexico, Chile, and South Africa. I also add Mauritius to this group for comparison. The per capita GDPs of all six of these countries have remained somewhat stagnant since the 1960s, reporting approximately 20–40% per capita income of that of the United States for more than five decades. Although per capita income in Argentina exceeded 40% of US levels in the 1960s, it subsequently began to decline, eventually dropping below 40%. Given

---

[7] I excluded those that possess too few patents to be reliable, such as Puerto Rico, Mauritius, and the oil-exporting country of Equatorial Guinea.

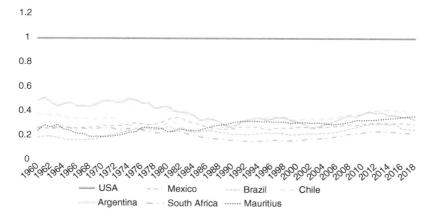

FIGURE 2.1 Per capita income as percentage of that of the United States: Mexico, Brazil, Chile, Argentina, South Africa, and Mauritius
Source: Drawn using data from the Maddison project: www.rug.nl/ggdc/historicaldevelopment/maddison/releases/maddison-project-database-2020

the homogeneous record of these countries' slow catch-up, one may hypothesize that if their NIS can explain their performance, then they should belong to the same NIS cluster.

Next, I turn to the long-term performance of Asian economies. Figure 2.2 clearly shows that they have displayed a steady catch-up trend, regardless of whether it is slow or fast. This contrasts sharply with the overall trend of stagnation or even decline in Latin America. All the economies in Figure 2.2 started with a per capita income below 20% of that of the United States, which is the threshold for the low middle-income level. Hong Kong is an exception, however, as its income levels were approximately 30% of those of the United States. However, their speed of catch-up displayed some variation. For example, the four East Asian tigers showed faster catch-up, with their per capita GDPs reaching 60% or even 100% of that of the United States. Meanwhile, Thailand and Malaysia remained within the 20–40% range (or the so-called MIT range) until the 2000s. Although China was the only economy classified as a low-income economy in 1960, it has rapidly caught up, reaching 30% of US per capita GDP by the late

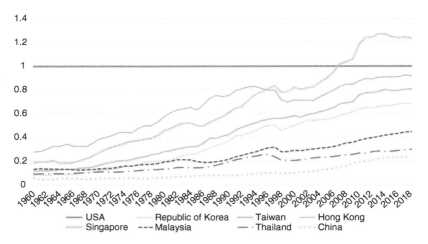

FIGURE 2.2 Per capita income as percentage of that of the United States:
Korea, Taiwan, China, Hong Kong, Singapore, Malaysia, and Thailand
Source: Drawn using data from the Maddison project: www
.rug.nl/ggdc/historicaldevelopment/maddison/releases/
maddison-project-database-2020

2010s. Given the somewhat slow catch-up in Thailand and Malaysia
and considering that some studies suggest that these countries may
be stuck in the MIT (Yusuf & Nabeshima, 2009), one can hypothesize
that these two economies belong to a different NIS type than their
Asian neighbors called Asian tigers. That is, they may belong to the
same NIS type as other trapped economies in Latin America. I will
provide more evidence for this argument in the next section.

I also compare the long-term performance of peripheral
European economies and Israel, which belong to the group of thirteen, with that of the very high-income economies of Hong Kong and
Singapore. On closer inspection, some divergence is observed among
them, with the economies of Singapore, Ireland, and Hong Kong nearly
reaching or exceeding US per capita GDP levels and Israel and Spain
reaching 60% of US levels. Finally, Greece and Portugal show very
weak performances, recently dropping back down to 40% of US per capita GDP. Given this divergence, one can hypothesize that these economies belong to different NIS group types. This hypothesis, of course,

is premised on the notion that there is a correspondence between economic performance and NIS, as argued by Schumpeterians.

The above discussion suggests the possibility of multiple NIS groups that each correspond to different catch-up performances. Given the variation in catch-up and stagnation between countries, we can assume that there are one or more catching-up NIS types and at least one trapped NIS type. Indeed, there is one group of economies that has achieved a very high level of per capita GDP, approaching 100% of US levels, and there is another group composed of economies above 60% but below 90% of US levels. There is a third group of economies still below 40% (MIT) or close to 40% (stagnation) of US levels. Of course, there are some outliers, such as Japan, which has a large GDP and a very high number of US patents, and also China, which has a huge GDP and only began catching up in the 1980s, albeit rapidly. Given the intense heterogeneity among these economies in terms of innovation-related aspects, it is interesting to examine how closely the NIS types correspond with growth performance. Additionally, it is notable that Chile and Malaysia have recently shown some signs of growing beyond the MIT to exceed the benchmark of 40% of US GDP levels (Figures 2.1 and 2.2). It would be interesting to investigate the recent catch-up performances of these two economies and their leading sectors. I will turn to these countries in Section 2.5.

The next section discusses NIS measurements and typologies to determine how well they can explain the economic performances of economies according to NIS type.

2.3   VARIETIES OF NIS AND THEIR LINKAGES TO ECONOMIC GROWTH

This section first discusses the varieties of NIS around the world.[8] This book uses a narrowly focused measure of NIS that highlights the NIS mechanisms that generate, diffuse, and use knowledge, that

---

[8] This section is a shortened version of a longer discussion in Lee, Lee, & Lee (2021).

is, a single dataset consisting of patents filed in the United States.[9] The advantage of using such a dataset is that the data sources are homogeneous, and the variables can be easily and consistently collected and measured for different countries over a long period of time. NIS is measured using the following five variables: knowledge localization (diffusion), technological diversification, decentralization of innovators, originality, and the CTT.[10] These variables cover various dimensions, such as creation and diffusion (*intra*-national vs. *inter*-national) of knowledge for innovation, decentralization or concentration of innovator distribution, technological diversification (width), wide or narrow sourcing of knowledge (originality), and longevity of knowledge (cycle time) in each economy. In general, the higher the per-capita income of an economy, the higher the values of these five NIS variables of an economy.

The analysis focuses on thirty-two economies around the world, including seventeen economies from Europe and North America and fifteen emerging economies. Among the emerging economies, we first considered the five large economies, or BRICS countries, of Brazil, Russia, India, China, and South Africa. Second, we considered five other economies that are relatively large and at the upper middle-income stage but may be stuck in an MIT: Argentina, Mexico, and Chile in Latin America, as well as Thailand and Malaysia in Southeast Asia. This study includes all the major economies, including the G7, BRICS countries, Southern European countries (Portugal, Italy, Greece, and Spain), the four East Asian tigers (Hong Kong, Singapore, South Korea, and Taiwan), the two second-tier tigers (Thailand and Malaysia), four major Latin American countries, one African country, and one country from the Middle East (Israel). The thirty-two economies adequately represent

---

[9] The United States Patent and Trademark Office releases patent datasets on a weekly basis. This bulk data has been turned into a user-friendly form by data mining. The data mining followed the method suggested by Potter and Hatton (2013). See Lee, Lee, & Lee (2021) for details.

[10] Some of these variables were first proposed by Jaffe et al. (1993) and Jaffe and Trajtenberg (2002), among others.

the world in terms of income groups and their combined share of US patents in the world.[11]

Table 2.1 presents the recent values of the five NIS component variables for the thirty-two economies – that is, the average values for the period from 2008 to 2015. Using these five NIS component variables, my colleagues and I conducted a cluster analysis, which has also been applied in the literature on VoC.[12] The objective of this cluster analysis was to classify the thirty-two economies into several clusters using statistically derived measures of similarity and difference based on the five variables. Our analysis identified five clusters, with the United States and Japan remaining as outlier economies given the larger sizes of their economies and their high number of patents.[13] The five clusters and their corresponding countries are listed below, together with group names, which will be explained in the following discussion.

(1) Balanced mature NIS (6): Canada, Germany, France, Italy, Switzerland, and the United Kingdom
(2) Balanced small NIS (4): Sweden, Finland, Israel, and the Netherlands
(3) Balanced mixed NIS (8): Ireland, Spain, Singapore, Hong Kong, Denmark, Norway, Russia, and India
(4) Imbalanced catching-up NIS (3): China, South Korea, and Taiwan
(5) Imbalanced trapped NIS (9): Argentina, Brazil, Chile, Malaysia, Mexico, South Africa, Thailand, Greece, and Portugal

[11] The representativeness of these thirty-two economies is appropriate given that they accounted for more than 97% of US patents on average during the 2015–2017 period (Lee, Lee, & Lee, 2021).

[12] The cluster analysis tests the sample units for the degree of structural commonality among all units. Its outcome is a categorization of the units analyzed that enables the maximization of the coherence of each group (or cluster) and the heterogeneity across different clusters. The cluster analysis initially determines which variables (characteristics) are used, measures the distance between units using the selected variables, and finally classifies the units on the basis of the calculated distance (Rokach & Maimon, 2005; Milligan & Cooper, 1985). See Lee, Lee, & Lee (2021) for details of the cluster analysis conducted.

[13] To demonstrate the robustness of the results of the clustering analysis, clustering was done in two steps or in two sets of countries. The twenty-two representative economies were analyzed in the first round, and all thirty-two economies were analyzed in the second round by adding ten more countries. The results are largely consistent, in that the analysis with thirty-two economies just added more members to the four existing clusters while identifying one more cluster consisting of small high-income economies plus two outliers of the United States and Japan.

Table 2.1 *Values of the five NIS variables in the sample economies, average 2008–2015*

Countries/economies	Decentralization (1-HHI)	Knowledge localization	Technological diversification	Originality	Relative cycle time	Average no. of US patents, 2015–2017
United States	0.9946	0.2507	0.9392	0.5119	1.0142	140,523
Japan	0.9808	0.4042	0.8562	0.3792	0.9349	51,347
South Korea	0.8399	0.1316	0.6861	0.3637	0.8427	19,555
Germany	0.9856	0.1444	0.8425	0.4727	1.1027	14,968
Taiwan	0.9769	0.1366	0.6812	0.3456	0.8323	10,523
China	0.9510	0.0451	0.5976	0.3691	0.8514	8,923
France	0.9811	0.1124	0.7215	0.4316	1.0850	6,226
United Kingdom	0.9940	0.0675	0.6924	0.4845	1.1332	3,980
Canada	0.9558	0.0710	0.6955	0.4979	1.0290	3,912
Switzerland	0.9858	0.0626	0.6164	0.4562	1.1545	3,749
Netherlands	0.9096	0.0712	0.5511	0.4704	1.0555	3,645
Sweden	0.8793	0.1019	0.5508	0.4345	1.0306	3,216
Israel	0.9906	0.0657	0.4341	0.5101	1.0267	2,017
Italy	0.9840	0.0897	0.6190	0.4321	1.1639	1,762
Singapore	0.9329	0.0353	0.2977	0.4562	0.8998	1,694
Finland	0.7587	0.0919	0.3904	0.4593	0.9754	1,632
Denmark	0.9774	0.0799	0.3542	0.4691	1.1667	1,002
India	0.9708	0.0271	0.2614	0.4030	1.0044	808
Ireland	0.9475	0.0244	0.2235	0.5010	0.9992	734

Hong Kong	0.9715	0.0469	0.2974	0.4134	1.0070	530
Spain	0.9875	0.0395	0.3219	0.4287	1.1015	492
Norway	0.9860	0.0698	0.2660	0.5061	1.1878	478
Brazil	0.9714	0.0234	0.1658	0.4231	1.2178	165
Russia	0.9394	0.0431	0.1418	0.4644	0.9717	154
South Africa	0.9678	0.0620	0.1296	0.4612	1.2503	86
Mexico	0.9543	0.0193	0.1036	0.5113	1.2109	84
Malaysia	0.9142	0.0337	0.1045	0.4228	1.0527	80
Portugal	0.9431	0.0236	0.0414	0.4234	1.1558	48
Chile	0.9429	0.0169	0.0391	0.4368	1.2233	34
Greece	0.9248	0.0123	0.0417	0.3782	1.1764	32
Thailand	0.8751	0.0091	0.0380	0.4501	1.0924	22
Argentina	0.9400	0.0376	0.0417	0.3959	1.1776	17
Mean	0.9473	0.0766	0.3982	0.4426	1.0665	
Standard deviation	0.0509	0.0778	0.2798	0.0460	0.1160	

Source: Adapted from Lee, Lee, and Lee (2021), Table 1.

These five NIS clusters appear reasonable, particularly considering the VoC literature, which also discusses three or four types of capitalism, including East Asian capitalism. Roughly, the first cluster seems to coincide with the mixed market economies of continental Europe and the liberal market economies of the United Kingdom and Canada. The second group corresponds to the coordinated market economies of Northern Europe, and the fourth group corresponds to East Asian economies.[14] The original literature on VoC tends to focus on advanced economies; the current study, however, grants increased representation to the emerging economies of groups 3, 4, and 5. We decided to focus on these three clusters (3, 4, and 5), as they include many emerging countries. Group 1 serves as a benchmark for the three emerging country groups. Thus, although all five clusters are represented in Table 2.2, our analysis and discussion avoid Group 2, which includes small high-income countries.

The main characteristics of these NIS clusters are evidenced by the values of the NIS variables for each cluster, as shown in Table 2.2. The four groups can be divided into two general groups: balanced and imbalanced NIS. The two balanced NIS groups (1 and 3) tend to have high values for all five of the NIS component variables. In contrast, the imbalanced groups show a very imbalanced, diverging distribution for the five NIS component variable values. Interestingly, the balanced groups include mostly high-income economies, along with Russia and India, whereas the imbalanced group is mostly emerging economies and the peripheral European economies of Greece and Portugal. This implies that having similarly high NIS values may be one attribute of a high-income economy or an attribute of large countries, as demonstrated by India. Let us turn to each of these clusters for further detailed analysis.

First, the cluster of the four major European economies of Germany, France, the United Kingdom, and Italy also includes Canada and Switzerland. This group is referred to as the "balanced

---

[14] See Storz et al. (2013) and the other articles in the special issue of the *Socio-Economic Review* on Asian capitalisms.

Table 2.2 *Comparison of NIS by selected groups*

Group	Nations	Decentralization (1-HHI)	Localization	Diversification	Originality	Relative cycle time	NIS5	Average no. of patents per year	Coefficient of variation (five NIS indicators)	Growth of per capita income (%)
Balanced mature NIS	Canada, France, Germany, Italy, Switzerland, UK	0.9811	0.0913	0.6979	0.4625	1.1114	3.394	4,725	0.285	0.04
Balanced mixed NIS	Denmark, Hong Kong, India, Ireland, Norway, Russia, Singapore, Spain	0.9641	0.0458	0.2705	0.4552	1.0423	2.423	493	0.530	1.51
Balanced catching-up group	Hong Kong, Ireland, Singapore, Spain	0.9599	0.0365	0.2851	0.4498	1.0019	2.291	533	0.580	1.52
Balanced small NIS	Finland, Sweden, Israel, Netherlands	0.8846	0.0827	0.4816	0.4686	1.0221	2.651	1,804	0.221	0.21

Table 2.2 (cont.)

Group	Nations	Decentralization (1-HHI)	Localization	Diversification	Originality	Relative cycle time	NIS5	Average no. of patents per year	Coefficient of variation (five NIS indicators)	Growth of per capita income (%)
Imbalanced catching-up NIS	China, South Korea, Taiwan	0.9226	0.1044	0.6550	0.3595	0.8421	2.489	8,426	0.628	4.39
Imbalanced trapped NIS	Argentina, Brazil, Chile, Greece, Malaysia, Mexico, Portugal, South Africa, Thailand	0.9371	0.0264	0.0784	0.4336	1.1730	2.109	58	0.714	0.74
Imbalanced trapped group	Argentina, Brazil, Chile, Malaysia, Mexico, South Africa, Thailand	0.9380	0.0289	0.0889	0.4430	1.1750	2.173	67	0.685	1.51

Note and sources: Adaptation of Table 2 in Lee, Lee, & Lee (2021). NIS5 index values are a summation of the five NIS components values after normalization (Lee & Lee, 2019).

All values are average values for the 2008–2015 period. Coefficients of variations are calculated using the normalized values of the five NIS component variables.

mature NIS" cluster because all these economies are high-income economies and because, most importantly, the values of the five variables are all equally high and thus balanced. We can measure and compare varieties of NIS using the five variables and make a composite index by taking a summation of the five component variables after performing normalization and assigning the variables a value from 0 to 5. The actual values in Table 2.2 clearly indicate that the first group, which is the balanced mature NIS cluster, boasts the highest index value, which is indicated as variable NIS5 (3.39) in Table 2.2. The low variation is indicated by the very low values for the coefficient of variation (0.29 in Table 2.2) of the normalized values for the five NIS variables. The equally high values of the NIS variables as well as the high value of the composite index (NIS5) in this group are consistent with the results of the growth regression in my previous work with colleagues (Lee & Lee, 2019), confirming a robust relationship between composite NIS indices and economic growth.

Group 3 is somewhat mixed, in that it includes India as well as the high-income economies of Singapore, Hong Kong, Denmark, and Norway. This group is referred to as the "balanced mixed NIS" cluster. India might look strange in this group given its low-income level; however, it has a similar number of patents to other countries in this group (see Table 2.1). India is included in this balanced group due to its strength in both short-cycle and long-cycle technology-based sectors (IT and pharmaceuticals respectively). By comparison, the balanced mixed NIS has a smaller NIS5 value of 2.42, and thus, if we were to draw a radial graph, it would be nested inside the boundary of the large balanced NIS. In this mixed NIS group, the values of the five NIS variables tend to be lower than the corresponding values in the first group (balanced mature).

Among the eight economies in the balanced mixed NIS cluster, we focus on the four economies of Hong Kong, Ireland, Singapore, and Spain. These four countries belong to the list of thirteen economies provided by the World Bank (2012), meaning that they have successfully transitioned from middle- to high-income status. These four economies show an NIS5 value of 2.29 in Table 2.2, and although they are still balanced, they are nested inside the boundary of the balanced mixed NIS economies. We refer to this group as the "balanced catching-up" group, given the countries' successful catch-up performance (see Figure 2.1 and the discussion in Section 2.2).

The remaining two clusters (Groups 4 and 5) tend to consist of emerging economies, and both can be said to have imbalanced NIS based on the considerable differences among the values of the five NIS variables, with their coefficients of variation above 0.6 and, in some cases, even 0.7. Group 4, which is the "imbalanced catching-up NIS" cluster. This cluster is comprised of the three East Asian economies of China, South Korea, and Taiwan, which have demonstrated rapid growth and catch-up. Group 5 includes other emerging economies, namely Argentina, Chile, Thailand, Malaysia, Brazil, and Mexico, and this group is called the "imbalanced trapped NIS" cluster.

An interesting contrast exists between the imbalanced catching-up cluster and the imbalanced trapped cluster: The former corresponds to high localization and diversification yet very short CTT and low originality, and the latter corresponds to very long CTT and high originality yet very low localization and diversification. That is, these two clusters are exact opposites, except that both share a similar level of decentralization and an equally higher concentration compared with the balanced NIS clusters. However, the gap in the composite NIS5 values of these two imbalanced groups is quite substantial, with values of 2.49 for catching-up and 2.11 for trapped, which is consistent with their divergent growth records (Figures 2.1 and 2.2).

In other words, one of the reasons why we use the terms "catching-up NIS" and "trapped NIS" is because they reflect the different performances of each of the two clusters in terms of economic growth, especially their performance in catching up (or not) to the per capita income levels of those in the balanced mature clusters, which are composed of the traditional high-income economies. The simple growth rates in Table 2.2 show that the imbalanced catching-up NIS cluster boasts the highest rate of per capita income (4.39% per annum), followed by the balanced catching-up group (1.52%) and finally the imbalanced trapped group (0.74%).

We have also conducted a similar cluster analysis that used the multi-period NIS values of thirty-two economies to analyze a longer period of time: the thirty-two years from 1984 to 2015.[15] A key finding from this dynamic analysis is that there used to be a big mixed group in the mid-1980s, which comprised most of the thirteen economies that escaped the MIT, as well as other economies stuck in the MIT. Then, gradually over time, two catching-up clusters, balanced and imbalanced, emerged. For instance, in the mid-1980s the economies of South Korea, Taiwan, and China all belonged to the same group as other emerging economies. Then, during the second period (1992–1999), South Korea exited this group to create a new group, which was then joined by Taiwan during the third period and finally by mainland China in the mid-2000s, with the three of them eventually forming this imbalanced catching-up NIS cluster. Another pathway is that taken by countries in the balanced mixed NIS group, which include Hong Kong, Singapore, Spain, and Ireland. This group was created by Singapore during the second period, which was soon joined by Ireland and then Hong Kong and Spain.

The above discussion suggests two alternative pathways to a high-income economy status, ultimately avoiding the MIT. Given that they have displayed rapid growth, it is important to identify the key variables that drove them to achieve this feat. On the one hand, simply looking at the number of patents cannot fully explain the emergence of these two groups, because the average number of patents of the balanced catching-up group (533 a year) is considerably lower than that of the balanced mature NIS group (4,725 a year;

---

[15] We used eight-year average values by dividing the thirty-two years into four subperiods for every eight years. The analysis was conducted using several methods to test the robustness of the results. For details, see Lee, Lee, & Lee (2021).

Table 2.2). On the other hand, the other catching-up group, consisting of China, Korea, and Taiwan, has maintained a quite imbalanced NIS and thus is distinct from the advanced economies. Nevertheless, these countries have been catching up rapidly in terms of number of patents (reaching 8,426 a year).

Finally, to confirm the divergent growth performances of various NIS groups, my colleagues and I (Lee et al., 2021) conducted cross-country panel regressions. We created a dummy variable for each NIS cluster and conducted growth regressions to match these dummies to their growth performance for the eight four-year subperiods (1984–2015). Economic growth rates were shown to be higher for the two catching-up NIS groups. Compared to the benchmark group, which is comprised of the major advanced economies with balanced NIS, the imbalanced catching-up NIS displayed the highest rate of growth, followed by the balanced catching-up group. In contrast, the trapped NIS economies tended to show no catch-up, with growth rates lower than that of the benchmark group.

2.4 CONTRASTING PATHWAYS OF THE TWO IMBALANCED NIS: CATCHING-UP VERSUS TRAPPED

The preceding section demonstrated the superior economic growth performance of the two catching-up NIS. Thus, it is now necessary to ask how these catching-up NIS emerged, overcame the trapped NIS condition, and progressed to catching-up NIS status. A clue to answering this question can be found in an examination of the dynamic evolution of economies belonging to each NIS cluster. The variable of the CTT trend seems to be the key driving force in the transition to the catching-up NIS.

Figure 2.3A shows the trend of CTT over time for the four NIS groups. We can see that in the 1980s, the imbalanced (short cycle) catching-up group (China, South Korea, and Taiwan) maintained a level of average CTT similar to those of other middle- or high-income economies; however, they have substantially reduced their average CTT since the mid-1980s by specializing in short-CTT sectors, such as IT. This is consistent with the fact that their catch-up started in the mid-1980s, although this new NIS cluster did not emerge until the 1990s. In comparison, the average CTT of advanced economies remained high, which is consistent with their strength in long-CTT sectors, such as pharmaceuticals, machine tools, and high-tech materials.

South Korea and Taiwan underwent similar processes of take-off, which relied on the so-called original equipment manufacturing (OEM) mode in labor-intensive sectors (Hobday, 1995) in the 1960s and 1970s.[16] In China, this process began in the 1980s and 1990s. However, countries that industrialize based on the OEM mode cannot maintain competitiveness in the long term because the country's wage rates will continue to rise relative to other lower-tier emerging economies, which is exactly the symptom of the MIT. Korea, Taiwan, and China all belonged to the same trapped group at one time. However, in the 1980s, Korea and Taiwan began to move into high value-added, short-CTT sectors, such as IT, with the help of various industrial policies, including public–private R&D consortiums involving public research institutes, such as the Industrial Technology Research Institute in Taiwan and the Electronics and Telecommunications Research Institute in Korea.[17] China made a similar transition into high value-added, short-CTT sectors in the 1990s.

The CTT of a patent is measured by the average backward citation lag of the patent. This involves such factors as the age of other patents cited by the patent and whether the innovation represented by a patent relies on old or recent knowledge. Specialization by a firm or nation in short CTT-based technologies means that innovation can be conducted with less need to cite or rely on old or existing patents owned by incumbents. Thus, this specialization is reasonable and can be a niche strategy for latecomers because short-CTT areas

---

[16] Hobday (1995a, 1995b) defined original equipment manufacturing as a form of sub-contracting in which a complete and finished product is produced in accordance with the specifications of the buyer.

[17] For details, please refer to Hou and Gee (1993); Kim (1993); and Lee (2013c, chapters 7–8).

have lower entry barriers, given that technologies tend to be quickly outdated or disrupted in short-CTT-based sectors (Lee, 2013c). This specialization into short CTT also helps latecomers to quickly increase their knowledge localization, especially because short CTT relies less on the knowledge base of advanced economies that have a strong reliance on long CTT. Furthermore, if a latecomer repeatedly enters newly emerging technology sectors, it will also be technologically diversified. Specialization into short CTT also implies improved growth prospects due to the frequent arrival of innovations and increased opportunities.

Figures 2.3B and 2.3C show the increasing trend (or catching up to the level of mature advanced economies) of technological diversification and knowledge localization in the imbalanced catching-up group, which includes China, South Korea, and Taiwan. This catching up contrasts with the stagnation of these variables in the imbalanced trapped group. This contrast is the key difference between the two NIS groups. In other words, there seems to be some correspondence between short (or long) CTT specialization and a high (or low) degree of technological diversification and knowledge localization, at least in the context of latecomer economies. This can be further discussed with reference to the specialization pattern of the trapped economies. In contrast to catching-up economies specializing in short-CTT sectors, the trapped economies have pursued specialization into extremely long-CTT sectors that are even longer than those found in advanced economies. The reasons for the stagnation of localization and diversification, as well as the associated slow economic growth of trapped NIS countries, can be explained using the same logic. In other words, because these countries specialize in extremely long CTT, they must continually cite and rely on patents owned by incumbent high-income economies. This reliance corresponds with a low possibility of increasing knowledge localization, as shown by the stagnant trend of this variable in Figure 2.3C. Moreover, by entering long-CTT sectors, these countries are necessarily engaging in activities similar to those of

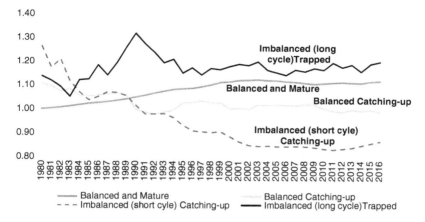

FIGURE 2.3A Dynamic changes of NIS variables: relative cycle time of technologies
Notes: (1) Balanced mature: Canada, Germany, France, Italy, Switzerland, and the United Kingdom
(2) Balanced catching-up: Hong Kong, Ireland, Singapore, and Spain
(3) Imbalanced (short cycle) catching-up: China, South Korea, and Taiwan
(4) Imbalanced (long cycle) trapped: Argentina, Brazil, Chile, Malaysia, Mexico, South Africa, and Thailand
Source: Author's adaptation of a table from Lee, Lee & Lee (2021).

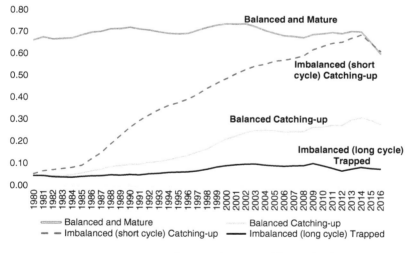

FIGURE 2.3B Dynamic changes of NIS variables: technological diversification
Notes: The same as for Figure 2.3A

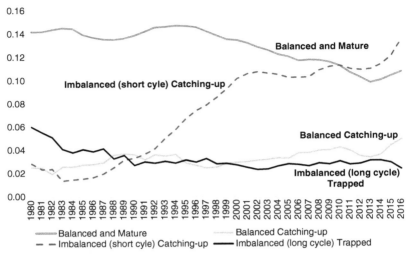

FIGURE 2.3C Dynamic changes of NIS variables: knowledge localization
Notes: The same as for Figure 2.3A

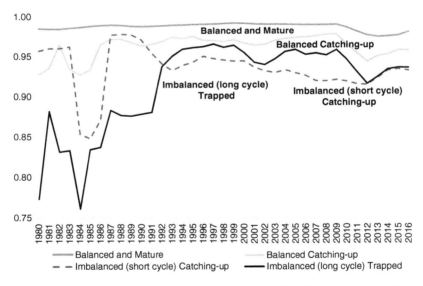

FIGURE 2.3D Dynamic changes of NIS variables: decentralization of innovations
Notes: The same as for Figure 2.3A

incumbent economies. Therefore, they are unable to identify any niche and face high entry barriers to new, successive innovation and commercialization. This pattern is consistent with the observation that there exists a decoupling of academic research and industrial commercialization in Latin America, which has been highlighted as a weakness of NIS in Latin America (Katz, 2001).

Notably, the average CTTs in China, South Korea, and Taiwan stopped decreasing around the mid-2000s, and even reversed to show a slight increase (Figure 2.3A). As China, South Korea, and Taiwan move into long-CTT sectors, there is an increased likelihood that their respective innovation systems will converge with those of mature NIS countries.[18] In other words, the catching-up NIS economies initially pursued a path opposite that of the balanced or mature NIS by specializing in short-CTT sectors. However, they have now begun to move into long-CTT sectors, similar to incumbent economies. I refer to this pattern as a "detour" in the sense that these economies may eventually come to resemble mature balanced NIS countries via a catching-up NIS.

This detour is a variant of a nonlinear economic catching up by latecomers in the sense that an economy taking this detour does not go in the same direction (of long CTT sectors) as incumbent economies. Rather, it goes in the opposite direction and pursues short-CTT sectors during the catching-up stage of economic development. In other words, although the long-term destination of these countries may be long-CTT specialization, they take a nonlinear or U-shaped path, as indicated in the Figure 2.3A. Another example of this nonlinearity is found in the concentration of innovation in a small number of big businesses rather than the dispersion of innovation among many entities. This can be discussed in terms of Figure 2.3D, which shows the decentralization of innovation trends of different NIS groups. As expected, the advanced economies display the highest level, indicating that a wider or more dispersed

---

[18] For instance, the Samsung Group in South Korea declared biomedicine as its future growth engine, and created two subsidiaries. This organization's production capacity is already in the top two or three in the world.

innovation base is desirable. The balanced catching-up group displays the second-highest value, which is also expected.

The next highest values belong to the imbalanced trapped and imbalanced catching-up NIS groups, which display relatively low levels of decentralization. In Figure 2.3D, the long-term trend, not the relative level of the imbalanced catching-up group, is of particular importance. It displays a U-shaped, nonlinear path. This downward trend continues. That is, innovation becomes increasingly centralized during the 1990s and 2000s, only to reverse in the 2010s. This reversal is more pronounced when we look at a graph for an individual economy, such as South Korea in the 2010s.[19] The U-shaped curve indicates that these catching-up economies experienced increased concentration of innovation among a small number of big inventors or businesses during the rapid catching-up period and then experienced subsequent decentralization after more recently becoming mature countries in the post-catching-up period.

In sum, the nonlinear pattern of transitional specialization into short-CTT sectors led by big businesses is an important element of the imbalanced catching-up pattern. What necessitates such a pattern? One answer is the need to circumvent entry barriers to high-end and value-added segments by seeking niches and concentrating resources and competencies in the hands of leading big businesses. Big businesses, especially in the form of business groups, benefit from the ability to mobilize and share resources among affiliates, which, in turn, facilitates entry into new business areas. This advantage is well documented in the literature.[20]

2.5   THE BALANCED SYSTEM AND THE INDIAN PATHWAY

The economic growth of the balanced catching-up NIS group (Singapore, Ireland, Hong Kong, Spain) is characterized by a steady increase in the five NIS indicators and a steady, linear catch-up with

---

[19] Such a figure is available as Figure 1 of Lee & Lee (2021).
[20] For instance, in Lee (2019, chapter 4) and Amsden and Hikino (1994).

the economies of the balanced mature NIS group. The levels of the five NIS variables in this group range between those of the balanced mature group and those of both imbalanced groups. For instance, their levels of diversification and localization are below the values of the mature group but between those of the two imbalanced groups (Table 2.2). While the level of technological diversification of the balanced catching-up group is 0.3, which is half that of the imbalanced catching-up group, it is more than three times higher than that of the trapped group. Meanwhile, the level of localization of the balanced catching-up group is lower than that of the imbalanced catching-up group, which implies that the countries of the balanced catching-up group are pursuing more open innovation, which contrasts with the more closed innovation model of the imbalanced catching-up group.

In comparison, the average CTT of the balanced catching-up group is again between that of the mature advanced economies and the imbalanced catching-up economies; however, it is much shorter than that of the trapped NIS group (Figure 2.3A). In other words, the economies of the balanced catching-up group have not pursued extreme specialization into either short or long CTT. Economies in the balanced catching-up group pursued some specialization into short-CTT sectors beginning in the early 1980s and into the mid-1990s. From the mid-1990s onward, their average CTT levels remained consistent or close to the average value of 1.0. This medium level of CTT is also consistent with their intermediate technological diversification. However, a detailed analysis reveals that each country within the group has experienced a steady increase in technological diversification, from 0 to 0.1 in the 1980s and 1990s, and from 0.23 to 0.33 in the mid-2010s. Despite some variations in other aspects among these four economies, this steady increase in diversification is one of the strongest shared attributes of the balanced catching-up group. In contrast, the trapped economies have experienced a stagnation (never above 0.1) of diversification for the last four decades.

Given that this group of balanced catching-up NIS includes both peripheral European countries (Ireland, Spain, and Russia) and the city-economies of Hong Kong and Singapore, which opened their economies early, one can conjecture that countries in this group succeeded because they were relatively early starters and faced lower entry barriers amidst a more fluid international division of labor. That is, these economies did not inherit a "heavier degree of imbalances" (Hirschman, 1958) and thus faced lower entry barriers to possible sectors. The four balanced catching-up economies started as middle- and upper-income countries in the early 1960s; in contrast, the imbalanced catching-up economies began as low- or low-middle-income economies (see Figure 2.1).

Furthermore, one commonality of the trajectories of economies in the balanced catching-up NIS seems to be the emergence of not only manufacturing but also decent high value-added service sectors, such as IT services, engineering, and banking services. This is different from immature deindustrialization or servicization into low value-added services. Notable cases are the IT service sectors in Ireland and Singapore and engineering and banking services in Spain. In contrast, Hong Kong, which was once a British colony, is an extreme case of a service and trading hub for manufacturing in mainland China.[21] Thus, the economies of the balanced catching-up group have managed to maintain a certain amount of manufacturing relative to services; Hong Kong, with its special relationship with mainland China, is the exception. For instance, Singapore and Ireland kept their manufacturing as a percentage of GDP in the range of 20–25% until the mid-2000s.[22] In particular, Ireland featured a strong medical technology industry, which may be considered a long-CTT sector, whereas Singapore has featured strong innovators not only in manufacturing sectors, such as electronics (short CTT) and precision and transport engineering (long CTT), but also in knowledge-intensive business services.

---

[21] Discussion here relies on Breznitz (2012) and Cunningham et al. (2020) for Ireland, Sharif and Baark (2008) for Hong Kong, on Wong and Singh (2008) for Singapore, and Garcia Calvo (2014, 2016) for Spain, which has experienced the rise of high value-added service sectors and the fall of capital- and skill-intensive manufacturing.

[22] Calculations using the WDI (World Development Indicator) data of the World Bank.

In sum, these balanced and catching-up economies share a certain degree of overlap in their active industrial policies. That is, by relying early on foreign direct investment and multinational enterprises, these economies successfully generated indigenous businesses in various manufacturing and service sectors.[23] Thus, it is also possible to compare balanced and imbalanced pathways by examining countries' tendencies to either specialize in a few niche areas or broaden their specialization to include more diverse areas, such as service sectors. Thus, while Nurkse (1953) emphasizes the need to balance agriculture and manufacturing, economies at the middle-income stage may actually need to strike some balance between manufacturing and services, as exemplified by the case of the balanced catching-up economies in our sample. In fact, Fagerberg and Verspagen (1999) indicate that manufacturing only acted as an engine of growth for developing countries but not developed ones.[24]

One can compare the relative productivity of services and manufacturing using the ratio of the relative productivity of services versus manufacturing, where the relative productivity of each sector is measured by the share of services (manufacturing) in GDP to the share of services (manufacturing) in employment. Then, if we calculate the ratio of the relative productivity of services to the relative productivity of manufacturing, the ratio variables can serve as a measure of the productivity of services relative to that of manufacturing. Calculations then show that this relative productivity of services tends to be highest (or higher than 1) in the balanced catching-up NIS group, whereas it is lowest in the imbalanced trapped group.[25] This may suggest that decent service sectors may have been the engine of catch-up growth in the balanced group, whereas the imbalanced trapped group was less successful in promoting high valued-added services.

---

[23] Refer to information from Cunningham et al. (2020) and O'Malley et al. (2008) for Ireland, as well as Wong and Singh (2008) for Singapore.

[24] This view is slightly different from that of Haraguchi et al. (2017), who reported the continuing importance of manufacturing globally.

[25] For details, see Lee et al. (2021), table 5.

2.5.1   The Case of India

It is notable that India also belongs to the balanced mixed group despite still being a low middle-income country. Although India is not yet a high-income economy, its increasing rate of economic growth and balanced (between short and long CTT) industrial structure means that it will likely join the balanced catching-up group in the future. India also differs substantially from other trapped economies, given its high level of technological diversification. In terms of the evolution of NIS types, India was grouped with other trapped countries in the first two subperiods before 2000. Since 2000, India, alongside Ireland, joined the balanced mixed group that began with Singapore. This transition coincided with India's entrance into IT services beginning in the 2000s. Only during the most recent period (2008–2015) was this group joined by Russia, Denmark, Spain, Norway, and Hong Kong. The per capita GDP of India grew at the rate of 5.1% per annum during the 2008–2017 period compared with the 32-country average of 1.1% per annum; this growth rate is comparable to that of China. Therefore, if India sustains its current economic growth beyond the middle-income stage, its path can be defined not as an imbalanced catching-up NIS but as a balanced catching-up NIS.

India has recently registered a large number of US patents. Figure 2.4 shows the relative composition of six major categories of US patents filed by India. India was once strong in the long-cycle technologies of drugs and chemicals; however, the shares of these two classes have declined sharply since the 2000s as India has gained strength in IT services, which consequently increased its number of patent filings.[26] The share of patents related to computers and communication rose from less than 15% in the early 2000s to over 60% by the mid-2010s. Subsequently, India became a more balanced, medium-cycle, and tech-based NIS comprised of both long- and

---

[26] For the rise of IT services in India, refer to Porto et al. (2021), Rao et al. (2017), and Lee et al. (2014).

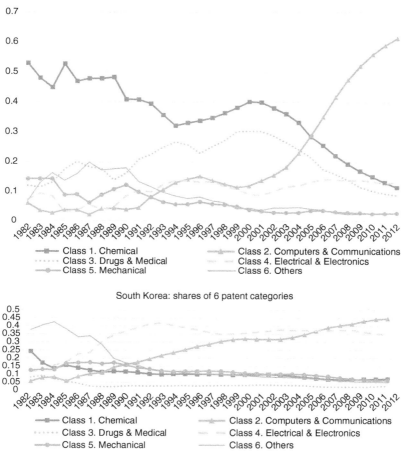

FIGURE 2.4   Relative distribution of patents by six categories:
A: India and B: South Korea
Source: The author calculations using the US patent data.

short-cycle technologies. It has also steadily increased its level of technological diversification. In contrast, the graph for South Korea in Figure 2.4 is completely different from that of India. Figure 2.4 indicates the absolute dominance of short-cycle technologies in Korea (e.g., IT and telecom), and likewise, it shows a very small number of patents in long-cycle technologies. Consequently, South Korea has been classified as an imbalanced short-cycle NIS. Despite this narrow specialization, South Korea's level of technological diversification is high in terms of three-digit level classifications because many sub-classes exist within the same short-cycle, tech-based classes. Indeed, the above pattern illustrates why and how India and South Korea differ from each other.

In addition to its existing strength in pharmaceuticals, India has also enhanced its IT services since the 1990s. This has been led by three extremely big businesses: Infosys, Wipro, and Tata Consultancy Services, two of which are listed on US stock markets and have generated numerous US patents. India's rise in IT services is also considered a case of leapfrogging, in the sense that India did not follow the traditional evolution from agriculture to manufacturing and finally services but instead skipped the stage of manufacturing-led growth to leapfrog into service-led growth.[27] The size of India's service sector has surpassed that of the manufacturing sector, and never in India's post-war history did the manufacturing sector command the largest share of GDP. India's entrance into the service sector is also different from premature servicization in Africa, as India's service sector is not based on low value-added sectors or the urban informal sector; instead, it is based on high value-added sectors and is globalized. India has specialized in the niche area of IT services and has taken advantage of its population of highly skilled workers with engineering backgrounds and English-speaking skills. IT services are also a short-cycle technology sector with low barriers to entry. Thus, it makes sense for latecomers at the middle-income stage to specialize in IT services.

Overall, India's economy is an interesting case, in that it contains both an element of aggregate or macro-level leapfrogging and a balanced technological structure consisting of both short- and long-CTT sectors.

---

[27] India as a case of leapfrogging is first discussed in my own work, Lee et al. (2014).

2.6   A PATHWAY OUT OF THE TRAP: RESOURCE-BASED DEVELOPMENT IN CHILE AND MALAYSIA

The cluster analysis in Section 2.2 grouped eight emerging economies into the imbalanced trapped NIS cluster, which includes economies with per capita incomes less than 40% of the United States level that fall within the range of the MIT. As shown in Figures 2.1 and 2.2, many emerging economies, including Mexico, Brazil, and South Africa, have not closed the gap with the United States. However, upon closer inspection, the figures reveal that Malaysia and Chile have recently exceeded 40% of the level of US per capita income despite belonging to the imbalanced trapped group. Unlike other trapped countries, Chile and Malaysia have been growing at faster rates over the past decades. In 1990, both countries shared a similar per capita income level that was approximate to those of Brazil and Algeria yet lower than Mexico. By 2017, however, Chile and Malaysia surpassed Mexico and reached a per capita income of $23,000 or higher, placing both countries far ahead of Brazil and Algeria, whose per capita income remained below $15,000. According to Figure 2.2, Malaysia's per capita income reached 40.8% of the US level in 2013. Throughout the late 2010s, it remained at about 44% of the US level. According to Figure 2.1, Chile reached 40.7% of US per capita income in 2012 and stayed in this range up until the late 2010s. It can therefore be hypothesized that Chile and Malaysia seem to have grown beyond the MIT.

This begs the question of how both countries were able to escape the trap and which sectors, in particular, led economic and export growth. In research I undertook with colleagues (Lebdioui et al., 2021), we demonstrated that Chile and Malaysia were able to sustain economic growth not because of manufacturing but rather because of several leading resource-based sectors, such as petroleum, rubber, and palm oil in Malaysia and salmon, fruit, wine, and wood-based products in Chile.

To determine which sectors were responsible for growth beyond the MIT, colleagues and I compared the contribution of different sectors to the export performance of Chile and Malaysia according to several indicators, such as each sector's share of the country's total exports, trade balance, and their revealed comparative advantages (RCAs) over time. We focused on export performance because, compared to a factor such as trade openness (trade to GDP ratio), it is a much stronger binding factor for economic growth in the Global South.[28] Developing countries must earn hard currency by exporting to pay for the imported capital goods that are required for investments and sustained economic growth. Without strong exports, developing countries cannot be free from the balance of payment (BOP) deficit problem, which is a chronic problem in the Global South.

When we compared the export performance of the resources-based sector with the traditional leading sectors in Chile and Malaysia, we found that resource-based industries have been driving exports in both countries. In Chile, the combined export share of new resource-based industries (salmon, wine, fruit, and forestry) reached 28% in 2017, becoming the second-largest contributor to exports after mining (55%).[29] In Malaysia, the combined export share of resource-based industries (petroleum, palm oil, and rubber) reached 21% in 2017, which was second only to the electrical and electronic (E&E) sector (38%).[30]

More importantly, the ratio of trade surplus to total trade values in Chile in 2017 indicates that these resource sectors all achieved very high ratios (78% on average). This contrasts sharply with typical manufacturing sectors, such as machinery and transportation goods (−85%) and chemicals (−38%), which recorded very high deficit ratios. In Malaysia, the ratio of trade surplus to total trade in palm oil in 2017 reached as high as 87%, and in the combined resource sectors (palm oil, petroleum products, and rubber products), it reached 26%, which was still higher than the E&E sector (16%). In contrast, other

---

[28] This point is made in Brenton et al. (2010) and Ramanayake and Lee (2015).
[29] These figures are from UN trade data as cited in Lebdioui et al. (2021).
[30] These figures are from UN trade data as cited in Lebdioui et al. (2021).

manufacturing sectors, such as machinery and transport equipment (–33%) and chemical products (–13%), recorded very high deficits.

A similar analysis of the trends of trade surplus by sector over time confirms the rising contribution of the new resource sectors. Indeed, since 2007, the combined trade surplus of the key resource sectors in Malaysia has become bigger than that of the E&E sector.[31] Since 2007, the contribution of the E&E sector has been mostly stagnant. Additionally, in Chile, the contribution of mining to the total trade surplus peaked in 2011 and has declined since then, whereas the combined share of key resources has been steadily increasing, reaching almost half of the amount of mining. The steady rise of trade surpluses in these resource sectors is in stark contrast to the ever-increasing deficits in the machinery and equipment sectors and other manufacturing sectors in Chile.

Lastly, I discuss Chile and Malaysia's RCA by sector.[32] RCA values larger than 1 indicate that the products of that country are internationally competitive. The RCA values in key sectors of Malaysia confirm the international competitiveness of new resource sectors. First, the RCA value of palm oil products has been extremely high at 30. Rubber and fuels were below 1 in 1995; however, since the mid-2000s, both of their RCA values exceeded 1. In contrast, throughout this period, the automobile sector has always recorded an RCA value below 0.2. The RCA values in the resource sectors in Chile, including wine, fish, fruit, and wood-based products, have stayed above 6 since 1995, meaning that these sectors are extremely competitive internationally.[33] The most dramatic increase was achieved in wine, which increased from an RCA of 6 in 1995 to over 15 in 2017. In

[31] The details are from figures in Lebdioui et al. (2021).
[32] Detailed figures are available upon request. The RCA metric can be used to provide a general indication of a country's competitive export strengths. The RCA for country z in product g is defined as the ratio of the share of goods g in total exports of country z to the share of goods g in total exports of the world.
[33] Wood-based products here correspond to the sum of products with the following SITC Rev. 3 (Standard International Trade Classification) codes: 63, 64, 24, and 25. Wood-based sector and forestry sector are used interchangeably in this paper.

contrast, Chile's RCA in the mining sector (ores and metals) is much lower and has remained around 4 since 1995.

The above discussion has confirmed the rising contribution of resource sectors to exports, trade surpluses, and RCA. However, at this juncture, it is worth asking whether it is unprocessed resources that are generating less domestic value added. Therefore, we provide evidence that a progressive downstream value addition has taken place in the exports of these three sectors in Malaysia since the 1960s. The share of crude rubber and crude petroleum decreased from over 90% of total petroleum products in 1960 to less than 30% in the 2010s (Lebdioui et al., 2021). In contrast, rubber-based manufactured products as a share of total rubber exports increased to over 50% by 2012, while petroleum-based processed products as a share of total petroleum products increased from less than 10% to over 70% by 2014. The same shift from exporting crude to processed palm oil occurred in Malaysia, but an equivalent shift did not occur in Indonesia during the same period (Sato, 2016).

With regard to Chile, the new resource sectors are very sophisticated and technology intensive. For example, salmon production requires technologies such as cold storage systems and vaccines as well as the infrastructure to transport fresh products to distant markets (Lebdioui, 2020). Chile produces premium-quality fresh salmon and fresh berries that are exported to Japan and the United States. They are more value-added, knowledge-intensive, and technologically sophisticated than typical fish or fruit products. Wood-based products are not logs but rather include various kinds of value-added products such as pulp, paper, paperboard, cork, and furniture.

Successful catching up through specialization in resource-based sectors is consistent with the key argument of this study that latecomers should identify low barrier-to-entry sectors in the international division of labor. In fact, these resource-based sectors represent low barrier-to-entry sectors for many resource-rich emerging economies. Growth that relies on domestically available resources makes more sense in the post-pandemic era when countries are seeking more resilient development pathways that are less constrained by the risk of GVC disruption. One OECD report argued that strategies to recover from the COVID-19 crisis should include a strong structural component to reduce dependence on external financial flows and global markets and that countries should develop more value-added, knowledge-intensive, and industrialized economies (OECD, 2020). Latin American scholars (Perez, 2008) argued that emerging economies could use resource-based development to leapfrog into emerging technologies, such as IT. In contrast, my colleagues and I are of the view that resource sectors can serve as leading sectors that generate intra-sectoral diversification and the deepening of value chains. This contrasts with the existing argument that resource sectors are merely transitional sectors that generate financial revenue that can be utilized to promote economic diversification into non-resource sectors.

The next question to answer is how these two countries have been able to promote the upgrading of resource-based sectors as their respective engines of growth. In Malaysia, these resource-based industries have shown great degrees of linkage development, competitiveness, and technological sophistication, notably achieved through governmental support for R&D activities, which contrasts sharply with the weak performances of the Malaysian electronics and automotive sectors. In Chile, the emergence and growth of resource-based sectors into competitive export industries are related to long-term policies designed to strengthen local capabilities in production and innovation through both vertical and horizontal interventions. Section 3.2 of Chapter 3 will elaborate on the role of industrial policy and local ownership.

2.7 SUMMARY AND CONCLUDING REMARKS

This study used US patent data for 32 economies to measure, classify, and analyze the evolution and performance of their NIS, with a focus on economies that sustained economic growth beyond the middle-income stage. Cluster analysis identified several varieties of NIS that are comparable to the various types of capitalist econo-mies. The analysis showed that in the NIS of advanced economies, the values of the five NIS component variables are all similarly high (and thus balanced), whereas the NIS values of emerging economies tend to be imbalanced and relatively uneven across the five NIS vari-ables. These findings are consistent with existing studies (Cirera & Maloney, 2017), indicating that multiple parts of typical developing countries' NIS are underdeveloped.

Importantly, this study identified multiple pathways for achieving economic catch-up from middle-income status to high-income status. One of the identified pathways corresponded to the balanced catching-up NIS cluster, which includes the countries of Ireland, Spain, Hong Kong, and Singapore, as well as the two large economies of India and Russia. The other pathway corresponded to the imbalanced catching-up NIS cluster, which includes the two Asian tigers of Korea and Taiwan and, more recently, China. This bodes well for the future of China in terms of the prospect of the country growing beyond middle-income status. We also identified a third group, the trapped NIS cluster, consisting of economies per-ceived to be stuck in the MIT.

The imbalanced catching-up NIS in East Asia is character-ized by an imbalance of very short CTT and low originality yet very high localization and diversification. The trapped NIS, in contrast, displays the exact opposite attributes. In comparison, the balanced catching-up cluster has equally balanced medium values for all of the NIS variables. The rapid economic catch-up of the countries in the imbalanced NIS group can be explained by the fact that these econo-mies have increasingly specialized in short CTT, thereby increasing their respective levels of knowledge localization and technological diversification.

In comparison, the alternative pathway of the balanced catching-up group shows that extreme specialization in either long- or short-CTT sectors is not always necessary for achieving a decent degree of technological diversification and decentralization. The long

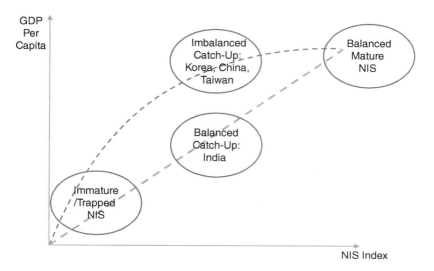

FIGURE 2.5 Two alternative pathways of catching up: balanced and imbalanced

CTT is a desirable feature, as shown by all long-CTT specialization in advanced economies; however, long CTT specialization is risky at the transition stage because it is associated with high barrier-to-entry sectors. In sum, these various patterns are still consistent with some correspondence between levels of CTT, localization, and diversification in latecomer economies. In other words, short-CTT specialization corresponds to high localization and diversification, whereas long-CTT specialization corresponds to low localization and diversification. Meanwhile, medium CTT corresponds to a medium level of localization and diversification.

The existence of two catching-up paths (balanced and imbalanced) corresponds to the classic debate about the two development strategies, namely the balanced (Nurkse, 1953) and the imbalanced strategy (Hirschman, 1958). Figure 2.5 illustrates these two alternative pathways. The graph indicates first that at earlier stages of economic development, the latecomer economies all tend to possess and start from an imbalanced trapped NIS. After this, either a linear or nonlinear pathway becomes available for them to develop into balanced mature NIS. The linear path is a path of balanced development that corresponds to the balanced NIS.

The nonlinear path is the path that East Asian economies have followed. That is, it is the imbalanced catching-up NIS pathway of specializing in short-cycle technologies, which is different from the long-cycle technologies of mature NIS economies. This path is thus a detour that begins with short-cycle sectors and then transitions to long-cycle ones. Imbalanced development also includes a detour from centralization to decentralization in terms of firm size distribution. In other words, these East Asian economies experienced the increasing importance of big businesses during the catching-up stage, given that these economies had experienced an increase rather than a decrease in the concentration of innovators within big businesses. In sum, the nonlinear pattern of transitional specialization into short-CTT sectors led by big businesses is an important element of the imbalanced catching-up pathway. This detour is necessary to circumvent entry barriers to high-end and value-added sectors and enable countries to seek out niches and concentrate resources and competencies in the hands of leading big businesses.

One important observation of this chapter is the correspondence between various NIS types and experiences of catching up or falling behind. The five NIS clusters were shown to correspond largely with various economic outcomes.[34] On the basis of these findings, one important policy implication is that the currently trapped economies may have not just one but several alternative pathways to overcome the MIT. India is also an interesting case because it is still a low middle-income economy and a member of the balanced NIS cluster, which may bode well for the future of its economy. India's catch-up is currently driven by both long-cycle

---

[34] Of course, there are outliers like Japan and Israel, which did not join either of the two catching-up NIS groups. It is interesting to note that whereas in a previous study (Lee, 2013c). I put all four Asian tigers in the same group, this study now shows that they followed two different paths at later stages, with Korea and Taiwan following the imbalanced NIS path and Hong Kong and Singapore following the balanced NIS path.

sectors, such as pharmaceuticals, and short-cycle sectors, such as IT services. India entered the pharmaceutical sector at a very early stage when entry barriers were relatively low.

While the balanced catching-up group features some balance between manufacturing and services, another possible combination may be a balance between manufacturing and resource-based sectors. This possibility is discussed in relation to the outstanding success of Chile and Malaysia, which both show signs of escaping the MIT not through manufacturing success but through the emergence of several resource-based sectors that are leading exporters of high value-added goods. Growth that relies on domestically available resources makes more sense in the post-pandemic era when countries are seeking more resilient development pathways that are less constrained by the risk of GVC disruption.

Based on the above discussion, we can make a final observation about a possible way out for economies now in the MIT. For countries with a national economy of a certain size and some resource endowments, such as Brazil, South Africa, and Argentina, one option may be a "balanced catching up" that promotes not only manufacturing but also resource-based sectors and IT services. These countries can learn from the experiences of Russia and India, which belong to the balanced catching-up NIS cluster, as well as from Chile and Malaysia. This option might also be applicable to countries such as Mexico, Thailand, and Turkey, which have had some experience in traditional manufacturing. Like Malaysia, they have also encountered difficulty in upgrading into high-end or value-added segments of manufacturing owing to high entry barriers.

3 From Global–Local Interfaces to Local Value Added, Knowledge, and Ownership

3.1 INTRODUCTION

By definition, latecomer economies from the developing world are late entrants in the global economy and are relatively lacking in capital, skill, and technologies. Thus, they have to rely on foreign sources for these resources and capabilities in the form of FDI, licensing and importation of capital goods, and so on. Furthermore, given the lack of stable sources of export earnings and convertible currencies, competitiveness in the world export market is most vital for latecomer economies to earn the dollars to pay for imported capital goods and technologies. Because FDI firms are always ready to move to other production sites offering lower wages, and tend to become increasingly reluctant to transfer or sell technology as latecomers keep catching up, local ownership of knowledge and technologies is important in the middle-income stage or later. In this sense, the ultimate challenge for latecomer economies is how to eventually create domestic sources of innovation and economic growth.

While all the latecomer economies have been open to inviting FDI for their development, they have found it hard to take advantage of FDI to bring up indigenous capabilities in production and innovation. Marin and Bell (2006) observe that the spillover effect of FDI does not occur if host countries do not focus on the linkages between FDI and the domestic economy. While Taiwan has been seen to rely more on MNCs than South Korea, the success of the Taiwanese catch-up is also supported by the eventual rise of indigenous firms (Amsden & Chu, 2003).

These observations are consistent with the so-called "in–out–in again" hypothesis (Lee et al., 2018), so that while latecomers are to be open to GVCs by inviting FDI or MNCs at an early stage of development, they have to create locally owned production and innovation capabilities and thereby increase domestic value added and reduce the backward linkage to GVCs (share of foreign value added in gross exports); then, at the final stage with enhanced local capabilities, they may be open or engage with more GVCs again.

If this dimension of the global–local interfaces is wrongly managed, latecomers often fall into the liberalization trap where local capabilities fail to grow after international liberalization but MNCs become and remain dominant in local economies (Bresser-Pereira et al., 2020). The worst consequence of this trap is premature de-industrialization which often leads to an MIT. Thus, one important argument in this book is that managing the global–local interfaces is a key determinant of building up the technological capabilities and long-term success of latecomer economies. This chapter will elaborate the importance of local value added, knowledge, and ownership, drawing upon several cases, such as resource sectors in Chile and Malaysia (Lebdioui et al., 2021), the auto sectors in four countries (Lee, Qu, & Mao, 2021), and three regions specializing in the same IT sector in Asia (Kim & Lee, 2022). Although the cases in the three sections are originally based on a separate regional, sectoral, or national innovation system perspective, they will be reinterpreted in terms of a new focus on the global–local interfaces and the roles of local ownership and knowledge.

First, section two will elaborate on how local sources of innovation and value added have been created to serve as new engines of export and growth in several resource sectors in Chile and Malaysia (Lebdioui et al., 2021), using the GVC framework. As mentioned in the last section (Section 2.6) of the preceding chapter, these resource sectors are important because they show that achieving growth beyond the middle-income stage has become possible not owing to traditional manufacturing, but to the emergence of new globally competitive resource sectors as exporters. These two economies may be the first example of escaping the MIT after the early incidence of South Korea or Taiwan. Thus, the emergence and growth of several resource sectors in Chile (wine, fruit, and wood products) and Malaysia (palm oil, rubber products, and petroleum products) as the leading export engines will be discussed to show that this success is led by the emergence and growth of locally owned firms, and that their emergence and growth did not occur spontaneously but because of policy intervention by the government.

Section three will focus on the auto sectors of Thailand, Malaysia, and China in comparison with Korea (Lee, Qu, & Mao, 2021). It will be argued that local ownership and knowledge should also be subject to global market discipline to be able to grow into competitive forces for innovation and growth. The auto sector in Malaysia led by a local brand, Proton, used to be tightly locally owned and controlled but was not export-oriented and lacked global market discipline, and eventually failed to rise. In comparison, the auto sector in Thailand has been doing fine, but is still a limited success with regard to domestic value added due to the lack of local ownership. In contrast, China's automotive sector is neither monopolized nor dominated by foreign joint ventures (JVs). Strong entries by locally owned firms since WTO membership provided fierce competition to incumbent foreign JVs. Support policies have also become more consistent and confident in the 2000s, combined with the aggressive firm-level responses of in-house technological efforts (Chu, 2011; Lee et al., 2017). Overall, China is the case most similar to South Korea in terms of local ownership and support policies, with a slight difference, in that the former relies on discipline from huge domestic markets, whereas the latter relies on discipline from global markets.

Section four discusses the three regions of Penang, Shenzhen, and Taipei in Asia (Kim & Lee, 2022), which all feature the same short CTT-based IT sector but have experienced different paths of development, such as fast catching up in Shenzhen vs. slow catching up in Penang. These deviant pathways will be explained by the various patterns of ownership of firms in the regions, such as the emergence of strong local ownership of firms in Shenzhen vs. persistent dominancy by MNCs in Penang, besides the role of industrial policy.

3.2 GLOBAL–LOCAL INTERFACES AND INDUSTRIAL POLICY IN CHILE AND MALAYSIA

3.2.1 *New Resource Sectors in Chile: Salmon, Forestry, Fruit, and Wine*

Section 3.6 in the preceding chapter observes that Chile has been achieving growth beyond the middle-income stage, not owing to the mining sector, but to the emergence of new globally competitive tradable sectors such as salmon, fruit, wine, and forestry. Regarding the growth of these sectors, first, they have not grown naturally and gradually by market forces but are promoted by public intervention, in particular by long-term investments in each of these sectors (Lebdioui, 2019b, 2020; Pietrobelli, 1998). For example, the comparative advantage Chile developed in the salmon and fresh fruit industries was not natural, but instead was acquired through the planned cultivation and accumulation of human capital, technology, and learning, combined with favorable natural endowments. Second, foreign knowledge that was transferred in various modes and further cultivated and developed in the local context played an important role. Third, there was the eventual emergence of local ownership of firms in these sectors, although there were more FDI firms than locally owned firms at the initial stage.

A brief explanation of these three points is provided as follows, relying upon Lebdioui et al (2021) and others.

First, **salmon** was not in the seas near Chile but was cultivated through a series of efforts since 1969 (first through the Japan–Chile Salmon Project) and has been more successful since the 1980s with efforts by Fundación Chile (FCh). It stepped in to acquire Domsea Farms, transfer technology from Norway to Chile, and experiment with the farming of various salmon species under different conditions to identify ways to make salmon farming commercially viable. Salmones Antártica, the company created by FCh, reached production levels of around 1,000 tons by 1988 and transmitted a clear message to potential entrepreneurs that the salmon industry was indeed profitable (Lebdioui, 2019a). The experience of this company was then copied by nascent firms, which increased in number from around four in 1980 to 219 in 1997 (Iizuka & Gebreeyesus, 2017). The FCh has also played a key role in experimentation in new activities with latent comparative advantage, developing pioneers and then promoting their role as examples, and in technology diffusion. The FCh's mandate as a nonprofit semipublic agency enabled it to treat R&D and technology as "public goods" to be widely diffused among local entrepreneurs to stimulate emulation and reduce entry barriers to new industries (Hosono, 2016; Lebdioui, 2019a). As local capabilities developed, firms started to develop their own technologies to meet their unique challenges and environment (Hosono, 2010, 2016; Iizuka & Gebreeyesus, 2012). For example, alongside salmon farming, Chile has developed patents for salmon vaccines and biotesting, and developed quality control labs (Hosono, 2010). Currently, the salmon industry in Chile is a thoroughly internationalized activity, with the strong presence of both local and foreign firms.

Regarding the **fruit** sector, Chile has also become successful in exporting more than twenty types of new fruit, including berries, whereas it used to export mainly grapes and apples in the 1960s; these changes were made by planned action including the founding of Corporación de Fomento de la Producción (CORFO), a national production development corporation (Bravo-Ortega & Eterovic, 2015), followed by the Chile–California Program in 1965 between the Universidad de Chile and the University of California and funded by the Ford Foundation. The program entailed sending more than eighty Chilean graduate students to study agricultural economics in California in order to learn how to cultivate and export fresh fruit; the FCh also pioneered the cultivation of berries in the south of Chile, showing entrepreneurs that berry cultivation in Chile was possible. This role of public entrepreneurship resulted in the introduction and development of a new product as well as new transversal technologies and capabilities, including cold storage systems, which are required to ensure product quality (Lebdioui, 2019a). In the fresh fruit export sector, ProChile, an export promotion agency, helped export market access, while other state agencies played an important role in the development of standards and logistics. Finally, in contrast to the widespread view that fruit cultivation in Chile has been dominated by MNCs, foreign firms only controlled about 23.6% of fresh fruit exports in 1984 and 30.5% in 1991 (Korzeniewicz et al., 1995; Lebdioui et al., 2021).

In the case of **forestry**, CORFO has subsidized investments in the planting of pinus radiata, a non-native tree, since the 1960s (Pietrobelli, 1998). In the forestry sector, technological and industrial upgrading took place as a result of subsidies for plantation activities, bans on exports of raw wood and debarked logs, as well as the attraction of investments from leading producers of wood fiber and forestry-based products (Lebdioui, 2019a, 2019b). The forestry sector is the one that the Chilean government has targeted most explicitly since the 1960s (Pietrobelli, 1998). At the time, the government made "a strategic bet on a nonexistent but potentially profitable sector," as it was known that radiata pine grew faster in certain parts of Chile than the rest of the world (Agosin et al., 2010, p. 7). Nowadays, forestry exports constitute the fourth largest exports of Chile with 9% of the total. In forestry, a majority of foreign companies carried out investments in Chile through alliances with domestic companies already established in the sector. Since the mid-1990s, foreign investment in the sector has continued to exist, but on a small scale (Borregaard et al., 2008).

In the **wine** sector, the role of the state has been key, but mostly through horizontal policies, instead of vertical ones, as in the salmon and fruit sectors (Giuliani et al., 2011). That said, while the wine sector's emergence in the export basket and its technological upgrading are mostly the result of foreign investments, it is worth noting that

Chile was already a producer in this industry at the time. Therefore, while it is a successful instance of export "discovery" favored by foreign investment, it is not a case of product discovery, as in the cases of the salmon and fruit sectors. The wine industry has constantly relied on flows of foreign oenologists and technology experts (Giuliani et al., 2011) as well as companies. In the wine sector, FDI enabled knowledge transfer related to upgrading production functions such as grape growing, wine making, and wine marketing. This favored access to distribution channels in the major markets and the improvement of the image of Chilean wine (Björk, 2005; Kunc, 2007; Kunc & Bas, 2009). Since then, over 200 globally competitive Chilean-owned firms have emerged in the wine sector, with more than USD 1 billion in exports (Pallares-Barbera et al., 2012).

In summary, public institutions and industrial policy have been key in the process of capabilities accumulation that shaped the emergence of these new industries in Chile, through R&D support, funding for technical training and human capital accumulation, regulatory and quality control for export markets, trade promotion, and technology diffusion. Owing to intervention by foreign and public agencies, one essential feature of these nascent industries is the integration of imported knowledge and technologies with local knowledge. Following this, the eventual emergence of local ownership in these new resources sectors had an influence on value addition outcomes in Chile, which became the basis for the sustained growth of exports and per capita income of the whole economy.

In contrast to these new resource sectors, copper, a traditional resource sector, was different in terms of the role of local knowledge and ownership. In the early stages of mining development, foreign-owned firms had no impact on the technological catching up among local suppliers. The situation changed with the nationalization wave in the 1970s, which led to incentives and expectations for local suppliers to collaborate with the state-owned firm, Codelco (Bravo-Ortega & Muñoz, 2015, p. 12). Codelco's vertical disintegration during the 1980s allowed local suppliers to join the supply chains and increase their technological capabilities. However, the situation has now been reversed; foreign firms produce two-thirds of Chile's overall mining output and local suppliers still struggle to compete with foreign providers. The limited success of the mining sector in Chile is also compared with the sector in Australia where local ownership is dominant; 84% of mining suppliers in Australia are domestically owned, and have accumulated domestic capabilities to produce various technologically sophisticated inputs for mining production (Bravo-Ortega & Muñoz, 2015).

3.2.2 New Resource Sectors in Malaysia: Rubber, Palm Oil, and Petro Products

As one of the second-generation Asian tigers, Malaysia had promoted IT manufacturing or the E&E sector since as early as the 1970s, initially led by the Penang area, which served as one of the earliest manufacturing hubs for MNCs in Asia[1]. In the E&E sector, the government adopted a rather "minimalist" approach, mostly providing basic infrastructure and government services, and promoting FDI by offering tax incentives and low wages (Rasiah, 2017). The initial outcome was the successful growth of low value-added, labor-intensive, FDI-led manufacturing. However, the long-term sustainability of this strategy was not certain, because Malaysia also faced rising wage rates, while other neighboring countries were offering lower wages to attract FDI. This forced Malaysia to move into high-end goods in order to be able to afford high wages for its workers.

In the meantime, the E&E sector in Malaysia was not innovative enough to compete with high-wage innovators from the top, and, at the same time, their wages were already too high to compete with low-wage manufacturers. This is a typical symptom of the middle-income trap (World Bank, 2012), and some studies discussed this possibility with regard to Malaysia (Rasiah, 2006; Yusuf & Nabeshima, 2009). In other words, the E&E sector achieved some form of catch-up

---

[1] This sub-section relies heavily on this author's work, namely Lebdioui et al. (2021).

with regard to sales and capital accumulation, but not much in terms of technological innovation (Rasiah, 2006).

This situation is partly due to the fact that there was no explicit industrial policy aiming at developing indigenous technologies in the E&E sector until the 2000s. The initial objective underlying the promotion of the E&E sector was indeed employment generation. It is only since the 2000s that more efforts have been made to move domestic firms toward more value-added activities with industrial master plans, tax incentives, R&D grants, and state investments. For example, in the semiconductor segment, targeted investments in high-end activities such as chip design, wafer fabrication, and support R&D have taken place since 2005 (Rasiah, 2017). Despite recent attempts to increase local content and manufacturing value added, the results remained limited (Yean, 2015; Lebdioui, 2019b, 2020). Malaysia's shares of global high-tech exports have decreased in recent decades, and the country is losing its labor cost advantage to neighboring countries (e.g., Vietnam). In the meantime, technology diffusion and domestic linkages remain constrained by the lack of technology transfer by MNCs in Malaysia (Cherif & Hasanov, 2015; Raj-Reichert, 2020).

In summary, the mixed success of E&E can be attributed to a combination of a lack of explicit industrial policy and a critical mass of locally owned firms vis-à-vis the continuing dominance of MNCs in the sector. Again, the dominance of MNCs implies less room for state intervention and less interest in building local capabilities, suppliers, and linkages.

Thus, as pointed out in Section 2.4 of Chapter 2, the driving forces for Malaysia beyond the MIT are not traditional E&E sectors, but the resource-based sectors of petroleum, rubber, and palm oil. Resource-based manufacturing in Malaysia consists of the production and export of rubber-based products (such as latex goods and tires), petroleum-based products (such as petrochemicals, plastics, fuel, and synthetic rubber) and palm oil-based products (such as kernel cake and oleochemicals). In what follows, we elaborate on these sectors, focusing how this success has been possible, relying upon the literature (Lebdioui, 2019a, 2020; Lebdioui et al., 2021).

First of all, it can be argued that the rise of these sectors as producers and exporters of high value-added goods seems not to have been due to free market forces, but to purposeful plans and promotion by the government, such as fiscal and R&D incentives, and quality control services (Lebdioui, 2019b). In these sectors, the role of state-owned firms has been critical, such as Petronas in the petroleum sector, or that of other public agencies, such as the Malaysian Rubber Board (MRB) in rubber, and the Federal Land Development Agency (FELDA) and Malaysian Palm Oil Board (MPOB) as a merged entity of the former Palm Oil Registration and Licensing Authority (PORLA) and Palm Oil Research Institute of Malaysia (PORIM) (Oikawa, 2016). What follows is an elaboration of each sector.

The **petroleum** sector in Malaysia was initially dominated by multinational oil companies, which remained the main providers of upstream technology in the early periods of resource exploitation, especially given the context of Malaysia's technology-demanding offshore and deep-water fields. To overcome this situation, the government of Malaysia established a state-owned enterprise, Petronas, in 1974, which became possible by proclamation of the Petroleum Development Act (PDA), and the associated Production-Sharing Contracts (PSC). The objective of the PDA was to gain greater national control over petroleum resources, to provide affordable petroleum resources to the local market to form the basis for capital- and energy-intensive industries, and to encourage production linkages in both upstream and downstream activities (Nordås et al., 2003). Petronas has also gradually developed capabilities and upgraded to higher-value activities.

The government also initiated a holistic approach to industrial policy combining local content requirements, tax incentives, skills transfer (through technical and specialized universities), and state-led investments and opportunities for learning by doing (Lebdioui, 2020). These tools have been successful in enhancing the industrial capabilities of local suppliers by allowing local firms to benefit from more stable intra-industry relationships, exposure to best practices, and improved quality standards, as well as marketing capabilities. This holistic approach led to the accumulation of the capabilities needed for knowledge-intensive activities along the petroleum value chain.

Petronas was a key vehicle for this industrial policy drive as it ran programs such as the Petronas Vendor Development Program to promote local suppliers. Petronas' partners are required to pay it an annual research contribution, the "Research Cess," to promote joint R&D (PSC, Arts 9.1 and 9.2). Thus, the growth of local companies followed that of Petronas, and 74% of the total value of contracts in upstream activities in the petroleum sector was granted to local companies by 1995 (Tordo & Anouti, 2013). Given the key role in promoting production linkages through several initiatives, it is doubtful whether similar value addition results would have been achieved if international oil corporations controlled the sector. Petronas itself has grown into a fully integrated international oil and gas company, which operates in more than thirty countries. It is now on the list of the global Fortune 500 companies.

The plantations in both the **rubber** and **palm oil** sectors were all foreign owned since the colonial period, and there was no interest in increasing domestic value added compared to foreign value added. The largely European-controlled plantation companies preferred to export crude palm oil and did not see many gains in relocating their vegetable oil processing facilities in Malaysia. After the initial entry point into the foreign-dominated GVCs during colonial times, Malaysia broke up those foreign-led GVCs through nationalization of ownership as it executed a hostile takeover of three British palm oil and rubber plantation conglomerates listed on the London Stock Exchange by Malaysian public capital in 1981 (Lebdioui, 2019b; Oikawa, 2016). The interest in processing palm oil and natural rubber locally has increased since then. In addition, in the rubber sector, a large difference in purchasing behavior between domestic and foreign firms can be noted. Foreign-owned firms have fewer forward and backward linkages to other manufacturers in the Malaysian economy than domestically owned firms.

Interestingly, Malaysia's efforts to stimulate industrial upgrading were met with counter-attacks from the incumbent firms. For example, Malaysia's exports of processed palm oil in the 1970s were blocked by the European common market, which practiced tariff escalation to make sure that refining capacity would remain in Europe. In order to counter the EU import duty structure, the Malaysian government had initially decided to introduce an export duty on crude palm oil. After further tariffs escalation in the EU in the 1990s from about 100% in the 1970s to more than 200% in the 1990s (Gopal, 2001), most of the market deals for Malaysian processed palm oil were signed through government-to-government partnerships under so-called barter arrangements.[2] As a result of this barter trade that enabled export markets to be secured, palm oil refining activities in Malaysia considerably increased and became the most competitive internationally within ten years, achieving both economies of scale and scope. Such upgrading into exporting processed palm oil, rather than crude oil, would not have been possible if there was no change of ownership from foreign to local. Another incentive for processed palm oil rather than crude oil was higher export taxes on crude oil and lower taxes for more processed oil, which made domestic prices of crude and processed oil deviate from the international market prices (Jomo & Rock, 1998; Oikawa, 2016).

This upgrading in the palm oil sector has been backed by increased R&D efforts, which were also led by the MPOB or PORIM before it was merged with PORLA to become the MPOB in 2000 (Oikawa, 2016). The Board or PORIM established in 1979 has been responsible for R&D on all palm oil-related activities, starting with chemistry, quality, analytical techniques, transportation and handling of palm oil products, and later expanding to R&D in oleochemicals and processed palm kernel oil, following the recommendations

---

[2] Barter grade is a system of trade in which participants in a transaction directly exchange goods or services for other goods and services of equivalent value without the use of money.

of the Industrial Master Plans (Oikawa, 2016).[3] Financial support for R&D from the government also targeted these activities, ranging from oleochemical byproducts to environmentally friendly cultivation and manufacturing methods. Such R&D efforts enabled firms to increase value added in existing products, as well as the introduction of new products in markets (such as biodiesel, specialty fats and vitamin A) (Rasiah & Shahrin, 2006). Government-funded R&D through the MPOB has also been conducted to stimulate innovation toward oil palm biomass, but it is too soon to assess whether those efforts will be fruitful. Indeed, while considerable ground has been covered to pursue value addition to processed palm oil and oleochemicals, further efforts are required to move toward highly sophisticated value-added palm oil-based products (such as biodiesel and specialty oleochemicals).

In the **rubber** sector, the MRB has become the world's leading authority in rubber-related R&D, and has accumulated expertise across the whole rubber value chain from cultivation to plantation management and rubber manufacturing techniques and rubber product marketing (Goldthorpe, 2015). Several Malaysian-owned firms have become world-leading producers of rubber-based products such as latex gloves and prophylactic goods, in highly competitive markets with low-cost producers (i.e., China and India) and other natural rubber producing countries (i.e., Thailand and Vietnam).

3.3 GLOBAL–LOCAL INTERFACES AND INDUSTRIAL POLICY IN AUTO SECTORS IN ASIA

The three countries of Malaysia, Thailand, and China all desired to promote their automotive industries, which are usually regarded as an important industry, with strong backward and forward linkages. They are considered latecomers given that their automotive sectors started in the post-war period or even the 1960s. Therefore,

---

[3] Research grants in the palm oil industry amounted to around US$565 million between 2000 and 2010 (Rasiah & Chandran, 2015).

these countries have to rely on foreign technology by either importing licensed technology or joining GVCs. Although all of them used
industrial policies to increase local value added, their actual growth
paths have diverged.[4] This section elaborates on these cases, relying
upon my work with colleagues.[5]

A comparison of Malaysia, Thailand, and China would be of interest because they all attempted to implement local content requirements
(LCRs) in their automotive sectors before they joined the WTO and
later cancelled the policy, resulting in divergent outcomes.[6] Thailand
has approximately fourteen automakers, but all of them are majority
owned by foreign companies, especially Japanese. Although Thailand
has become the largest automobile exporter among the Association of
Southeast Asian Nations (ASEAN) countries, the amount of domestic
value added generated is unclear, given the dominance of MNCs (Tai &
Ku, 2013). This question can be answered by examining several GVC
indicators (Lee, Qu, & Mao, 2021). By contrast, Malaysia has focused on
establishing a local brand and is the only one that has a national brand
in the ASEAN. The first Malaysian car – the Proton Saga – has successfully occupied the domestic market. However, the brand failed to
compete in the international market. Thus, the question for Malaysia
is why locally owned carmakers, such as Proton, have not been able
to maintain that advantage, failing to increase not only the domestic
value added but also the export orientation.

In contrast, the automotive sector in China now features
fierce competition among foreign JVs and indigenous manufacturers, despite the initial dominance of the former, including one with
Volkswagen (Chu, 2011). Indigenous automakers, such as Chery and

---

[4] Baldwin (2016) observed that, different from the failed "build strategy" in Malaysia,
a successful case is the "join strategy" of the automotive sector in Thailand, where
Japanese firms established factories in Thailand that focused on the assembly and promotion of Thai component suppliers under LCRs (pp. 250–254).

[5] This sub-section relies on this author's work, namely Lee, Qu, & Mao (2021).

[6] LCR policy is to increase local content ratio or localization rate, which is defined as
the percentage of the value of domestically produced parts or components in the value
of finished products (Thuy, 2008).

Geely, entered the market after China joined the WTO and rapidly captured market shares in the 2000s (Hu, 2009; Lee et al., 2017). So, the question is how China has been able to upgrade its automotive sector with domestic value added increasing remarkably over time.

3.3.1 Three Factors for Successful Upgrading

In what follows, we focus on the question of what has brought about divergent outcomes in the auto sectors of the three countries. Determining the success (or failure) conditions of industrial policy is of particular interest. Our focus is on the following three factors: ownership of target firms (local vs. foreign), market structure (discipline from market vs. entrenchment from monopoly), and firm-level effort and strategies.

First, given that LCRs are oriented toward independent industrial development imposing restrictions on foreign-made goods in a national economy, they are often compared with a liberal policy stance emphasizing the positive roles of FDI. Amsden's research (1989) is one of the early studies that emphasize the importance of promoting local ownership rather than passive reliance on FDI. Lee et al. (2017) and Lee and Lim (2001) observe that FDI can be an important channel for gaining foreign knowledge, but tends to interfere with the eventual growth of indigenous technological capabilities. These observations are based on comparable examples in the automotive sectors of China and Korea (e.g., Geely and Chery vs. Shanghai Volkswagen and First Auto Works in China; and Hyundai Motors vs. Daewoo, a JV with GM in Korea). Indigenous ownership becomes more important at a later stage because foreign firms tend to become increasingly reluctant to transfer or sell technology.[7]

---

[7] An example from Lee et al. (2017) is the mobile handset sector in China. To take advantage of the large market, MNCs formed various JVs with indigenous firms to produce mobile phones in China. Nevertheless, in 2001, most MNCs stopped their JV collaborations after China joined the WTO. The same occurrence was observed in Korea when Korean IC chip firms caught up with foreign firms, and the latter became increasingly reluctant to provide designs for chip production (Kim, 1997a; Lee & Lim, 2001).

Specifically, in terms of upgrading in GVCs, Lee et al. (2018) argue that national ownership is eventually necessary to build local value chains for upgrading.

Second, we determine that LCRs are effective when combined with discipline from either domestic or global markets. Aghion et al. (2015) regard competition as a precondition of an effective industrial policy, including LCRs. Greenaway (1992) also considers market structure as a key factor that affects the successful implementation of LCRs. Hao et al. (2010), in a study on the British wind power sector, state that a stable and sizable domestic market is an important factor that can determine the success of LCRs. In the case of Korea, fierce competition is observed mainly among four carmakers, Hyundai, Daewoo, Kia, and SsangYong, although foreign ownership remains limited (Lee, 2011). Furthermore, these brands have been oriented toward the global market from the beginning. Given the oligopolistic market structure protected by high tariffs during the 1970s and 1980s, certain rents are associated with such protection but are used to pay for capital investments that are required to survive in the global market (Jung & Lee, 2010); one of the key elements of industrial policy in Korea is the close linkage between export performance and privileged access to cheap loans and other support measures. The effects of such a combination of oligopolistic rents and discipline from the global market on productivity growth are confirmed by econometric studies by Jung and Lee (2010).

Third, the effectiveness of LCRs is also affected by how firms respond to such policies, along with supplementary ones. Lahiri and Ono (1998), Davies and Ellis (2007), and Hao et al. (2010) also observe that LCRs cannot be effective when implemented alone without support policies, such as other taxations and preferential loans. However, the most critical factor should be the firms' right response to these policies in the form of putting increasing effort into building their technological capabilities. One might reason that the combination of local ownership and pressure from market competition may result in firms exerting more effort for technological innovation and their own capabilities. Therefore, we still consider additional firm-level responses and strategies as one of the three factors to be considered.

The three requirements mentioned above for a successful upgrade to GVC by industrial policy, such as LCRs, can be discussed with the Korean automotive sector as an example. Over the past fifty years, the Korean automotive industry has grown from a small auto parts supplier to a global center of automotive companies (Lee, 2011; Ravenhill, 2003). Independence in terms of ownership is considered a factor that helps Korean automotive firms achieve industrial upgrades from OEM to original brand manufacturing (OBM) (Lee & Lim, 2001). Hyundai, one of the leading Korean brand cars, chose an independent R&D strategy to develop its own engines after Mitsubishi refused to provide the engine technology. According to Ravenhill (2003), the reason why Hyundai can increase their localization rate faster than other Korean automotive producers is their explicit strategy to avoid dependence on partners and integrate licensed technology from various countries to develop its own technology, including their engine. Although Hyundai Motors was initially a JV, foreign ownership (by Mitsubishi) was limited or less than 20%, and eventually bought out by the Hyundai side. An interesting contrast can be made with the case of Daewoo, a former JV with GM with a share of 50%. In this JV, the perception of Daewoo was that GM was reluctant to transfer core technologies to Daewoo and was not willing to allow Daewoo's foreign expansion plans (Auty, 1994; Ravenhill, 2005). This experience underscores the limitation of the JV strategy without local ownership and control. A similar story of a failure involving a JV is the case of Guangzhou-Peugeot in China (Lee, Qu, & Mao, 2021).

3.3.2   Common Starts with Divergent Ends in Malaysia and Thailand

3.3.2.1   Common Starts

The automotive industries in Thailand and Malaysia began in the 1960s. Initially, both countries aimed to build their own automotive industry, thus restricting importation of CBUs (completely built units, namely fully assembled cars) by complicating its process, charging high import taxes, and charging lower tariffs to CKD (complete knock down) cars.[8] Given such policies, the local automotive assembly industry achieved rapid development in both countries in a short time, although the main carmakers are foreign JVs (Tai & Ku, 2013). Both countries desired to restrict foreign ownership in such JV cases to allow domestic partners to have majority ownership. In the 1980s, the direction of the two countries diverged, with Malaysia heading on a nationalist road of promoting locally owned brand cars and Thailand relying on foreign (mainly Japanese) carmakers.

In 1982, the Malaysian government declared the "National Car Project" to establish a national champion brand, Proton, through cooperation among national enterprises, the Heavy Industries Corporation of Malaysia Berhad (HICOM) and Mitsubishi Corporation. With the government's support, Proton became the leading brand in the Malaysian car market at that time (Athukorala, 2014; Wad & Govindaraju, 2011; Fujita, 1998). By contrast, Thailand took advantage of the eagerness of Japanese carmakers to establish assembly lines overseas, seeking low labor costs to offset the cost increases associated with yen appreciation after the 1985 Plaza Accord. The Thai government initiated a series of favorable tax incentives to attract Japanese investment (Tai & Ku, 2013). They also loosened the former policy of restricting foreign ownership in assembly manufacturers in the early 1990s. In 1997, the government officially cancelled the restriction of majority ownership to be held by a Thai national (Intarakumnerd & Gerdsri, 2014). Consequently, Ford, Chrysler, and GM from the United States established assembly factories in Thailand. Their suppliers of parts and components then followed. Japanese manufacturers also built new factories in Thailand in the 1990s. After

---

[8] Before the 1990s, the Thailand government used to charge import tariffs as high as 300% for passenger vehicles larger than 2,300 cc. Imports of passenger vehicles lower than 2,300 cc were not allowed (Natsuda & Thoburn, 2013).

several years of promotion through policies, the MNC automotive suppliers in Thailand increased to 300 manufacturers from 1987 to 2005 (Wad, 2009). Foreign ownership has taken over Thailand's domestic market not only in assembly, but also parts and supplies to a lesser degree.

3.3.3   Strong Exports with Less Domestic Value Added in Thailand

Ownership in the Thai automotive sector is basically characterized by foreign dominance in parts suppliers and final assemblers. Most of the leading firms in Thailand's automotive industry are JVs with majority shares owned by Japanese carmakers. For example, Toyota Motor Corporation holds 86.4% of Toyota Motors Thailand; Mazda Motor Corporation holds 96.1% of Mazda Sales (Thailand) and 100% of Mazda Powertrain Manufacturing (Thailand); foreign ownership also includes Nissan Thailand and Mitsubishi Thailand (Intarakumnerd & Charoenporn, 2015). By the end of 2005, sixteen car assemblers and 1,800 component suppliers could be found in Thailand. Among the assemblers, Japanese firms dominated the market with a 91% market share (Busser, 2008).

Without national carmakers to monopolize government support or the issue of entrenchment by any carmakers, foreign JVs faced the same market competition. They were also eager to enter the global market or the Southeast Asian market using Thailand as a hub. Thus, the production and export volume of Thailand became the largest among ASEAN countries (Tai & Ku, 2013). However, industry policies for domestic suppliers were not sustained in Thailand; for example, tariffs on the importation of CKD and CBU and on vehicles with various sizes increasingly declined year by year, whereas more incentives were given to foreign JVs (Tai & Ku, 2013).

Given their own need to enhance productive efficiency, Japanese carmakers attempted to train and upgrade the skills of Thai workers and to conduct more technologically sophisticated activities (Intarakumnerd & Techakanont 2016; Lee et al., 2020), and these efforts may have translated into increasing domestic value added in the industry to a certain extent. However, given that nearly half of their suppliers were also foreign owned, the eventual influence on locally owned suppliers in terms of local value added may have been limited. For example, all the assemblers are foreign-controlled JVs, and among the 635 first-tier part suppliers, almost half are foreign JVs, while local ownership is dominant only by second- or third-tier suppliers as of the mid-2010s (Intarakumnerd & Techakanont, 2016). Thus, even though some trucks use engines locally produced by foreign JVs, their local value added must be limited.

One measure of local value added is the share of foreign value added (FVA) embodied in the gross exports of a country, which is one of the backward linkages in GVC (Banga, 2013; Koopman et al., 2014; OECD, 2017; Wang et al., 2013). The inverse of FVA serves as a measure of upgrading with regard to increasing the domestic value added, because the higher this value is, the lower the share of domestic value added will be. If we compare the FVA trend in the three countries, only China shows a decreasing period from the mid-1990s to the late 2000s, which is similar to that in the mid-1970s to 1990s in South Korea. The rapid decline to a low value like 15% implies that China is engaged in the "made in China" policy. Such a period of decreasing FVA or increasing domestic value added is not clearly observed until the 2010s in Thailand or Malaysia, except for a short period of decline from 2000 to 2003 in Malaysia.

Furthermore, the foreign partners in Thailand do not seem to have pursued globalization in terms of setting up factories abroad. This tendency is not surprising, as it also happened to GM-Daewoo in Korea; GM did not want this JV to go for globalization (Lee & Lim, 2001). This is why Thailand has ended up showing low values of the share of domestic value added embodied in foreign exports as a share of the gross exports of a foreign country (hereafter, DVAFXSH), which is a measure of forward linkages in GVC and of upgrading the capabilities and competitiveness of intermediate goods (parts and components); higher values of this ratio indicate higher competitiveness of a country's intermediate parts and components in international markets.

3.3.4 National Ownership without Discipline in Malaysia

With regard to ownership, the National Car Project in Malaysia resulted in two national car brands, Proton and Perodua, with majority equities of 70% and 68%, respectively, although their Japanese partners Mitsubishi and Daihatsu owned 30% and 32% of the equity shares, respectively (Athukorala, 2014; Wad & Govindaraju, 2011). In 2004, Proton became a fully Malaysian-owned company when Mitsubishi sold its stake to Khazanah National BHD (the government's investment arm).

To support the growth of the two national carmakers, various policies have been implemented. First, tariffs on CKD kits for national vehicles were exempted to lower the price of national vehicles (Athukorala, 2014; Tai & Ku, 2013). Second, the "Vendor Development Program" was also implemented to boost the development of local SME parts suppliers. Through this program, the parts manufacturers of national cars were provided with production subsidies, which allowed their parts prices to decrease by 10–12%. The number of parts suppliers of Proton increased rapidly from 17 in 1985 to 186 in 1999 (Tai & Ku, 2013).

However, the Malaysian automotive industry lacked competition in the domestic market, and no effort was exerted to export to the global market. The government has forbidden other manufacturers to produce models that could result in direct competition with Proton (Athukorala, 2014; Tai & Ku, 2013). Even the other national carmaker, Perodua, was only allowed to produce cars with an engine capacity of less than 1,000 cc (Athukorala, 2014), despite enjoying the same tariff concessions, tax relief, and other government supports as Proton (Athukorala, 2014).

Before national cars appeared, Toyota and Nissan dominated the Malaysian market. Proton seized the market in an extremely short time with the help of a series of discriminatory policies, occupying an 80% share of vehicles under the 1,500 cc range by 1987 (Nizamuddin, 2008). In 1991, the Malaysian government made a partial reform to reduce the restrictions of the automotive industry, which allowed new entrants, such as Hyundai, Citroen, Rover, and other international car manufacturers into the Malaysian market. By the mid-2000s, despite having fifteen car manufacturers in Malaysia, the major market share remained occupied by the two national carmakers (Wad & Govindaraju, 2011). The two national carmakers thus faced no discipline in the market to upgrade their innovation capabilities, such as the localization of engines and other key parts, as indicated by the high FVA ratio. Furthermore, they did not compete for the larger markets of other countries, which prevented them from achieving economy of scale and from enjoying the discipline from global markets. These firms should have devoted the financial resources from near-monopoly profits to upgrading their technological capabilities to produce their own engines, which did not actually occur.

Eventually, after Malaysia joined the WTO and abolished LCRs in 2004, the dominance of national carmakers weakened steadily over time, and they failed to enter the global market (Tai & Ku, 2013). Proton's market share declined after high-quality models produced by Japanese manufacturers with lower prices were launched in Malaysia (Wad, 2009). National carmakers were not ready to compete with foreign carmakers once the market was open because they lacked technological capabilities. Given its ever-weakening performance, Proton has become a problem for Malaysia. As a solution, it was sold to DRB-HICOM Berhad in Malaysia in 2012. In 2017, DRB-HICOM transferred its 49.9% stake to Geely, a rising Chinese carmaker that also acquired Volvo.[9]

[9] Source: www.thestar.com.my/business/business-news/2017/05/24/drb-hicom-to-sell-49pt9pct-in-proton-to-geely-holding/

3.3.5   Ownership, Competition, and Policies in China

3.3.5.1   Mixed Outcome or Even Failure with JVs in the Early Period

China's automotive industry started earlier than those of Malaysia and Thailand. Before the 1960s, the country had five assemblers with an annual production capacity of 60,000 vehicles. China also intended to build its own automotive industry despite its low level of technology (Yu et al., 2008). This situation led to a change in policy in the 1980s toward inviting foreign JVs with the expectation of technology transfer from the so-called "market for technology," which was also applied to other industries, such as telecommunication equipment (Mu & Lee, 2005). One of the first JVs was the Beijing Jeep Company, signed in 1983, followed by Shanghai Auto Industry Corporation (SAIC)-VW (SVW) in 1984 and Guangzhou-Peugeot in 1985, while more came in the 1990s.[10] In 1988, the government proposed a strategy of supporting three majors and three minors among JVs. With this series of JV agreements, the production of automobiles increased rapidly as new brands were launched, given no competing locally owned brands (Wang, 2007). In these JVs, the cap of foreign ownership was regulated to be 50% or less (Liu et al., 2014) and they were also requested to establish R&D centers (Yu et al., 2008).

However, this strategy of relying on FDI or JV did not lead to the expected outcome in terms of technology transfer and eventual enhancement of technological capabilities of automakers in China (Chu, 2011). In the early efforts, the size of the country was not considerably an advantage; rather, it was a source of information and coordination failure associated with complex politics involving the central and local government that resulted in difficulty in conducting

---

[10] The 1990s saw a joint venture agreement between SAIC and GM in 1997, followed by Guangzhou-Honda (1998), Tianjin-Faw-Toyota (2000), Changan-Ford (2001), Beijing-Hyundai (2002), Brilliance-BMW (2002), and Dongfeng-Nissan (2002); the Chinese auto market became a global battlefield (Chu, 2011).

Japan- or Korea-style centralized industrial policy (Brandt & Thun, 2010; Huang, 2002; Thun, 2004; Thun, 2006).[11]

Although the central government attempted to achieve economy of scale by limiting the number of automakers (e.g., the so-called three majors and three minors policy) in the nation, provincial governments often circumvented such regulations and actually allowed entries by local or foreign JV firms. Thus, China ended up with more than 110 car assemblers, with about half being foreign JVs (Chu, 2011). The problem in the auto sector in China has been summarized as "outdated products, high prices, and no R&D capabilities," and "too many production sites, indiscreet project approval, redundant investment, and slow localization" (Chu, 2011). In particular, a policy by the central government that allowed only state firms to form JVs with foreign firms is responsible for the situation where each JV adapted an old mid-market design from the foreign partner and concentrated on fulfilling government-mandated localization requirements, rather than trying to develop their own engines (Thun, 2018).

Guangzhou-Peugeot Automobile Company (GPAC) is a representative case as one of the first foreign–Chinese JVs to fail in China. It was established in 1985 as a JV between Peugeot and the Guangzhou Automobile Group. After some success until 1992, sales plummeted due to low competitiveness, and total losses reached RMB 10.5 billion before it was closed in March 1997 (Lassere & Zeng, 2002). Peugeot was unwilling to promote local value chains but kept relying on imported parts, which ultimately raised the final cost of the products (Harwit, 1994). The reliance on CKD kits caused

---

[11] The size of domestic market can be a strong source of bargaining power in dealing with foreign companies about technology transfer negotiation; however, this does not imply that it is actually used as such unless the local government has an effective plan and will to promote the local industry. Thus, the so-called "trading market for technology" idea is used effectively in the case of the telecommunication switch development, which is not the case in the auto sector. Local government failed to provide an effective coordination to promote a parts supplier network until the 2000s (Chu, 2011).

troubles. For example, production stopped for more than two months in late 1986 when Peugeot and the Chinese company could not agree on the prices the JV should pay for the CKD kits (Harwit, 1994; Peng, 2000). Although the Guangzhou area lacked high-quality parts suppliers, officials there prohibited the purchase of high-quality parts at a low price from suppliers in other areas of China. Instead of using profits to upgrade their products, GPAC had an extremely high dividend payout ratio (Sun et al., 2010); thus, the Chinese side believed that Peugeot focused on obtaining short-term profits from selling CKD kits without facilitating localization.

3.3.5.2   *Success with Indigenous Ownership since the Mid-2000s*

Only after China joined the WTO in 2001 were locally owned carmakers allowed to enter the market (Lee et al., 2017; Zhao, 2013), causing a rise in competition. Before 2000, JVs dominated the Chinese market (Tian et al., 2010). Since then, locally owned manufacturers, such as Great Wall, Chery, and Geely, rapidly emerged and continued to increase in market share, reaching 30% in 2009 (Tian et al., 2010). In passenger cars, shares by indigenous brands already reached approximately 40% in the 2000s, and for sport utility vehicles, seven of the top ten best-selling models in 2015 were produced by indigenous firms (Lee et al., 2017).

These new companies pursued slightly different strategies from those of foreign JVs in building technological capabilities and acquiring foreign technology. They conducted in-house R&D activities, filing more patents than foreign JVs, and relied on active licensing and international mergers and acquisitions (M&As). For example, Chery bought the used assembly line of the SEAT company (a Volkswagen subsidiary in Spain) and the engine factory of the Ford company based in England in 1997 (Lee et al., 2009). With the imported assembly line, they recruited engineers from foreign JVs; the CEO of Chery (Tongyao Yin) used to be a manager in First Automotive Works-VW (FAW-VW), and more than 100 engineers left FAW-VW to join Chery.

Moreover, thirteen key engineers from Dongfeng-Nissan joined the development team for the popular Tonga QQ model, which took off from Chery (Lee et al., 2007). These key engineers left the JVs in disappointment because the JVs had no ambition to be independent innovators, and they wanted to build an independent automaker in China (Lee et al., 2009).

Given the strong motivation for success associated with private or nonstate ownership and facing tough market competition, indigenous firms, including BYD, invested aggressively in new facilities and technologies to build their technological capabilities. These firms frequently tested and improved their ideas in the market to learn rapidly, launching more than 170 models from 2003 to 2007 (Chu, 2011; Lee et al., 2017). Indigenous firms further built their capabilities through global outsourcing and even acquired foreign companies (Lee et al., 2017). Chery established a JV with Jaguar Land Rover to enhance its brand reputation and technological capabilities. In 2007, Geely set up an overseas factory and bought a stake in UK cab firm Manganese Bronze Holdings (Guo et al., 2017). In 2009, Geely acquired Australia's Drivetrain Systems International, the world's second-largest gearbox manufacturer, and Geely further improved its technological capabilities with the M&A of Volvo.

Currently, given the rise of indigenous firms, the size of domestic market segmented into low and high ends had a role in facilitating the growth of such firms first based on the low-end segment while avoiding direct competition with JVs targeting the high-end market (Thun, 2004, 2018; Tian et al., 2010). Eventually, these indigenous firms, such as Geely, achieved stage-based upgrading, from imitation to innovation, from low end to middle and high end, and from the domestic market to the global market. The rise of indigenous firms also indicates more competition between these local firms and JVs, which further contributes to the deepening and widening of local supply chains in China as an additional factor other than the LCR policy. Given the dominance of local firms in the low-end segment and of foreign JVs in the high-end segment, the competition for the medium segment forced foreign JVs to attempt to reduce cost, while forcing local firms to improve quality by building their own local supplier network and increasing localization (Brandt & Thun, 2010).

Other than LCRs, three categories of policy initiatives have been implemented for the automotive sector in China, namely, import restrictions, entry control, and market discrimination. First, according to the "Automotive Industry Policy" issued in 1994, import quota licenses are used to regulate the import of auto parts and assembled cars. Even the types of cars allowed for import are determined in consideration of the nationwide policy of automotive sector promotion. Thus, used cars or parts for car assembly are forbidden, which implies that automotive manufacturers are not allowed to import kits to produce cars via semi-knocked down or CKD (Chen & Han, 2007). Second, foreign enterprises are not allowed to establish more than two JVs in China for one specific type of car. For investment projects with regard to such parts as CBU and engines, foreign automotive manufacturers are required to collaborate with indigenous manufacturers (Nan, 2005). Third, foreign cars are discriminated against with higher registration fees and taxes than those for domestic cars (Chen & Han, 2007).

3.4 GLOBAL–LOCAL INTERFACES IN INNOVATION SYSTEMS OF TAIPEI, PENANG, AND SHENZHEN

Scholars from the Schumpeterian School observed that differences in NIS may lead to variations in innovation performance and economic growth[12]. However, the question of why innovation activities and economic development are unevenly distributed over space, even in the same nation, remains unanswered (Asheim et al., 2019, p. 1). This question justifies the concept of regional innovation systems (RIS) and the analysis of innovation and economic performance of regions and cities. Cooke et al. (1998) defined RIS as a region-level "system

---

[12] This section is a compact rewriting of an article by the author of this book and a colleague, Kim and Lee (2022).

in which firms and other organizations are systematically engaged in interactive learning through an institutional milieu characterized by local embeddedness" (p. 1581). This section looks at this question of uneven development of regions in the context of Asia, focusing on the role of local ownership.

While the Asian economic takeoff has been associated with international integration via FDI or MNCs, we still see some divergence among regions, for instance, Shenzhen versus Penang. Shenzhen in South China was one of the first special economic zones to attract FDI and has spearheaded the economic development of China since the 1980s. Penang in Malaysia has also been one of the first regions in Southeast Asia to attract FDI since the early 1970s, but its growth was somewhat slow compared to that of Shenzhen. The size of the surrounding nation might not be the dominant factor in this difference, given that Taipei has also achieved fast growth while relying on FDI since the 1960s, even though it is a city on the small island of Taiwan.

Among the three regions, Taipei has the highest GDP per capita. Shenzhen and Penang are catching up with Taipei at different speeds (i.e., Shenzhen is catching up rapidly, but Penang is doing so slowly). The innovation performances of these two regions also differ. Shenzhen is more innovative than Penang in terms of the number of US-filed patents. This correlation between innovation and economic performance in the three regions served as a motivating justification of this study to apply the RIS framework and explain their divergent economic performance. Thus, a comparison of these regions in Asia with regard to the broad framework of uneven development of regions would be interesting (Yeung, 2021) given a common initial condition of growth dependent on FDI in their early development stage.

Various studies on cities and sub-national units in East Asia have applied the concept of RIS (Hassink, 2001; Wong et al., 2018; Yang, 2015; Yoon et al., 2015). Among the various dimensions of RIS, this study focuses on the local–global interfaces, namely, where and how local actors and their learning interact with foreign actors and knowledge sources. Thus, the focus of this study can be justified because the three regions, as latecomers from emerging economies (EEs), share the common initial condition of heavy reliance on FDI in their early stage of development. However, the question is "why and how" these regions have evolved to eventually correspond to divergent outcomes.

3.4.1 Taipei, Shenzhen, and Penang in Asia

Taipei, Shenzhen, and Penang belong to the dynamic economies in Asia, that is, Taiwan, China, and Malaysia, respectively. They can also be regarded as representing the fast economic growth of their respective economies.

Taipei has served as the central city that has greatly contributed to the overall economic growth of Taiwan's economy. Taipei has not only been the center of Taiwanese enterprises but also the headquarters of foreign multinational corporations (Huang, 2008). Several foreign MNCs established their headquarters or subsidiaries in Taipei as early as the late 1950s. But since the 1960s, the vast majority of export-based manufacturing headquarters have flocked to Taipei in order to take advantage of the administrative and policy support from the central government, as Taiwan started to adopt the mode of export-oriented industrialization more aggressively (Chou, 2005; Hsu, 2005; Li et al., 2016). However, the weight of foreign firms has steadily decreased as some indigenous firms have grown into large giants, such as Acer (Amsden & Chu, 2003; Hsu, 2005). In the present study, the term "Taipei City" covers the former Taipei County (New Taipei) and the former Taipei City proper, with its formal merging and recognition in 2010;[13] its population grew slowly from 2.2 million in 2000 to 2.6 million in 2017.

Shenzhen was one of the first four special economic zones that represented the open-door policy of China initiated by Deng Xiaoping.

---

[13] Since Taipei City and Taipei County were confusingly used in patent data, we designate both Taipei City and New Taipei City as "Taipei City" in our analysis below.

Although it used to be the home of labor-intensive manufacturing that used low-cost labor and supplied to Hong Kong, it has grown into a high-tech region (Chen & Kenney, 2007; Yang, 2015). Reflecting its prosperity, Shenzhen's population has increased from less than 5 million in the 1990s to more than 12 million in 2017.

Penang was one of the earliest manufacturing hubs in Asia to attract foreign MNCs because of its strategic location, low labor costs, and low taxes in areas involving various electronic parts and components (Ariffin & Figueiredo, 2004; Diez & Kiese, 2006; Rasiah, 1988). The operations of MNCs in Penang started in 1972 when the Bayan Lepas free trade zone was launched and initially hosted seven MNCs.

One of the common features of the three regions is that they initially invited and promoted FDI through MNCs by setting up industrial parks, such as the Free Industrial Zone (FIZ) in Penang in 1972, and then the Special Economic Zones in Shenzhen in 1980 (Hsu, 2005; UNDP, 2006). In particular, despite starting later than Penang, Shenzhen has shown faster long-term growth in its income and the number of patents, which makes an interesting puzzle to pursue in this study.

In terms of the trends of per capita GDP in each region and per capita GDP relative to that in the United States, the three regions have a decent record of economic growth and catching up with the level of the United States. Among them, Taipei has reached the highest level, and Penang has reached the lowest level. Since 2000, Taipei has successfully caught up with a per capita GDP of over 80% of that of the United States. Its per capita GDP is more than $50,000 in PPP terms, and it reached almost 97% of that of the United States in 2017. In 2017, the per capita GDP of Shenzhen was $39,245 in PPP terms, ranking second among the three regions, and this level was approximately 72% of the per capita GDP of the United States. In 2017, the per capita GDP of Penang was $27,569 and reached more than 50% of that of the United States. It was even less than 40% before 2000. In this sense, all three regions have a decent record of catching up, although their speeds differ. In particular, the speed of Shenzhen is faster than that of Penang.

Let us first look at the number of patents, especially those registered in the United States, for fair comparison. The number of US patents registered with the inventor's address in Taipei has increased dramatically since the late 1990s. In 2017, the number of patents was 3,780. Similarly, this parameter has increased remarkably since the late 2000s in Shenzhen, that is, from zero in the 1990s to about 2,500 in 2017. However, this rapid catching up is not realized in Penang, whose number of patents is only 100. This comparison of the three regions remains valid in terms of patent count per person.

This discussion therefore raises one interesting question: "Why has Shenzhen caught up with Taipei faster than Penang?" This study aims to explain the sources of this performance gap among the regions by analyzing their respective RIS beyond a simple count of patents. More specifically, we explore the possibility of different development trajectories among the three regions with regard to the different local–global interfaces or the role of indigenous firms and their contribution to innovation in these regions.

3.4.2   Local–Foreign Interfaces in RIS of the Three Regions

In the context of emerging economies, the concept of peripheral or immature RIS is characterized as being heavily reliant on external knowledge, given its lack of an indigenous knowledge base (Asheim et al. 2019, p. 73; Rodriguez et al., 2014). Similarly, the concept of the dirigiste systems is proposed to refer to a low level of regional embeddedness (Hassink, 2001, Park & Markusen, 1995). The latecomers' reliance on foreign knowledge makes sense, given that typical latecomer economies tend to achieve economic growth by relying on FDI and learning from foreign MNCs (Amsden & Chu, 2003; Bernardes & Albuquerque, 2003; Lebdioui et al., 2021). This pattern indicates that latecomer regions show a low level of patenting at early stages and more citations of foreign patents than indigenously owned patents, even after they start to conduct their own R&D and file patents (Wong & Lee, 2021).

This characterization of RIS in emerging economies in terms of a low level of indigenous knowledge is consistent with national-level studies involving the NIS concept of emerging or catching-up economies. Lee (2013c) and Lee, Lee, & Lee (2021) also found that one of the important attributes of the NIS of an economy showing a performance of rapid catching up is the initially low and increasing level of knowledge localization or degree of intranational creation and diffusion of knowledge, as measured by national-level self-citations. Therefore, during the early stage of economic development, emerging economies are likely to rely on knowledge from foreign or more advanced economies rather than creating and diffusing their own indigenous knowledge. During the stage of economic catching up, latecomer economies can adapt foreign knowledge to a local context to conduct imitative creation (Kim, 1997b) and move on to the stage of proper innovation, which is characterized by an increasing level of knowledge localization and local ownership.

In the context of this research, this specific process and mechanism of "localization of knowledge creation and ownership" would be the key mechanism of more successful or less successful performance of the innovation systems of the different regions of Taipei, Shenzhen, and Penang. Thus, our answer to the question of why Shenzhen has been doing better than Penang is that the former has increased the degree of localization of knowledge creation and ownership more rapidly than the latter, and that in the former region indigenous firms have eventually emerged to become the dominant players of knowledge creation and diffusion within the region, whereas they used to rely on foreign firms as sources of knowledge.

Given the discussion above, first, this study proposes to determine the specific pattern of dynamic changes in the role of foreign knowledge at the regional level. Specifically, given that the highest per capita income is recorded in Taipei and the lowest is in Penang, we hypothesized that Taipei would show a high and increasing level of intraregional knowledge localization and a low and decreasing level of internationalization (or degree of relying on foreign knowledge). As a rapidly upgrading region, Shenzhen would correspond to an increasing level of intra-regionalization and a decreasing level of internationalization. This pattern of decreases in internationalization corresponds to the decreases in backward participation at GVC measured by the share of foreign value added in gross exports (Lee et al., 2018).

For this purpose, this study develops its own measures of RIS and focuses on three dimensions, namely, intraregional, interregional, and international. This approach is different from the two-dimensional approach in NIS, which is only divided into intranational and international, that is, the former is the exact residual or opposite of the latter. Unlike an NIS study, RIS analysis needs another dimension, the interregional dimension of one region's reliance and interaction with other regions in the same nation. Therefore, this study considers this interregional dimension of how much a region relies on or interacts with other regions in the same nation. In general, one may hypothesize on the basis of a similar logic described above that an advanced or catching-up region would show a high or increasing level of inter-regionalization (high or increasing citations of patents by other regions). We measured these variables by exploring the citation patterns of all patents with the inventors' addresses in localities, regardless of legal ownership, that is, foreign or local ownership.

Second, this study focuses on the role of local/foreign ownership of patents representing knowledge creation and diffusion. This dimension is important because simply relying on foreign-owned knowledge (patents) is insufficient in sustaining the upgrade to the later stages as foreign firms become increasingly reluctant to transfer or sell their technologies to latecomers who are catching up and getting close to the frontier (Lebdioui et al., 2021; Lee, Qu, & Mao, 2021). Amsden and Chu (2003) recognized this point in their study on Taiwan. They emphasized that one of the factors for Taiwan in joining the ranks of high-income economies beyond the middle-income stage is its ability to create a critical mass of locally owned firms, although it used to rely on FDI in its early stage of development. In this sense, South Korea and Taiwan share a common formula for successful upgrades; therefore, economies attempting to catch up should acquire an indigenous technological capability (Mazzoleni & Nelson, 2007). We will be looking at Shenzhen and Penang from this perspective or in comparison with Taipei when we examine the extent and trend of ownership of patents filed in each region.

Thus, our analysis tests the hypotheses that Taipei has a high level of local patent ownership or a high share of patents filed by locally owned firms, and that Shenzhen shows an increasing share of locally owned patents compared with Penang. One of the causes for the slow catching up of Penang, even though it started earlier than Shenzhen, is its failure to enhance the degree of local ownership in its innovation activities measured by patent ownership in this context.

We can start by looking at the extent and trends of the intra-regionalization index of the three regions. As expected from the hypotheses in the preceding section, the level of intra-regionalization in Taipei is much higher than that of Shenzhen and Penang. In the meantime, Shenzhen and Penang have an increasing pattern, which is consistent with their increasing per capita income that is catching up steadily with the United States' level over time. The degree of intra-regionalization in Taipei has increased from 4% in the 1980s to >10% in the 2000s, indicating a self-citation rate of about 10% at the regional level. By contrast, the level of intra-region self-citation in Shenzhen or Penang is only half of the level in Taipei, or 6% in Shenzhen and 4% in Penang in the 2010s. Less than 10% of intra-regionalization implies that the majority of citations by these regions is attributed to foreign patents. This finding is expected for a region in EEs.

Also available are the extent and trends of internationalization, such as the degree to which patents by inventors in the region tend to cite foreign patents, that is, patents with inventors' addresses in foreign nations. As we expect and hypothesize, the internationalization or reliance on foreign patents of Taipei clearly decreases, which reflects the enhancement of its own indigenous technological

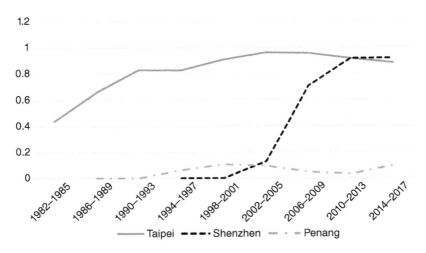

FIGURE 3.1 Local ownership of innovation: Taipei, Shenzhen, and Penang
Source: Figure 6 of Kim and Lee (2022)

capabilities and RIS. The absolute degree of internationalization decreased from 95% in the early 1980s to less than 82% in the early 2000s, although it increased again slightly in the 2010s (Kim & Lee, 2022). By contrast, this trend is unclear in the cases of Shenzhen or Penang, and their level of internationalization remained higher than 90%. However, the level of Shenzhen is lower than that of Penang. This finding is consistent with a higher level of development or catching up by Shenzhen than that of Penang.

Figure 3.1 shows the time trend of the local firm ownership of the three regions. The shares in Taipei rose from about 40% in the 1980s to almost 100% by the mid-2000s. The share of local ownership in Shenzhen reached a similar level by the mid-2010s within a shorter time because it used to be close to zero in the mid-1990s. By contrast, the local share in Penang did not show such a sharp increase, but has remained around 10% since the 1990s.

One can also discuss a more detailed picture by looking at the cross-country decomposition of the top ten assignees in each region.[14]

---

[14] Refer to the Figures in Kim and Lee (2022).

The trends in Taipei have confirmed the dominance of Taiwanese firms since the mid-1990s. In Shenzhen, the share of domestic or Chinese-owned firms in the top ten assignees has kept increasing since the late 1990s and reached almost 100% in 2013–2015. This trend is matched with a decrease in shares by the United States and Taiwan. Unlike Shenzhen and Taipei, Penang has remained dominated by US firms with 50–70% shares since the 1990s. This value is matched with a decrease in shares by Malaysian firms from 20% to zero in the mid-2010s. Further detailed information about the specific names of the top firms in each region since the 2000s is available.[15] In Shenzhen, the two Taiwan-origin firms, Hong Hai Precision and Foxconn, ranked as the top one and two in 2005. In 2011, the top four ranks were dominated by indigenous Chinese firms such as Huawei, followed by the Taiwanese firm Hong Hai Precision, which ranked fifth. By 2015, all the top ten firms were Chinese-owned companies led first by ZTE, and then Huawei. In contrast, Penang is still dominated by US firms, including Intel, Motorola, and Altera.

Taipei and Shenzhen have steadily reduced their dependency on the knowledge of foreign firms, which is contrary to the situation in Penang. The considerable creation of knowledge by the indigenous firms in Shenzhen seems to be one of the reasons why it has made a transition from a peripheral to catching up in RIS compared to Penang. The increased indigenous knowledge in Taipei and Shenzhen is the knowledge pool in the region and likely affects the increase in the intraregional and interregional localization of knowledge, as shown above.

3.4.3 The Different Roles of Industrial Policy in the Three Regions

Now let us turn to the burning question of how Shenzhen, following Taiwan, has been able to promote locally owned firms out of their interaction with and learning from foreign MNCs. By comparison,

---

[15] Refer to the Appendix Tables for Shenzhen and Penang in Kim and Lee (2022).

Penang is more slowly catching up and has remained reliant on MNCs. Broadly speaking, the question of "how" can be placed in the context of a larger question of how to sustain economic growth in emerging economies, thereby overcoming the possibility of the MIT.

First, the Taipei model can be characterized by a high degree of intra-regionalization and the lowest degree of internationalization. However, Taipei also used to be dominated by foreign MNCs and faced a crisis as foreign vendors switched to other lower-wage economies, such as Malaysia, for their OEM orders (Amsden & Chu, 2003, pp. 70–79; Li et al., 2016), as the wage rate in Taiwan increased in the 1980s. This phenomenon is a typical symptom of the MIT. In this situation, many engineers who used to work in foreign-owned television factories left to start their own firms in related areas (Amsden & Chu, 2003, pp. 23–24). For them, the source of technology changed from FDI to technology licensing agreements with foreign entities. Eventually, a more effective model appeared, and that was a combination of firm-level R&D efforts and industrial/innovation support policies by the government, including public–private collaboration (Lebdioui et al., 2021; Lee, Lee, Meissner, et al., 2021; Lee, Qu, & Mao, 2021).

Specifically, public research organizations such as the Industrial Technology Research Institute (ITRI) played the role of a "new developmental state" because they developed high-tech parts and components that were formerly imported and had private firms to produce them (Amsden & Chu, 2003, p. 77). Furthermore, for an important upgrading transition from making small (analog) calculators to laptop PCs, ITRI led a public–private R&D consortium to develop a common machine architecture for laptop PCs and prototypes, which could be easily translated into a series of standardized components produced by manufacturers through mass production. The consortium represented a watershed after some previous failures, indicating the potential of an R&D consortium to help establish new "fast follower" industries (Mathews, 2002b). Despite collaborative relations with foreign entities for technology licensing, the acquisition of innovation (design) capability required an active learning effort from the Taiwan side. For example, in making circuit chips, Taiwanese engineers went around the world to study large-scale integration applications. Eventually, by combining their observations and knowledge gained from Japanese suppliers, they became good at integrating a large number of parts and components sourced globally at the lowest prices into a small space (Amsden & Chu, 2003, pp. 28–32).

Second, the Penang mode is somewhat the opposite of the Taipei mode in terms of the continuing dominance of foreign MNCs in production and innovation. In the past, MNCs were attracted to Penang's low-cost wages and tax haven. Despite increasing income and wage rates, the share of MNCs in total investment ranged from 60% to 70% from 2014 to 2015. It also fluctuated but had no clear declining trend; conversely, the local investment contributed approximately 30–40% in the same period (Figure 5 in Lee et al., 2020). A new cycle of development is emerging, and the economy of Penang has been diversified from labor-intensive manufacturing operations to high-value-added manufacturing, including services from them, such as software, engineering design, R&D, and industrial system-based services, as well as new service industries such as medical tourism, education, and shared service centers (Penang Institute, 2015, pp. 10–15). These structural changes have also been a response to the rise of China as an alternative location for MNCs (Diez & Kiese, 2006). Penang witnessed some downsizing and exits of MNC manufacturing operations and M&A among multinationals to rationalize their resources and reduce redundancies over the past few years. However, many MNCs maintained certain operations in Penang, as they are provided with strong supply chains, allowing them to produce advanced technologies and services. Some locally owned firms have emerged to advance their high value-added activities in Penang (Diez & Kiese, 2006; Lee et al., 2020). A key factor of this positive scenario is a local institution that has enabled the training and upskilling of their local force, such as the Penang Skill

Development Center, a nonprofit institution that provides technical knowledge and training programs to engineers in the region (Lee et al., 2020).

Third, Shenzhen between Taipei and Penang in terms of the levels of per capita income and of intraregional and international localization of knowledge, although it is closer to Taipei with regard to the share of the local ownership of innovation. The leading companies in terms of the number of patents are Huawei and ZTE. How did these firms grow and become dominant? The answer, which is the same as for Taipei above, is a combination of firm-level R&D efforts and industrial/innovation support policies by the government, including public–private collaboration (Lebdioui et al., 2021; Lee, Qu, & Mao, 2021, Yang, 2015).

Specifically, the industrial policy in China has been called a "trading market for technology" (Mu & Lee, 2005), that is, the Chinese government used its huge bargaining power associated with the size of China's market to require foreign joint venture firms to transfer important parts of technologies. A famous example is the indigenous development of the fixed-line telephone because of the technology transfer and diffusion from a JV, Shanghai Bell, with the Chinese side owning 60% or a majority of shares. The transferred key technologies were later diffused to a local R&D consortium to develop Chinese-owned fixed telephone switches. This consortium finally transferred the technologies to ZTE, two other SOEs, and one private firm (Huawei) to be in charge of the actual production. When these four indigenous Chinese firms started to compete directly with JVs, the role of the Chinese government was to provide market protection and give financial and moral incentives for the adoption and use of domestic products (Mu & Lee, 2005; Xin & Wang, 2000).

Given its status as a special economic zone (SEZ), Shenzhen City has enjoyed many privileges in various policy initiatives (Yang, 2015). In the most recent case of Tencent, the help of the local government was critical to guarantee funding from venture capital and other financial investors at the initial growth stage (Breznitz &

Murphree, 2011, pp. 175–178). To strengthen the local firm owner-ship of knowledge, Shenzhen promoted the growth of local firms, such as Huawei and Tencent, by investing in universities and large research institutes (Breznitz & Murphree, 2011; Yang, 2015). The Shenzhen municipal government made efforts to encourage higher education and attracted advanced manpower, where universi-ties and their research institutes, such as Shenzhen University in 1983, Shenzhen Polytechnic in 1993, the THU Shenzhen Tsinghua Research Institute, and the research base of Peking University, CAS, the Chinese Academy of Engineering, and Hong Kong University of Science & Technology, were established by providing incentives or benefits (Chen & Kenney, 2007). These initiatives must have helped a large, diverse pool of human resources from other regions in China and other countries to come to Shenzhen. For example, Huawei runs R&D centers in Beijing, Shanghai, Nanjing, Shenzhen, Hangzhou, and Chengdu.

The above discussion suggests that Taipei in Taiwan and Shenzhen in mainland China have been more active or aggressive in terms of the degree of public intervention than Penang in Malaysia, which might be one of the reasons for the different degrees of local ownership of innovation in the three regions. Whereas the former two cities involved the direct intervention of the public sector in specific R&D projects to help indigenous firms, the role of the public sector in Penang seems to have been more in the matter of human capital development or re-skilling and up-skilling of the workforce, which is used by foreign MNCs.

3.5 SUMMARY AND CONCLUDING REMARKS

This chapter elaborates the importance of local value added, knowl-edge, and ownership in latecomers' catching up, drawing upon several cases, such as resource sectors in Chile and Malaysia, auto sectors in four countries, and the three regions or IT cluster cities in Asia. As was discussed, in the cases of more successful rises of latecomer firms and sectors, they have all seen the eventual consolidation of a system for the local creation of value added and knowledge supported by the rise of local ownership, although they have all tended to involve foreign entities and sources at their early stage. As the cases of the auto sector in Thailand, IT sector in Penang and mining sector in Chile show, continued reliance on foreign ownership is a recipe for a mixed success in terms of the limited or slow rise of domestic value added and innovation. In Thailand, this limited success (or upgrading) can be associated with a lack of local ownership under a less consistent industrial policy, which is given up after liberalization and WTO entry.

Continued dominance of foreign ownership corresponds to slow catching up, because it corresponds to lukewarm efforts to build domestic value added (e.g., Thai autos or Chilean mining) or even to hostile measures against the rise of high value-added (processed) palm oil exports from Malaysia. More importantly, foreign MNCs tend to source knowledge from R&D centers in headquarters and thus do not feel a need to cultivate R&D centers abroad, except for some development of skilled human capital (e.g., Penang in Malaysia and Thai autos). Malaysian and Chilean success in resource sectors all involved consistent efforts to build local R&D centers by public resources and initiatives, as shown by the role of catalyzing R&D and technology transfer by the Fundación Chile in the salmon and berry sectors of Chile, as well as R&D initiatives by PORIM or MRB in Malaysia.

The eventual rise of local sources of knowledge and firms is neither easy nor natural, given that they have all relied on foreign firms, technologies, and finances as the initial sources. The point is that this rise was possible owing to the involvement of the state in the various forms of industrial and innovation policies. This intervention is inevitable; otherwise, there will be a continuation of foreign dominance in ownership and knowledge sourcing. In the most extreme cases, such as the palm oil sector in Malaysia, local ownership was obtained by hostile takeovers of foreign firms. In some cases, there were asymmetric regulations and promotion of indigenous firms over foreign firms, such as the auto sector in China. The relative success in China is related to a combination of restricted foreign ownership, the competitive nature of markets among foreign and national brands, and an explicit firm-level effort to build techno-logical capabilities through in-house R&D and M&A of foreign firms and their technologies.

In other cases, there was a more gradual process of shifting from foreign to domestic entities, which was also possible with a long-term process of cultivation of local forces, which is shown by the cases of resource sectors in Chile, in particular the wine and wood sectors, where there is the coexistence of foreign and domes-tic firms. However, even in these sectors in Chile, the role of public intervention has been critical, as the government made a strategic bet on nonexistent but suitable and potentially profitable sectors, such as salmon, berries, and radiata pines, which were not natural to Chile. Of course, this cultivation of newly introduced products was made possible by an initial and coordinated inflow of foreign knowl-edge and skills and overseas learning opportunities.

It is also seen that promotion of locally owned firms and sectors goes together with discipline from global market competition, which is nothing but the principle of carrots and sticks. The failure of national cars in Malaysia points toward this simple principle. The failure of the automotive sector in Malaysia, despite its national brand ownership, is related to the lack of competition in markets and of specific strategies to localize imported parts and components, such as engines.

The cases in this chapter are all from various regions and sec-tors of different countries. Despite this, they all seem to indicate a common success formula of "learning from foreign sources at the initial stage, leading to the rise of local value added, knowledge, and ownership, owing to firm-level efforts and active industrial policies under market discipline." Overall, one important argument in this book is that managing the global–local interfaces is a key determi-nant of the successful rise of latecomers.

4 Coevolution of Firms with Sectoral, Regional, and National Systems

4.1 INTRODUCTION

The overarching theme of this book is alternative pathways for latecomers in catching-up development. This chapter addresses this question at the level of firms, whereas Chapter 2 does so at the level of nations. Overall, the book looks at the interaction of national and sectoral dimensions of innovation; sectoral and regional dimensions; and the interaction of corporate innovation systems with sectoral, regional, and national innovation systems. This chapter examines these interactions to derive the importance of firms, particularly big businesses, as the ultimate carrier of catching-up growth in the latecomer context.

Regarding the issue of alternative pathways, one way to raise this question at the firm level is to ask whether latecomers catch up and finally forge ahead by using "similar or different" technologies from those of the forerunning incumbent firms. Using similar technologies implies that the latecomer simply attempts to imitate, whereas using different technologies indicates the pursuit of creating new technologies and taking a different technological path or trajectory from the incumbents.

This contrast between similar and different technologies is interesting in terms of the literature on technological catch-up. Traditional or early studies, such as those of Lall (2000), Kim (1980), Westphal et al.(1985), and Hobday (1995a, 1995b), have observed that the latecomers attempted to catch up with advanced countries by assimilating and adapting the incumbents' more-or-less obsolete technology. A contrasting view has been expressed by Lee and Lim (2001) and Lee (2019) that the latecomer does not simply follow the advanced countries' path of technological development; instead, they sometimes skip certain stages or even create their own path that is different from those of the forerunners.

Accordingly, this chapter begins in the next section by exploring the issue of the path of latecomer firms in their effort and achievement in catching up with incumbent firms. Specifically, Section 4.2 addresses the question of whether latecomer firms will catch up with and eventually overtake the incumbent by merely imitating them, or by going beyond imitation but initiating their own technological innovation different from those of the incumbent. The answer will be sought by looking at and comparing the overtaking experiences in three pairs of latecomer and incumbent firms. We draw on the quantitative analyses of Joo and Lee (2010), Oh and Joo (2015), and Joo et al. (2016), which have each analyzed a latecomer vs. an incumbent pair, such as Samsung vs. Sony, Hyundai Motors vs. Mitsubishi Motors, and Huawei vs. Ericsson, respectively.

Section 4.3 then deals with the coevolution of firms and surrounding institutions in the context of post-reform China where firms with diverse ownership have emerged, forming an ideal setting to examine the different interactions of firm ownership and institution. Specifically, relying on my own study (Lee and Lee, 2022), we may compare privately owned local enterprises (POLEs) with foreign-owned enterprises (FOEs) or state-owned enterprises (SOEs) to show how POLEs catch up with other ownership firms by exploiting more effectively the surrounding institutional development. While the initial productivity of POLEs was lower than that of FOEs at the low levels of institutional development, POLEs are shown to eventually catch up with FOEs because institutions develop further over time to be better exploited by POLEs than FOEs. Hence, any policy design should consider this coevolving nature of institutions and firm ownership; whereas private firms cannot prosper without sound institutions, institutional development may be useless unless there are private firms that can benefit from this institutional development.

Section 4.4 will elaborate, relying on Wong and Lee (2021), the case of one region, Hsinchu City in Taiwan, to show that its long-term trajectory of upgrading and centralization is driven by the rise of a leading big business, namely TSMC, a world-class semiconductor foundry, although the region was initially characterized as the Marshallian industrial district with more equal distribution of differently sized firms and diverse sectors. However, with the growth of the leading firm of TSMC, the region has steadily become similar to a hub-and-spoke (HaS) type of industrial district with increasing centralization in the distribution of firms, particularly the increasing dominance by a single firm, TSMC.

This tendency of increasing centralization driven by the rise of leading firms is consistent with the national-level detour of increasing concentration of NIS at the catching-up stage, followed by the eventual decentralization at a later stage (see Figure 2.3D) discussed in Chapter 2. There, the imbalanced catching-up NISs are at relatively low levels of decentralization or high levels of centralization as economies with such NIS have shown a tendency toward increasing concentration of innovation during the last two decades of the 1990s and 2000s, only to turn around in the 2010s toward decentralization. This turnaround is clearer if we look at the graph of an individual economy, such as that of South Korea, for the recent period (Figure 1 of Lee & Lee, 2021a). This U-shaped curve means that these catching-up economies experienced an increasing concentration of innovation into a small number of big inventors or big businesses during the rapid catching-up period and then some decentralization only recently after they matured or entered a post-catching-up period.

Finally, Section 4.5 discusses, relying on Im and Lee (2021), a match between the micro and macro dimension of innovations by referring to the changes in the corporate innovation system of Korean firms. The behavior of Korean firms earlier corresponded with that of typical catching-up firms (e.g., prioritizing growth over profitability, borrowing and investing more, and specializing in short-cycle technologies) but currently show radical changes in their behavioral pattern to show signs of convergence toward the behavior of mature firms in the advanced economies, such as the United States; they now care more for profitability and dividend payment over sales growth and re-investment, and for moving into long CTT-based sectors such as biomedicals. Such change or a phenomenon of shift from catching up to convergence at the firm level is an exact match with the macro-level convergence of South Korea with respect to the Anglo-American economic systems in terms of the slowing down of growth and employment and rising inequality (Lee & Shin, 2021). Such changes in the firms are driven by the post-1997 crisis reform imposed by the IMF as a condition for emergency loans, which had forced the Korean firms to adopt the corporate governance measures found in the shareholder capitalism in the United Stares or United Kingdom.

This chapter deals with each of the above-discussed themes in sequence. Section 4.2 discusses the roles of similar or different technologies in catching-up. Section 4.3 deals with the coevolution of firms and surrounding institutions in the context of post-reform China. Section 4.4 discusses region-level concentration by the rise of a big business, and Section 4.5 discusses convergence of Korean firms toward the Anglo-American system. Lastly, Section 4.6 summarizes the findings and provides the concluding remarks.

4.2   CATCHING UP BY SIMILAR OR DIFFERENT TECHNOLOGIES

This section digs into the question of whether latecomers catch up using "similar or different" technologies from those of the forerunning firms, and it will look at the three pair-cases of overtaking of incumbents by latecomers. The section draws on the research of Joo and Lee (2010), Oh and Joo (2015), and Joo et al. (2016), which has analyzed each pair of a latecomer vs. an incumbent, such as Samsung vs. Sony, Hyundai Motors vs. Mitsubishi Motors, and Huawei vs. Ericsson, respectively. In the three pairs of cases, one common pattern is that a latecomer firm overtook the incumbent in market shares.

In other words, our selection of the above pairs of companies is not arbitrary, because our objective is to compare an incumbent company and a latecomer firm which eventually overtook the incumbent company. This section focuses on these cases where overtaking in terms of market share is completed to determine the necessary conditions of a successfully completed catch-up, namely overtaking.

Such cases of finished catch-up or overtaking are quite rare around the world, and these cases may be considered the universe of the sample. Thus, the results of the analyses may be generalizable as important necessary conditions for overtaking. Other cases of latecomer firms that are also increasing market shares at diverse speed may exist, but they are not the target of our comparison.

The section will thus focus on the hypothesis that latecomers' consistent accumulation of technological capability rather than its cost advantage has been the crucial factor in its successful overtaking. Furthermore, latecomers' overtaking is hypothesized to be a result of its eventual success in creating its own technological trajectory, although it started by imitating the forerunner by integrating the same or similar technologies in the early stages. The empirical method to verify this hypothesis is quantitative analysis using patent and patent citation data. The focus is on the three specific criteria, namely, quantity and quality of patents with the latter measured by impacts (forward citations received) of patents, technological independence measured by self-citations, and technological dependence on each other measured by mutual citations, which will be further explained in the subsequent sub-sections.

4.2.1 Three Cases of Market Catch-Up by Technological Catch-Up

The three cases of overtaking introduced above are all noteworthy cases as they may represent both market and technological catch-up in different sectors and countries, namely, South Korea and China.

First, Samsung's catch-up with Sony is a symbol of Korean catching up with Japan, as Samsung Electronics has been a leading

IT firm in South Korea, whereas Sony previously represented the IT business of Japan. Samsung Electronics, which is the focal company in the section, is the leading affiliate of the Samsung business group, which is now the biggest business group in Korea. Although the early businesses of the Samsung group were textiles and refined sugar, it entered consumer electronics in the early 1970s by establishing Samsung Electronics as a new affiliate. In its early days, Samsung Electronics learned from the Japanese companies such as Sanyo. In the TV or display segment area, Sony was a paramount leader in the global market and had been the target of bench marking and imitation by Samsung Electronics (hereafter Samsung). Even by the early 1990s, Samsung's sales were less than half those of Sony. However, by the mid-2000s, Samsung's sales and firm values in the stock market overtook those of Sony. Thus, the question is, how was that phenomenon possible and, specifically, what was the role of technological capabilities in this overtaking?

The second comparison pair is Hyundai Motors and Mitsubishi Motors. Hyundai Motors represents Korea's auto industry as the leading company. The Hyundai business group earlier focused on the construction business and entered the auto business as late as 1967 or practically in the1970s. Thus, Hyundai was a latecomer and had to start as an OEM assembly maker to Ford. However, Hyundai soon separated from Ford as it wanted to sell its own brand cars and thus had a technology transfer/licensing contract with Mitsubishi in 1973. Since then, Mitsubishi had been a major source of technology for Hyundai, which almost fully relied on Mitsubishi for its engine, transmission, and exhaust systems (Oh & Joo, 2015). In 1982, Hyundai even had to give 10% equity share to Mitsubishi in return for the guaranteed supplies of key parts and components.

Mitsubishi is one of the top four business groups in Japan, with its long history dating back to 1917, when it began production of the Mitsubishi Model A, Japan's first mass produced car. Mitsubishi established its authority as an innovator in automotive technology, developing Japan's first diesel engine in 1931,

Japan's first four-wheel drive passenger car in 1934, and the world's first "Silent Shaft" technology in 1975. Only in 1970, Mitsubishi Motors was split off as an independent firm from Mitsubishi Heavy Industries (Oh & Joo, 2015).

Both companies were doing well in the 1990s, and their revenues kept increasing. However, both companies suffered seriously during the period of the Asian financial crisis in 1997. Nonetheless, since 1998 onwards, only Hyundai had rapidly increased its sales volume in both the US and Korean markets owing to improved productivity during the 1990s led by its own development and production of engines and transmission (Lee & Lim, 2001). Consequently, Hyundai's sales grew bigger than those of Mitsubishi after 2001, as the latter's sales had staggered in the 2000s and thereafter.

The third pair for our comparison is Huawei from China versus Ericsson from Sweden. Huawei was established in 1987 by Ren Zhengfei, a former People's Liberation Army officer. The firm was formerly a telecommunication equipment distributor with a barn on a Shenzhen farm as an office, from which the founders sold telephone switches imported from Hong Kong (Xu & Girling, 2004). In 1990, Huawei decided to risk transforming itself into a telecommunication equipment manufacturer by using in-house research and development, which was the strategy of typical Chinese manufacturers at that time. By using reverse engineering on an imported switching device and networking equipment, Huawei developed the HJD48 (a 512-line analog telephone switch) in 1991 (Mu & Lee, 2005). Huawei's cost advantage allowed it to gain access to the rural Chinese market, a market that was neglected by multinational firms. Eventually, by successfully developing a large capacity digital switch, Huawei increased its market share rapidly to become the largest digital switch supplier in China in 1998 (Mu & Lee, 2005). In the 2000s, Huawei began to reach out to the international market, starting from Hong Kong and extending to emerging and developing countries and regions. Huawei's international market revenues were sluggish during the first few years but surged from the late 1990s.

The telecommunication system industry has long been dominated by several Western firms. In particular, the industry has been led by the Swedish telecommunication giant, Ericsson, followed by Siemens, Nokia, Motorola, Alcatel, Nortel, and Lucent. In the early 2000s, the industry faced a drastic decline in market demand because of the IT bubble burst. Although many incumbents suffered, Huawei had accelerated its market shares since the mid-2000s. In 2012, it finally overtook the longstanding industry leader, Ericsson, in terms of annual revenue.

The impressive story of catch-up and overtaking by latecomers in market sales begs the question of how this became possible, and particularly whether the latecomers achieved such catch-up by cost advantages or technological capabilities. Our focus is on the latter aspect, exploring the hypothesis that gradual catch-up in the market would be possible merely by cost edges. However, sustained catch-up or eventual overtaking by latecomers would not be possible without technological catch-up. Thus, we have to measure the degree of technological capability and address the question of how the technological development path of latecomers is different from or similar to that of incumbents.

4.2.2 *Empirical Method*

For this purpose, let us first discuss a method to assess whether the technological path of the latecomers is the same or different from that of the forerunners. Three criteria are used to assess the same or different technologies or broad aspect of technological capabilities.

First, the quality of the two firms' patents, measured by the average number of received citations, is examined to determine if the latecomer's patent quality catches up with or even surpasses that of the forerunner. Second, the firms' degree of self-citation, which can measure their self-reliance on their own knowledge base, is examined (Lee, 2013c, Chapter 5). This study focuses on the latecomer's degree of self-citation to assess the extent to which it becomes independent of external knowledge sources and self-reliant on its own knowledge base. Third, the mutual citations between the two rival firms' patents are examined to establish the extent through which they rely on each other as their source of knowledge. For instance, if Huawei's patents cite many Ericsson patents, then, Huawei is imitating and relying on Ericsson.

The catching-up process has a dynamic nature. Hence, this study's grand hypothesis is that the latecomer firm may imitate the forerunner by incorporating the same or similar technologies in its early stages but should be able to create new or different technologies from the forerunner firm to achieve an overtaking. The logic behind this idea is simple. If a latecomer continues to follow the same path as its forerunner, the latecomer would always remain behind the forerunning company, unless it runs much faster than its target, which is not easy. Thus, an alternative for a latecomer is to explore a short cut or a different path. Lee (2019, p. xxi) referred to this idea as the so-called, "catch-up paradox," that is, you cannot catch up if you only keep catching up. This paradox implies that "just trying to emulate or replicate the practices of the forerunning economies is not enough, and catch up realizes only if you take a different path."

This section also addresses the question of whether latecomers rely more on recent or old technologies than the incumbents by examining the latters' citation lags, and whether the former relies more on scientific knowledge than the latter in terms of their patents' citation in scientific literature. These two aspects have already been verified by an analysis using a large sample of firms in Park and Lee (2015), and this study does a similar job for the case of these two comparable firms. A possible hypothesis is that the latecomer would rely more on scientific literature because science literature is not protected by any IPR forms and is freely available for use. Thus, the latecomer has a reason to explore fully useful knowledge from scientific commons in their catch-up efforts.

The latecomer may also attempt to rely less on old technologies protected by patents, which indicates a continued reliance on the incumbents. Such an attitude also makes sense in terms of the need to avoid any possible patent dispute with the incumbents. The latecomers therefore have a reason to explore a technological trajectory that is less connected to existing technologies. Thus, their citation pattern will be geared more toward recent patents. Therefore, the average cycle time of their patent portfolio would be shorter than those of the incumbents. This hypothesis is interesting given that some studies (Park & Lee, 2006; Lee, 2013c) have found that the latecomer countries tend to specialize in short-cycle technology-based sectors. These studies are concerned with across-sector specialization, whereas the present section explores a twisted question of whether a latecomer firm's patent portfolio would show a shorter average cycle time than those of the incumbents in the same sector.

4.2.3 Common Patterns in Overtaking in Technologies

Table 4.1 summarizes the patterns of catching up by the three latecomers of Samsung, Hyundai, and Huawei against the corresponding incumbents of Sony, Mitsubishi, and Ericsson. The first row shows the year that the latecomers overtook the incumbent in terms of sales volume or the years that market catch-up is completed to realize overtaking. Then, the remaining rows show diverse aspects of technological catch-up, such as quantity and quality of patents, self-citations, and mutual citations, among others.

First, the hypothesis that technological catch-up precedes market catch-up or that market catch-up tends to realize owing to technological catch-up, is mostly supported when we consider technological catch-up in terms of the number of patents only. While Samsung overtook Sony in 2005 in terms of sales volume, its number of US patents grew bigger than that of Sony in 1995 or nearly ten years before the sales catch-up. Whereas Hyundai overtook Mitsubishi in 2001 in sales, it filed more patents than Mitsubishi as early as 1998. Whereas Huawei overtook Ericsson in 2012 in sales, it filed more patents than Ericsson from 2007 onwards. In other words, the three latecomers all succeeded in filing more patents than the incumbent (which means technological catch-up) before they caught up with the incumbents in markets in terms of sales (which means market catch-up).

Now, the question of catching up by similar or different technologies can find answers by looking at three variables of patent quality, self-citations, and mutual citations. The answer seems to be that the latecomers have all developed their own technologies in the sense that their technologies tend to be of equal or higher quality, and that they have all become independent in terms of increasing self-citations and reducing citations to the incumbents.

Table 4.1 shows that Samsung's patents have enhanced quality to a higher level than that of Sony from 1992 or more than ten years before it overtook Sony in market sales. Similarly, Huawei's patents boasted a much higher quality than those by Ericsson from its early days or since the 1990s or more than ten years before it overtook Ericsson in market sales. Only Hyundai showed a slower catch-up in patent quality as its quality became similar to that of Mitsubishi as late as 2005 or several years later than its market catch-up in 2001. Such slower catch-up in automobile than in IT sectors is expected and makes sense, given that automobiles corresponds to more tacit knowledge and longer cycle time of technologies than IT and thus slow speed in learning and copying incumbents' knowledge by latecomers.

Next, the values of self-citations reflecting the degree of technological independence in Table 4.1 show that the latecomers have all overtaken the incumbents in this regard or several years before overtaking them in market sales. Samsung's self-citations increased to the level of Sony's in 2002 or two years before their market overtaking in 2004. Hyundai's self-citations have also kept increasing to become higher than those of Mitsubishi in 1998 or three years before market overtaking. Huawei's self-citations have also caught up with those of Ericsson in 2008 or four years before the market overtaking.

The final indicator of similar or different technologies is the degree of mutual citations. In this aspect, all the latecomers have reduced their reliance on or citations to the technologies owned by the incumbents (Table 4.1). In comparison, the citations from incumbent to latecomers indicating the degree of dependency on latecomers' technologies were increasing, although somewhat slowly. This pattern of asymmetry in mutual citations between the latecomer and incumbents is expected and is a part of the continuation of technological catch-up by the latecomers.

An emerging summary of the above would be that when the latecomers have succeeded in overtaking incumbents in markets (sales), they have also succeeded in technological overtaking in terms of quantity and quality of patents as well as self-citations and mutual citations. This analysis confirms the hypothesis that technological

Table 4.1 *Catching up by similar or different technologies: comparison between a latecomer (L) vs. incumbent (I)*

	Samsung vs. Sony	Hyundai vs. Mitsubishi	Huawei vs. Ericsson
Sales revenues, overtaking when? (year)	L > I (2004)	L > I (2001)	L > I (2012)
Patent quantity	L > I (1995)	L > I (1998)	L > I (2007)
Patent quality	L > I (1992)	from L < I to L = I (2005)	L > I from the beginning
Self-citation	increasing L to L > I (2002)	increasing L to L = I (1998)	increasing L to L = I (2008)
Mutual citations			
1) From L to I	decreasing	decreasing	decreasing
2) From I to L	increasing slowly	increasing slowly	increasing slowly
Short or long CTT	from L > I to L < I	from L > I to L < I	L < I from the beginning
Relying on science	L < I	L < I	L > I

Source: Author using the information from Joo et al. (2016), Oh and Joo (2015), and Joo and Lee (2010)

catch-up tends to be a basis for market catch-up, which sounds very similar to Schumpeterian theory.

Finally, Table 4.1 further provides information on the cycle time of technologies and the reliance on science. The literature, such as that of Park and Lee (2015), earlier discovered that the average CTT of latecomers' patents would be shorter than that of incumbents, particularly in the short-cycle sectors. Table 4.1 provides some evidence of this. Huawei's patents show a shorter CTT than that of Ericsson from the beginning or the 1990s. The average CTT of Samsung or Hyundai was previously longer than its corresponding incumbent and has eventually become shorter at a later stage of catch-up. These patterns are consistent with theoretical observation, in that the latecomers have all ended up having shorter CTT than the incumbents, as they all managed to finish the process of market catch-up or overtaking. The pattern also implies that the latecomers attempt to avoid reliance on existing or old technologies occupied by the incumbent during the process of catching up.

In terms of the degree to which patents cite scientific articles or technological innovation relies on scientific knowledge, only Huawei shows a consistently higher degree than that of the incumbents. By contrast, the patents by Samsung or Hyundai rely less on science than those of Sony or Mitsubishi, respectively. Huawei's strong reliance on science may be understood through its having to go through more patent disputes with incumbents such as Cisco from its early days.

4.3 LOCAL VS. FOREIGN FIRMS IN THEIR COEVOLUTION WITH SURROUNDING INSTITUTIONS IN CHINA

4.3.1 *Theoretical Perspectives*

Economic institutions refer to the rules and standards that make up all the business transactions of a region (Wan & Hoskisson, 2003). Subnational regions within a country may have different levels of institutions (Meyer & Nguyen, 2005; Porter, 1998). In particular, subnational regions in developing countries exhibit a high level of heterogeneity in the development of their products, capital, and intermediate markets (He, 2003). Some regions are more troubled by institutional voids than others (Khanna & Palepu, 1997; Ma et al., 2013; Wei et al., 1999). As a result, firms in less developed subnational regions face greater difficulty and uncertainty in doing business than those in developed regions because market transactions in subnational regions are not highly efficient (Ma et al., 2013). A subnational government can improve institutional conditions by developing market institutions and formulating formal rules of transactions in the region (Ma & Delios, 2010; Wan & Hoskisson, 2003). These rules can improve firm performance (Lee and Lee 2022).

Subnational regions within a country can also be dissimilar in terms of the abundance level of various forms of capital, such as infrastructure, human, and knowledge capital (Cantwell, 2009; Meyer & Nguyen, 2005). The level of capital in a region is highly related to the nature of firm production (Wan & Hoskisson, 2003). Therefore, local government investments in physical infrastructure, education institutions, and innovation systems can contribute to the productivity growth of firms (Driffield et al., 2002). For example, a highly educated workforce may help foster the absorptive capacity of a firm with regard to the generation of new product ideas and the acquisition of new knowledge, thereby contributing to firm productivity (Lee and Lee 2022).

In sum, subnational regions within an economy tend to be heterogeneous in terms of institutional factors. Such heterogeneity provides firms with differential opportunities and constraints that shape the cost and return potential of their business activities and ultimately lead to performance differences. In the meantime, as Schumpeterian theory (Nelson, 1991; Winter, 2006) suggests, business firms tend to be heterogeneous, with their heterogeneity often persisting due to the limitation in learning and benchmarking. One source and dimension of firm heterogeneity has to do with their ownership, such as locally or foreign-owned firms. Given that owners can also decide on how firms allocate resources in the process of production, the ownership types of firms should affect and alter their performance (Cuervo & Villalonga, 2000). Firms of different ownership types, namely, state, private, and foreign, may have different business goals and face different constraints. Such differences may result in different economic behaviors, particularly in the way institutions are exploited. Therefore, different ownership types can lead to different economic outcomes even though they face the same institutions (Lee and Lee 2022).

First, FOEs or affiliates of MNCs can access, and therefore share, technical and managerial knowledge of their parent companies located in their home or developed countries (Javorcik, 2004). According to the resource-based view of firm growth (Penrose, 1959), parent corporations in advanced economies have access to diverse resources within the firm, or they can easily acquire these resources from other firms, compared to firms in emerging economies (Mathews, 2002a). Thus, FOEs can bring a large portion of advanced resources from their parent companies to the production process in emerging economies, and this could be a source for their out-performance (Lee and Lee 2022).

However, FOEs have no strong desire to invest in regional resources transacted in local markets (Graham & Wada, 2001). Furthermore, MNCs, which are the parent companies of FOEs, invest and maximize profit on a global basis. Thus, MNCs tend to be more cautious with regard to huge long-term investments in a specific region than privately owned local enterprises (POLEs), which have roots in the area. On the one hand, MNCs can repatriate profits without expanding investment over time once they have successfully settled in their host countries (Seabra & Flach, 2005). On the other hand, MNCs tend to decrease their investment in a specific region in the long run if they lose location advantage because of rising wage rates or the lack of tax breaks (Dunning, 1998). FOEs may depend less on the subnational region in terms of acquiring the resources they need. For example, FOEs may not need to hire local human capital if they can bring in talented workforce from their parent companies.

Therefore, regional innovation systems and institutional development has minimal or less effect on FOE performance. The development of institutional factors in a region may also contribute to the performance improvement of FOEs (Lee and Lee 2022).

In comparison, POLEs, especially those in latecomer or emerging economies, tend to be lacking in diverse resources and competences for business (Mathews, 2002a). Thus, the main goal of firms in developing economies is to acquire these resources and to improve the availability of such resources over the course of firm operations. Therefore, profit is sought mainly to facilitate further the expansion of these resources (Lee & Temesgen, 2009). This type of backwardness is more serious for private firms than for SOEs and FOEs, which may have access to resources as a result of their networks with the state or parent corporations in their home countries. By contrast, POLEs must strive to fully exploit any available external resources (institutions) in a region because of the lack of support from the government or foreign parents (Xia & Walker, 2015). POLEs in China may have a high propensity to rely on the supply of resources from a subnational region (Nachum, 2000). Subsequently, the development of regional institutions and innovation systems may lead directly to the performance change of POLEs. For example, the evolution of market institutions allows POLEs to pay for the minimal costs associated with market transactions, which could have possible effects on the improvement of productivity over time (Lee and Lee 2022).

In summary, although the development of regional institutional factors is beneficial to all firms in the region regardless of ownership, POLEs are desperate and are likely to obtain more benefits because of their strong predilection for investing to acquire and benefit from regional resources in local markets. Thus, the effect of institutional development on a firm may vary depending on the type of firm ownership, because each type involves different incentives and business goals. So, my own study (Lee and Lee 2022) explore the hypothesis that institutional development is positively related to firm productivity and that the extent of the effect is larger in POLEs than in FOEs.

4.3.2 Exploring the Hypothesis in the Context of China

The subnational regions in China exhibit significant heterogeneity in institutional development (He, 2003). China comprises thirty-one subnational regions (twenty-two provinces, four municipalities, and five autonomous regions). Each region has its own market institution within which firms operate; meanwhile, each local government plays an important role in shaping the infrastructure, education, and innovation systems, as well as other public services in the region to stimulate regional economic development. Therefore, these regions tend to differ from one another in terms of the levels of institutional development, which exerts varying levels of influence on firms. Further, China has a unique industrial structure in which state-owned, private, and foreign-invested companies constitute a substantial portion of its economy in the twenty-first century (Bai et al., 2009; Sachs & Woo, 2001). Hence, testing the influence of such heterogeneity on firm productivity according to ownership type can be interesting and effective in the Chinese context. However, few solid empirical analyses of the effect of subnational institutions on performance of different ownership in China exist.[1] One notable exception is my own study, Lee and Lee (2022), and thus we present the main results of that paper in a summary form.

Lee and Lee (2022) use the Chinese Industrial Enterprises Database of the National Bureau of Statistics (NBS) of China, covering the period of 1998–2009, and include all industrial enterprises with annual sales of 5 million yuan or higher. Their descriptive table shows that in terms of labor productivity, the FOEs significantly outperformed the other types of firms on average, but the productivity gaps decreased continuously over time due to rapid catching up by privately owned local firms. The sales per worker of the POLEs in the sample increased from 202.1 Yuan RMB in 1998 to 568.8 in

---

[1] For instance, important works like Dollar et al. (2005), Chan et al. (2010), and Ma et al. (2013) have not dealt with the possibility of institutional effects varying according to ownership.

2009, whereas those of FOEs increased from 312.7 to 630.9 during the same period. The productivity gap decreased from 115.6 to 61.2. One reason behind the fast catching up by POLEs can be their different coevolution with surrounding institutions.

In Lee and Lee (2022), several dimensions of institutions are considered. The first set of institutional variables are about transportation (physical capital), high education (human capital), and invention patents (knowledge capital).[2] The second set is about market institutions, measured by the marketization index developed by the National Economic Research Institute (NERI) (Fan et al., 2011). The NERI index is a comprehensive catalog that captures regional market development in the following aspects: (1) the relationship between the government and the market, (2) the development of the nonstate sector in the economy, (3) the development of the product market, (4) the development of the factor markets, and (5) the development of market intermediaries and legal environment (Li et al., 2009). Measured at each province, three major regions of eastern, western, and central regions, as well as those for the entire country, all the average of these values exhibit an increasing trend over time, reflecting the rapid development of institutions in China.

4.3.3 Institutions Supporting Out-Performance of Local Firms over Foreign Firms

In Lee and Lee (2022), a robust econometric analysis is conducted to reveal the reason behind the differences in the relative performance of firms with different ownership types. The key interests are the effects of interaction between institutions and ownership, in addition to their separate effects. First, the benchmark results without

---

[2] First, we measure the development of physical capital through the expansion of public transportation, such as railways and highways. Our measure for each province is defined as the ratio of the total length of railway and highway to the gross area of the province. Second, this study determines the development of human capital through the number of college graduates per 10,000 population in each province. Third, the number of invention patents registered per 10,000 population in each province is used to represent the development of knowledge capital.

the interaction terms suggest that the coefficient of foreign ownership is positive and significant, indicating that foreign ownership
alone has a bigger positive effect on firm performance as compared
with private ownership. Second, the effects of the three institutional
factors, namely, market development, human capital development,
and physical infrastructure development, are all positive and significant as expected.

Finally, and most importantly, the results with the interaction
terms of ownership dummies and institutional variables show that
private ownership enjoys larger positive benefits from regional institutional development in comparison with the other types of ownership. For instance, the three institutional factors (human capital,
knowledge capital, and physical infrastructure) are positive and significant for foreign ownership but these coefficients are all smaller
than those for POLEs. Therefore, we can infer that POLEs tend to
derive and enjoy larger benefits from the same institutional development in comparison with FOEs.

Figure 4.1 illustrates the dynamic effect of the interaction of
ownership and institutional development on labor productivity. The
graph shows the different sizes of the effects of institutional development by ownership type of firms, and the differences are shown by
the different slopes of the two curves. The intercept term, referring to
the initial level of productivity, is lowest for the POLEs but the slope
is the steepest in POLEs, which reflects the larger effect over time of
institutional development on POLEs than on FOEs or SOEs. In other
words, the sizes of the curve slopes correspond to the capability of
firms of diverse ownership to exploit the institutions.

Figure 4.1 also reflects well the coevolution of firms and surrounding institutions. That is, the productivity of the POLEs lags behind that
of the FOEs or SOEs when the institutions are at low levels or in their
early stages of development. However, POLEs gradually catch up with
FOEs or SOEs as institutions develop over time because the POLEs
have stronger capabilities to use and exploit the institutions than FOEs
or SOEs; hence, POLEs eventually overtake FOEs or SOEs.

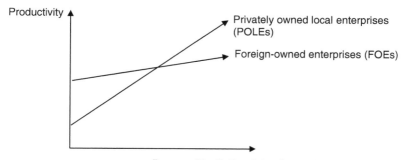

FIGURE 4.1 Productivity catch-up by interaction of firm ownership and surrounding institutions
Notes: adaptation of a Figure in Lee and Lee (2022).

The aforementioned results are consistent with the reasoning that POLEs tend to utilize the development of institutions more effectively and seize new business opportunities well. Local ownership translates into stronger incentives and capabilities to exploit regional institutions than other types of ownership. This capability comes from the strong incentive of local private ownership to exploit regional resources for profit and growth. FOEs have less need to exploit local institutions in comparison with POLEs because the former can rely on their parent companies abroad when seeking a large portion of productive resources; thus, they are not deeply rooted in the local economy. In comparison, SOEs are typically under government protection and network with bureaucrats; thus, they have fewer reasons to try to exploit the institutional development in their locality.

The results suggest that the influence of institutional factors on firm performance depends not only on the ownership type of a firm but also its interaction with institutions. In this light, these results may have some policy implications. Any one-sided promotion of institutional development or private entrepreneurship (start-ups) cannot be effective in fostering economic growth because these two elements tend to evolve together. On the one hand, private firms cannot prosper without sound institutions. On the other hand, institutional development is useless unless there exist private firms that can benefit from this development. Also, the results imply that POLEs may outperform FOEs in the long run as long as there is sound and steady development of diverse institutions including innovation systems, and thus they can be relied upon as a long-term determinant of economic growth.

4.4 CORE FIRM LEADING THE GROWTH OF A REGION: TSMC IN HSINCHU

National-level analysis in Chapter 2 discusses the idea of detour in two dimensions. One is a detour of first specializing in short TT sectors before going into long-CTT sectors at a later stage, and the other is that of becoming more centralized during the catching-up stage as innovation tends to be led by big businesses rather than a large number of SMEs. Thus, an important element of an imbalanced pathway of catching up is the nonlinear pattern of transitional specialization into short CTT sectors led by big businesses. A necessity for big businesses was to find a vehicle to circumvent entry barriers to high-end and value-added segments by seeking niches and mobilizing resources and competences. This section explores this issue further, now at the level of a region, exemplifying the growth of Hsinchu City led by the emergence of a core firm, TSMC.[3]

4.4.1 *Innovation Systems of Industrial Districts*

Centered on the question of why innovation activities and economic development are unevenly distributed over space (Asheim et al., 2019, p. 1), many studies have investigated industrial districts and RIS. Markusen (1996) and Park (1996) are two noteworthy classic works on the typologies of the industrial district. They focus on the interfirm network in the governing productive activities in a region. Markusen (1996) presented several industrial network structures, such as Marshallian, HaS, and satellite platform

---

[3] This section is a summarized account of the case of TSMC using the detailed information in a study by Wong and Lee (2021).

districts. The Marshallian district demonstrates high resiliency in sustaining the dynamics of productive activities because it primarily consists of small firms that often engage in cooperative competition (Markusen, 2003). By contrast, HaS districts, such as Toyota City in Japan, are led by a small number of large firms as the magnet for smaller firms that want to utilize proximity to resourceful anchored tenants. The satellite platform district consists of SMEs that supply diverse MNCs clustered in a region. The key players of the three structures comprise many firms, a few large firms, and firms supplying to MNCs, respectively.

Given our interests in the characteristics of the RIS of Hsinchu, a catching-up region in emerging economies, we combine the district typologies with the analyses of the innovation systems to identify the innovation-related counterparts that differentiate the dynamics of the industrial districts. In this sense, we are not only interested in the features of a Marshallian or HaS industrial district but rather in Marshallian or HaS innovation systems, specifically the patterns of knowledge creation and diffusion among firms and their concentration or decentralization. Such focus is justifiable because the firms in catching-up Asia have emerged not only as producers or suppliers but also as innovators that offer state-of-the-art technologies.

Given that Hsinchu is populated by SMEs, we may say that Hsinchu resembles a Marshallian network. Actually, Hsinchu shows a high degree of cooperation/linkages among local firms. An intriguing question then regards dynamic transformation and the possibility of convergence, namely, whether a tendency exists toward a gradual convergence to a HaS type of RIS, and to what extent it is associated with an increasing dominance by the core firm (TSMC) or ever higher levels of concentration in tems of innovator distribution. As the core firms continue to grow to reach the technological frontier, they tend to become responsible for a dominant share of innovation activities in the region while increasing the degree of self-citations and strengthening the linkages with nonfirm actors (e.g., universities or scientists). Such a possibility of eventually changing types of industrial districts is consistent with the early observation by Park (1996) on the emergence of the "advanced HaS" type from the Marshallian type.

4.4.2 Evolution of Hsinchu toward Centralization by a Leading Firm

The establishment of Hsinchu as a high-tech region originated from the plan of the National Science Council of Taiwan to construct the Hsinchu Science and Industrial Park (HSIP) in 1980, which envisions a tripartite collaboration between industry, academia, and government research institutes, such as the ITRI (Wong et al., 2015). Since its construction in 1980, HSIP has witnessed how six industrial sectors, namely, ICs, personal computers (PCs) and peripherals, telecommunications, optoelectronics, precision machinery, and biotechnology, formed a self-sufficient and closely integrated value chain from R&D to mass production (Hu, 2011). This origin can serve as a basis to propose that Hsinchu resembles the Marshallian district more than the HaS one. However, the semiconductor sector (IC chips) has replaced the PC and peripheral sectors since the 1990s as the core sector. The former has eventually become the focal sector of HSIP, dominating in terms of the number of employees and sales since the 2000s (Hu, 2011).

The rise of the semiconductor sector in Hsinchu is not simply a natural progression but was rather caused by the targeted promotion of this industry at the national level in the early 2000s under the "Two Trillion and Twin Star Project." In 1970, the government and pragmatic technocrats and entrepreneurs envisioned that the established semiconductor companies abroad would promote a fabless[4] business structure because globalization and offshoring movement were then gaining momentum. Therefore, they aspired to make Hsinchu the foundry hub for global fabless firms in

---

[4] Fabless manufacturing is the design and sales of hardware devices and chips while outsourcing their fabrication (fab) to a specialized manufacturer called a foundry.

the semiconductor production value chain. The government allocated ample resources to ITRI and two other research universities in Hsinchu to develop such capabilities and niches. In the 1980s, the segmentation detaching foundries from integrated device manufacturers was realized, and the firms that invested in foundry businesses in HSIP were then contracted to supply fabrication services to foreign firms in advanced countries.

Taiwan used its networking assets and mobilized its social capital to commit to specialized assets (i.e., sources of finances and technical skill) to develop a "pure-play" foundry[5] (Yeung, 2016, p. 138) and encouraged associated industries to realize an active ecosystem. These efforts led to the founding of TSMC as a spin-off in 1986 from ITRI as a joint venture with Philips as well as other fabless firms that provide designs and chips for telecommunication and multimedia products. As the firms gained sufficient capabilities to upgrade and mature, ITRI evolved as a platform that coordinates collaborative research and establishes R&D consortiums for new industries. Actually, laboratories of ITRI had acted as the prime vehicle for leveraging and modifying advanced technologies from abroad, and these technologies were effectively diffused among various Taiwanese firms including TSMC (Amsden & Chu, 2003, Mathews, 2002b). Thus, a patent citation analysis for the 1990s shows a high citation tendency of TSMC and United Microelectronics Corporation (UMC) to the patents held by ITRI (Lee & Yoon, 2010).

However, the rise of TSMC to global prominence occurred ten or fifteen years after its spin-off from the ITRI, which could be attributed to the firm-specific innovation effort beyond the initial government promotion in the 1980s (Yeung, 2016, p. 140). Specifically, between the two dominant firms, TSMC and UMC, TSMC eventually significantly outperformed UMC in revenue and technology capabilities after the mid-2000s. Such performance is attributable

---

[5] Pure-play foundry means a company that does not design but operates fabrication plants for other companies.

to the technological breakthrough TSMC made in 2005, unveiling its manufacturing capability in commanding 90-nm node process technology in 12-inch semiconductor wafer production. By contrast, other competing firms in Taiwan and abroad were operating via 0.5-micrometer (μm) to 110 nm process technology.[6] In sum, such development of the IC sector, which is led by TSMC, has been the driving force for Hsinchu to evolve toward a HaS structure.

Increasing dominance of TSMC in the region can also be captured by looking at the distribution of patents in the region. Except in the early years, the share of TSMC in the total number of US patents filed by the region was flat at 7% for most of the 2000s, when it faced regional competitors, such as UMC. TSMC eventually emerged as the frontrunner after the global financial crisis in 2008 and dominated the region, owning approximately 30% of the total patents in Hsinchu in 2017. Such a tendency toward centralization in innovation is consistent with the hypothesis that Hsinchu is shifting toward the HaS structure despite being a close Marshallian type prior to the 2000s or before the rise of the semiconductor sector as the main industry in the region (Hu, 2011). We can also discuss this observation in terms of the value of HHI (Herfindahl–Hirschman Index), which is a conventional measure of concentration used in analyzing NIS or RIS. Initially, the HHI level of Hsinchu is comparable to San Jose in the Silicon Valley area or 0.02 in 2018 (Wong et al., 2021). Later, Hsinchu showed a trend of increasing concentration, reflecting the increasing dominance of the core firms. For instance, the value of HHI hit the bottom at less than 0.05 in the late 2000s; then, it kept increasing in the 2010s and approached 0.20, which is a big jump.

4.4.3 Doubling Upgrading of the RIS Led by a Core Firm

Such a trend of centralization does not need to be considered bad, because it is accompanied by the upgrade of Hsinchu from a peripheral to a catching-up RIS at both the dimension of the leading firm

---

[6] See Wong and Lee (2021).

and the region excluding the core firm. First of all, as shown in Table 4.2, the number of US patents increased a couple of times from the early 2000s to the early mid-2010s in both the region and the region excluding the core firms; from 2,431 to 5,063 in the region excluding TSMC, and from 901 to 3,838 by TSMC.

Most importantly, in view of the literature on the peripheral RIS with a low level of regional embeddedness, upgrading or catching up of RIS in Hsinchu has been explained in terms of the reduction of reliance on external knowledge or increasing localization of knowledge creation and diffusion, which is further accompanied by increasing reliance on new sources of knowledge, such as scientific articles (science-based-ness) and universities (university–industry linkages). Specifically, in terms of upgrading in knowledge sourcing, not only the core firm but also the region excluding the core firm has realized increases in all the three dimensions of localization (over the 1990s to the 2000s period), university–industry linkages, and science-based-ness.

For instance, the degree of localization (share of local citation in total citations) in "Hsinchu without TSMC" has increased from an average of 5.3% in the 1995–1997 period to an average of 9.3% in the 2000–2002 period, whereas it remained around that level (or 8.3%) in the 2016–2018 period (Table 4.2). The corresponding numbers for TSMC are 3.6% in the 1995–1997 period, 7.8% in the 2009–2012 period, and 6.4% in the 2016–2018 period. In terms of science-based-ness measured by the share of patents citing one or more scientific article, the degree in the region excluding TSMC has increased from an average of 13.6% in the 2000–2002 period to 39.0% in the 2016–2018 period. In the case of TSMC alone, the increase was from 14.8% in the 2002–2002 period to 40.6% in the 2016–2018 periods.

Technological diversification has also increased at both levels of the core firm and the region excluding the core firm. The numbers indicating diversification have increased from an average of 0.26 in the 2000–2002 period to an average of 0.32 in the 2016–2018 period

Table 4.2 *Comparison of the core firms and the regions without the core firms, 2000–2002 and 2016–2018*

	Hsinchu	Hsinchu without TSMC	TSMC	Suwon	Suwon without Samsung	Samsung
1. Patent counts (filed in the United States)						
Total count: 2000–2002	4,846	2,431	901	1,772	116	1,581
Total count: 2016–2018	13,286	5,063	3,838	11,465	1,036	9,260
2. Localization of knowledge creation and diffusion						
Average of 1995–1997	0.036	0.053	0.036	0.00	0.00	0.01
Average of 2000–2002	0.075	0.093	0.078	0.001	0.003	0.032
Average of 2016–2018	0.060	0.083	0.064	0.032	0.046	0.042
3. Concentration of innovations (assignees): HHI						
Average of 2000–2002	0.09	0.096	–	0.826	0.336	–
Average of 2016–2018	0.13	0.02	–	0.67	0.15	–
4. University–industry linkage (share of patents with both firms and universities as co-assignees)						
Average of 2000–2002	0.00	0.00	0.00	0.00	0.00	0.00
Average of 2016–2018	0.007	0.003	0.003	0.022	0.006	0.016

5. Science-based-ness (share of citations with more than one citation to scientific articles)

Average of 2000–2002	0.147	0.136	0.148	0.126	0.16	0.127
Average of 2016–2018	0.405	0.39	0.406	0.493	0.453	0.500

6. Cycle time of technologies (backward citations lags in years)

Average of 2000–2002	5.15	5.92	4.77	6.52	8.16	5.65
Average of 2016–2018	7.98	10.04	7.19	7.94	11.963	6.51

7. Technological diversification
(no. of classes a region has filed patents divided by the total number of 3-digit patent classes)

Average of 2000–2002	0.316	0.256	0.07	0.22	0.056	0.186
Average of 2012–2014	0.343	0.32	0.073	0.316	0.153	0.246

Notes: The concentration (HHI) for Suwon considers Samsung Group as one of the top five assignees.
Source: Adaptation of Table 4 in Wong and Lee (2021)

at the level of the region without the core firm. In the case of the core firm, TSMC, the degree of technological diversification has increased from 0.070 to 0.073 during the same period.

If upgrading happens only at the core firms, it may not be called a proper upgrading. However, in Hsinchu, both the surrounding regions and the SMEs have experienced upgrading. Notably, Hsinchu without its core firm, TSMC, displays higher specializations in long-cycle technologies (associated with parts and components), distinct from the core firm specializing in short-cycle technologies (developing, assembling, and producing IC chips). Such growth of SME suppliers to the core firm with a different technological specialization from the core firm seems to have been possible because ITRI provided them with various technical services, consultancy, licensing, and workforce training; it also played an important role in fostering domestic industrial competencies by linking SMEs with large foreign corporations (Fuller, 2005; Mathews & Cho, 2000, pp. 258–259; Wong et al., 2015).

Given that such upgrading of the whole region has accompanied the region's centralization over the distribution of innovators, this mode of the RIS may not be called a mature RIS which is characterized by a more even or dispersed distribution of innovation but can be called a catching-up RIS along an imbalanced development path discussed in Chapter 2. Such conceptualization of an imbalanced mode of catching-up RIS is consistent with the idea of the two alternatives: balanced and imbalanced modes of catching-up NIS discussed in Chapter 2, which revived the classic debate on imbalanced development (Hirschman, 1958), in contrast to the balanced development of Nurkse (1953). In this sense, this study has identified at least one viable path of upgrading RIS in emerging economies. In such a mode of imbalanced RIS, upgrading may happen not necessarily through globalization associated with foreign direct investments or MNCs but through the emergence of large indigenous firms, although they have learned from MNCs at their early stage.

4.5 FIRM-LEVEL CONVERGENCE MATCHING THE MACRO-LEVEL CONVERGENCE: KOREAN FIRMS

4.5.1 How to Measure and Analyze the Firm-Level Innovation Systems

While the literature on innovation systems tends to focus on the national or sectoral level, one can also conceptualize and analyze corporate innovation systems (Granstrand, 2000). For instance, we can use the same variables measured at the level of a nation to analyze the firm-level innovation system as has been done in Lee (2013c, Chapter 5). Such extension is consistent with Schumpeterian theory of firms discussed in the research of Winter (2006) and Nelson (1991, 2008a, 2008b), which emphasizes the heterogeneity of firms and considers knowledge and imperfect learning as sources of interfirm heterogeneity. Given such emphasis on the knowledge base or innovation systems of firms, this section looks at several quantitative expressions of various aspects of the knowledge base of firms so that they may reveal the changing behavior and performance of South Korean firms. These knowledge-related variables are indicators of the nature of the knowledge pool each firm utilizes for its innovation and other activities. The property of the knowledge base thus relates to the firm-level innovation system underpinning the innovative activities of a firm.

Given our focus on catching-up firms, we address the aspects of knowledge that are shown to be markedly different between advanced and catching-up firms. Following Lee (2013c, Chapter 5), key variables are the CTT, self-citation (intra-firm creation and diffusion of knowledge), technological diversification, and originality. These variables are used to investigate their relationship with firm behavior and performance. Among them, we are particularly interested in the following two variables.

The first focal variable is CTT, which is about the speed of change in the knowledge base of technologies, and a short cycle time means a quick speed of change and thus means the underlying knowledge tends to be quickly outdated or becomes obsolete over time. The average CTT of a firm can be measured as the average time difference between the application year of the cited patent and of the citing patents which are owned by a firm (Jaffe & Trajtenberg, 2002). A sector-level analysis by Park and Lee (2006) found that technological catch-up tends to occur in sectors with a shorter cycle time, whereas advanced countries tend to be dominant in sectors based on long-cycle technologies (Lee, 2013c, Chapter 3). The firm-level analysis in Lee (2013c, Chapter 5) found that catching-up (Korean) firms tend to specialize in short-cycle technologies, which also lead to higher profitability. This is because short CTT on average means that such firms rely less on average on the old stocks of knowledge of which the patent rights are owned and dominated by the incumbent. Accordingly, the latecomers may avoid direct competition, or IPR disputes, with incumbents, and may find a niche, thus avoiding competing in the same markets. In other words, it makes more sense for the latecomer firms to conduct innovation relying on more recent technologies than the old technologies occupied by the incumbents.

Specifically, for the Korean and US companies in the 1990s, short CTT specialization had a significantly positive effect on Korean firms' performance but not on those of the United States, because US firms or advanced firms need not identify a niche in such short CTT but tend to be more diverse in their patent portfolio. Thus, if Korean firms became similar in the 2000s or 2010 to US firms and commanded a more diverse patent portfolio in diverse sectors, their profitability would also have been less affected by CTT as in the case of US firms.

The second focal variable is that of self-citations in Korean firms. The ratio of self-citation at the sector level represents appropriability, namely, the capability to protect one's innovations from being copied by others and thus monopolize profits from the innovation (Trajtenberg et al., 1997). By contrast, self-citation at the firm level is the degree to which the innovation of a firm builds upon its accumulated knowledge pool. In general, the literature finds that the more advanced or older the firm, the higher its patent self-citation ratio, or its self-citation can be a measure of technological capabilities, which is confirmed by comparing Samsung with Sony (Joo & Lee, 2010) and Huawei with Ericsson (Joo et al., 2016). In fact, Lee (2013c) found that self-citation ratios are much higher in US firms than in Korean firms, and they tend to have a significantly positive effect on firm performance (firm values) in US firms; conversely, such is not the case for Korean companies with a very low ratio in the 1990s. Then, if Korean firms have become similar to, or technologically as strong as, US firms over time, we may hypothesize that the self-citation ratio must have increased in Korean firms and should have a significant impact on firm performance, particularly firm values.

In summary, if Korean firms had entered the convergence phase in the 2000s or 2010s, the effect of CTT on corporate performance should be positive or insignificant. By contrast, it was negative in the 1990s. Next, whereas the self-citation ratio was insignificant to the performance of Korean companies in the 1990s, it is expected to be positive and significant for firm values from the 2000s onwards.

4.5.2 The Trend of CTT and Self-Citations and Their Effect on Firm Performance

If we investigate the trend of key innovation system variables of Korean firms since the 1990s and later, we can notice a clear-cut trend of continued catching up and even convergence, which is well presented in Im and Lee (2021). First, the average number of patents filed by each firm has shown a substantial increase since the 1990s, from less than 50 per firm in the early 1990s to more than 150 per firm in the 2000s and 2010. Second, the average ratio of self-citations has also notably increased about four times, from less than 2% in the early 1990s to approximately 8% by the mid-2010s. As discussed in Lee (2013c, Chapter 5) and Joo et al. (2016), high self-citation represents one aspect of strong technological capabilities. In fact, the level of 8% in the 2010s is somewhat close to the average level

(12%) of US firms in the 1990s according to the information in Lee (2013c, Chapter 5). Thus, this increasing number of patents per firm and increasing trend of self-citations reflect the increasing levels of technological capabilities of Korean firms over time.

Third, the trend of the average CTT of Korean firms has increased from six or seven years in the early 1990s to nearly twelve years in the 2010s, although some changes have occurred in recent years. Overall, this finding indicates that Korean firms have substantially reduced the degree of former specialization into short CTT-based sectors. The nearly double increase over a period of time can be considered a big change, although it might also reflect, to a certain extent, the increasing trend of CTT over time and over the nationality of firms as analyzed in Lee and Lee (2021b).

Table 4.3 presents the average values of key innovation variables of firms and their change over time in the three sub-periods of the 1990s, 2000s, and 2010s. The statistically significant changes over time are confirmed with regard to the two focal variables of self-citations and CTT. The subsequent regression analyses also showed that these two variables are the main drivers of change affecting the performance and behavior of Korean firms and their innovations.

We can discuss the regression results as reported in Im and Lee (2021) on the impacts of the CTT and self-citations on the two measures of firm profitability (return on assets and return on sales). The variable of the CTT is noteworthy and important. The CTT is shown to be negative and significant in the 1990s but insignificant in the 2010s. That is, the results for the 1990s are identical to the results for the Korean firms in Lee (2013c), but the results for the 2010s have become similar to those for the US firms in the 1990s as reported in Lee (2013c). An interpretation is that Korean firms have discontinued their earlier strategy of focusing just on short CTT for niche areas but are now more diversified in the 2010s. This find is consistent with what we hypothesized as one aspect of convergence of the Korean firms toward US firms.

Table 4.3 *Trends of innovation variables of the Korean firms over the three periods*

Variables	Mean value			T-test of the gap between periods: mean difference	
	sub-period 1: 1990–1996	sub-period 2: 2001–2006	sub-period 3: 2010–2015	Period 2 - period 1	Period 3 - period 1
Technological specialization (inverse of diversification)	0.601	0.483	0.516	-0.118**	-0.085*
Originality	0.333	0.343	0.268	0.01	-0.065**
Self-citation ratio	0.026	0.058	0.070	0.032**	0.045**
Cycle time (years)	8.815	9.797	13.385	0.982*	4.570**

** $p < 0.01$, * $p < 0.05$, + $p < 0.1$.

Note: Technological specialization is HHI over technological classes of the patents filed by firms and therefore an inverse of technological diversity of firms' patent portfolios.

Source: Adaptation of Table 7 in Im and Lee (2021)

The regression results for the determinants of firm values measured by Tobin's Q are also interesting with regard to the key innovation variable of self-citation. The variable of the self-citation ratio is now shown to be positive and significant in the 2010s whereas it was insignificant in the 1990s or 2000s. The results for the 2000s are a continuation of the results for the 1990s reported in Lee (2013c), whereas the latter part for the 2010s is consistent with the results for the 1990s US firms reported in Lee (2013c). The fact that the self-citation ratio now shows a positive effect on Korean firm value in the 2010s is indicative of the convergence of behavior of Korean firms toward US firms in terms of their level of technological capabilities and their importance in firm values. The results that the variables of self-citations are insignificant as a determinant of firm growth are also consistent with the US firm results reported in Lee (2013c).

4.5.3 A Partial Convergence?

The overall picture emerging from the preceding part is a thesis of ongoing convergence of Korean firms toward US firms. With a marked increase in self-citations and CTT occurring over time in Korean firms, the relationship between innovation variables and profitability and firm values in Korea has now become similar to that in the United States in the 1990s. In other words, we find some important evidence of convergence, such as no significant relationship between (short or long) CTT and firm profitability and a significant relationship between higher self-citation and firm values. This new pattern is exactly the same pattern found in US firms for the 1990s by Lee (2013c), which is a reflection of an increasing level of technological capabilities of Korean firms and is indicative of convergence in the innovation system of Korean firms. This aspect of convergence is also a deviation from the typical pattern of catching-up firms in the 1990s discussed in Lee (2013c, Chapter 5) when Korean firms sought niche-based strategies for profitability by specializing in short CTT, and their technological capability represented by self-citation is too low to significantly affect firm values. The unfinished part comes from the finding that although Korean firms are shown to be diversifying into non-short CTT-based sectors, their growth mechanism is still shown to have not considerably changed, still relying on fixed investment associated with a high capital–labor ratio rather than technological capability associated with self-citations.

The trend of firm-level changes in Korea analyzed in this chapter is consistent with the country-level pattern discussed in Chapter 2. Additionally, the finding of Lee and Lee (2021a) indicates that the economic growth (per capita income) of Korea is now positively associated with long CTT of the country, as it is now moving toward long CTT-based sectors, such as biomedicines and bioproducts and high-tech materials and components. Given that the overall level of CTT in Korea (nine years) remains notably shorter than that of Germany (twelve years) (Figure 1A in Lee & Lee, 2021a), the shift toward long CTT continues to be an ongoing process. Interestingly, this gap between Korea and Germany in average CTT is somewhat similar to their gap in per capita GDP in PPP terms such that per capita GDP of Korea has now reached the 70% level of the United States, whereas that of Germany is approximately 85% of the United States according to the more recent data from the IMF released in 2021.

4.6 SUMMARY AND CONCLUDING REMARKS

This chapter deals with the question of alternative pathways for latecomers' firms in their coevolution with regional or national innovation systems. Thus, it takes up a similar framework from the national level proposed in Chapter 2 and modifies it for the firm-level analysis.

Specifically, the first question at the firm level is about whether latecomer firms use "similar or different" technologies compared with that of incumbents. The discussion in Section 4.2 shows from the cases of latecomers overtaking incumbents in market shares that such market overtaking involved technological overtaking in terms of quantity and quality of patents as well as the level of technological capabilities (proxied by self-citations) and mutual dependency measured by mutual citations. We also find that the average CTT of latecomers' patents tends to become shorter than that of incumbents, which reflects their strategy of seeking niche areas different than those occupied by incumbents in long-CTT sectors.

Section 4.2 of this chapter deals with the important issue of coevolution of firms and surrounding institutions with an example of the Chinese context. It shows that POLEs tend to exploit the benefit from regional institutions rather than other types of ownership. This capability comes from the strong incentive of private local ownership to exploit regional resources for profit and growth. FOEs have less need to exploit local institutions in comparison with POLEs because the former can rely on their parent companies abroad when seeking a large portion of productive resources; thus, they are not deeply rooted in the local economy. The implication is that any one-sided promotion of institutional development or private entrepreneurship (start-ups) cannot be effective in fostering economic growth because these two elements tend to evolve together, and that POLEs may outperform FOEs in the long run, as long as there is sound development of institutions including regional or sectoral innovation systems.

Section 4.4 of this chapter discusses the role of the leading firms in a region going through the detour of centralization first or during the catching-up stage, probably to be followed by decentralization at a later stage, which is also an important element of an imbalanced pathway of catching up. The focus region is Hsinchu City in Taiwan, led by emergence and eventual dominance of a core firm, TSMC. Rapid development of the IC sector led by TSMC has been the driving force for Hsinchu to evolve from a decentralized Marshallian district in the 1990s toward a more centralized structure or HaS type since the 2000s. Such a trend of centralization does not need to be considered bad, because it is accompanied by the upgrade of the entire Hsinchu City. Specifically, in view of the literature on the peripheral RIS characterized as a low level of regional embeddedness, upgrading or catching up of RIS in Hsinchu has been documented in terms of the reduction of reliance on external knowledge or increasing localization, which is further accompanied by increasing reliance on new sources of knowledge, such as scientific articles and universities. Given that such upgrading has happened at the expense of increasing the region's centralization over the distribution of innovators, this mode of the RIS may not be called a mature RIS with more even or dispersed distribution of innovation but can be called a catching-up RIS along an imbalanced development path as discussed in Chapter 2.

Such conceptualization of the imbalanced mode of catching-up RIS is consistent with the idea of two alternative, balanced and imbalanced, modes of catching-up NIS discussed in Chapter 2, which revived the classic debate on imbalanced development (Hirschman, 1958), in contrast to the balanced development of Nurkse (1953). In this sense, this study has identified at least one viable path of upgrading RIS in emerging economies. In such a mode of imbalanced RIS, upgrading may happen not necessarily through globalization associated with continued dominance of FDI or MNCs but through the emergence of large indigenous firms, after they have learned from MNCs at their early stage. The role of big businesses in such upgrading can be understood as a vehicle to circumvent entry barriers to high-end and value-added segments by seeking niches and mobilizing resources and competences.

Finally, this chapter in Section 4.5 has dealt with the question of whether behavior and performance of catching-up firms would become similar to those of mature firms in advanced economies as they build up technological capabilities over time. Given that Chapter 2 has discussed the national-level detour or eventual convergence, a remaining issue is the match between the firm- and national-level innovation systems as discussed here. Based on the Schumpeterian theory of firms, Section 4.5 analyzes the innovation systems of Korean firms as a representative of catching-up firms to determine that their behavior has changed from the 1990s to the 2010s, indicating an ongoing process of convergence toward US firms. With a marked increase in average self-citations and CTT occurring over time in Korean firms, the relationship between innovation variables and profitability and firm values in Korea has now become similar to that in the United States in the 1990s. In other words, we find some important evidence of convergence, such as no significant relationship between (short or long) CTT and firm profitability and a significant relationship between higher self-citation and firm values. This new pattern is exactly the same pattern found in US firms by Lee (2013c).

This change is a reflection of an increasing level of technological capabilities of Korean firms and is indicative of convergence in their innovation systems. This aspect of convergence is also a deviation from the typical behavior of catching-up firms in the 1990s discussed in Lee (2013c, Chapter 5) when Korean firms sought niche-based strategies for profitability by specializing in short CTT, and their technological capability represented by self-citation is too low to significantly affect firm values. The trend of firm-level changes in Korea is consistent with the country-level pattern that the economic growth (per capita income) of Korea is now positively associated with long CTT of the country, as it is now moving toward long CTT-based sectors, such as biomedicines and bioproducts and high-tech materials and components.

5 Innovation–Development Detour in South Korea

5

5.1 INTRODUCTION

Following the country's dramatic political, economic, and socio-cultural transformation since the end of Japanese colonial rule in 1945, South Korea has emerged as an exceptional latecomer country and established itself as a fully fledged democratic market economy. However, this process has not been without friction, as the country also experienced decades of political authoritarianism and government-led economic development (Amsden, 1989; Johnson, 1982; Wade, 1990). Korea's achievement is often encapsulated by the term "catching-up," which derives from Abramovitz's (1986) seminal article "Catching-up, Forging Ahead, and Falling Behind."

Catching up can be defined as closing the gap between a country's current state and a predetermined benchmark. Korea is a paradigmatic example of a catch-up country: Korea joined the Organisation for Economic Co-operation and Development (OECD) in 1996 and achieved an income level equivalent to other high-income countries. Despite this remarkable catch-up, Korea experienced a major crisis in 1997 and nearly avoided another crisis in 2008 and 2009. Whereas the 1997 crisis was linked to excessive indebtedness and overinvestment by big businesses, the crisis of the late 2000s began in the United States and led to capital flight from Korea back to Wall Street. This, in turn, caused the Korean currency to depreciate substantially. It is interesting to note that Korea recovered remarkably quickly from both crises, prompting the investigation in this chapter into the sources of this resiliency. This chapter expands on my earlier work on the sources of South Korean growth beyond the MIT range since the mid-1980s. Motivated by these questions, this chapter seeks to reconceptualize the Korean model of catch-up development, aiming to suggest a consistent answer to both earlier and new questions.

Given Korea's miraculous catch-up, it is unsurprising that scholars and commentators hold diverse views on this achievement. Therefore, this chapter begins by evaluating existing views and myths regarding the Korean economy's miraculous growth and resiliency, such as the influence of initial conditions, while also reviewing debates on the role of markets versus the government, inclusive versus exclusive institutions, and import substitution versus export promotion. Based on an evaluation of various myths and misunderstandings regarding the Korean model, this chapter elaborates on and redefines the Korean model while focusing on elements that have seldom been mentioned in the literature.

The first element is the role of domestically owned big businesses and their capability building for export orientation; the second element is smart specialization into short-CTT and thus low entry barrier sectors during the upper middle-income stage. On this basis, this chapter redefines the Korean experience as an exemplary case of a country that took a detour from short-CTT to long-CTT sectors and from dominant big businesses to SME emergence. These two elements constitute a detour because advanced economies tend to be dominant in long-CTT and thus high barrier-to-entry sectors with sources of growth that are dispersed among both SMEs and big businesses.

This chapter explores the Korean experience to demonstrate that multiple catching-up pathways are possible for latecomers, and that latecomers do not necessarily follow the trajectories of incumbent advanced economies in a linear manner. Indeed, for latecomer economies, taking different or multiple paths is necessary for overcoming the entry barriers to high value-added and end goods sectors and other challenges at the middle-income stage. Additionally, I demonstrate that most successful economic catch-ups involve strategically navigating global–local interfaces to promote the emergence of big domestic businesses. Moreover, we show that no successful catch-up has occurred without generating a certain number of big businesses, which are needed not only to overcome the latecomers' disadvantages regarding entry barriers at the middle-income stage but also to ensure a certain degree of resiliency against crises. This observation differs from the existing development literature, which asserts that no country has successfully achieved a high-income economy without growing its manufacturing sector.[1]

To summarize, this chapter emphasizes that the promotion of domestically owned yet export-oriented big businesses – not foreign-controlled subsidiaries of multinational corporations (MNCs) – is an important feature of the Korean model. MNCs survey the globe, seeking cheaper labor and larger markets. Therefore, they cannot be relied upon to generate sustained growth in specific localities or countries, although they can serve as useful channels for knowledge transfer and learning at an early stage of development.

Section 5.2 provides a very brief summary of the history of Korea. Section 5.3 reviews existing views on the Korean model. Section 5.4 discusses the emergence and growth of big businesses and their export capability building. Section 5.5 discusses the issue of sectoral specialization by latecomers during the middle-income stage and Korea's strategy of entering short-CTT-based sectors. The main arguments in Sections 5.4 and 5.5, namely the roles of big businesses and their sectoral specialization, will be used to formulate my definition of the Korean model in Section 5.6. A brief summary follows in Section 5.7.

5.2 A VERY BRIEF HISTORY OF KOREA

Although Korea is often considered a latecomer or emerging country, the country has a long history stretching back nearly 5,000 years, according to records. Koreans as an ethnic group are distinct from the Chinese, and the Korean language is classified as an Altaic language.

---

[1] Indeed, this argument is primarily made by scholars who emphasize structural transformation, such as Szirmai and Verspagen (2015).

The borders of the ancient kingdoms of Korea at times reached Manchuria. Although the Korean language was distinct linguistically from Chinese, Korean lacked its own characters, and therefore, Korean texts were written using Chinese characters. Chinese characters, however, are logograms, making it cumbersome to memorize thousands of characters. Therefore, in the early fifteenth century, King Sejong and his scholars invented a phonetic alphabet called Hangul, which consists of five basic vowels and fourteen consonants. Koreans also invented printing. The *Jikji*, which is the world's oldest extant printed book, was first printed in 1377, which is seventy-eight years before Gutenberg's Bible in the West. In 2001, this copy was included in UNESCO's Memory of the World Register as the world's oldest metalloid type.

The last dynastic kingdom of Korea was the Chosun Dynasty, led by the Yi family. The dynasty began in the fourteenth century and lasted for five centuries; it is one of the three longest dynasties in the world. Although Chosun kings made many cultural achievements, such as inventing Hangul, they ruled over a feudal kingdom. Moreover, because the dominant philosophy of the dynasty was Confucianism, kings kept Korean society isolated from the West and modern civilization until the end of the nineteenth century. Consequently, the Chosun dynasty missed the opportunity to modernize and was annexed by neighboring Japan, a modern, constitution-based nation-state that had embraced modern civilization before Korea.

In 1945, following thirty-five years of colonial rule, Korea was liberated. After defeating Japan in the Pacific War, the United States and Soviet armies landed on the southern and northern halves of the peninsula, respectively. The US Army Military Government (USAMG) ruled South Korea for three years until the formal establishment of the Republic of Korea in 1948. The USAMG also initiated several reforms, including land reforms that returned farmland to peasants. However, the implementation of the land reform was disrupted by a civil war that broke out in 1950 with the communist regime in the North attacking the South. A cease-fire was declared in 1953, and despite subsequent US aid, the South Korean economy remained weak throughout the 1950s as the country recovered from the war. Nevertheless, a democratic political system with free and direct elections for the presidency took root in South Korea. South Korea's first president was Syngman Rhee, a civilian and former independence fighter against the Japanese empire. However, due to a poor economy and the unpopularity of Rhee, massive demonstrations led by students and civilians broke out, leading to Rhee's resignation in 1960. The subsequent transitional government, however, was weak and did not last for more than a year. The government ended when army general Park Chung-hee carried out a coup in 1961.

Park aggressively pushed an industrialization plan and achieved economic takeoff before being assassinated in 1979 by a former collaborator who had participated in the 1961 coup. Although Park established a harsh authoritarian regime in Korea, during his time in power Korean per capita income doubled. In 1960, Korean per capita income was below that of Thailand and Malaysia and a mere 10% of US per capita income; by 1980, Korean per capita income had exceeded Thailand and Malaysia and had reached 20% of US per capita income (see Figure 2.2). Following Park's death, ex-military general Chun Doo-hwan became president through the electoral system under his control. Korea in the 1980s maintained a system of not direct but indirect elections for the president, and became a quasi-democracy in that sense. Chun pursued an economic policy of increased economic opening with less government intervention. Owing to the successes of big businesses and chaebols (family-owned conglomerates), the Korean economy became stronger, with its per capita income reaching 30% of that of the United States by the late 1980s (Figure 2.2).

This economic prosperity also led to a reduction in inequality (Wong & Lee, 2018), which was associated with the rise of a well-educated, hard-working, and better-paid middle class. However, the newly rising middle class viewed rule by an ex-military president unfavorably, and the demand for democracy continued to increase

(Eichengreen et al., 2015, p. 27). Finally, in 1987, mass demonstrations broke out, resulting in the return of free and direct elections. However, another ex-military general, Roh Tae-woo, who was a classmate of Chun Doo-hwan at the Korean Military Academy, won the 1987 presidential election. Consequently, it took Korea another five years to elect a civilian government. In 1993, pro-democracy activist Kim Young-sam was elected president as part of a political coalition formed by merging his party with the party led by ex-military politicians.

President Kim Young-sam implemented further financial liberalization to meet the conditions for joining the OECD. In the mid-1990s, Korea achieved the status of a high-income country, with its per capita income surpassing 40% of US per capita income (Figure 2.2). As a result, Korea was permitted entry to the OECD. However, firms abused this liberalized environment to borrow excessively from foreign capital markets at rates that were below domestic rates; this became one cause of the 1997 Asian financial crisis. To escape the crisis, Korea accepted an IMF bailout agreement, which imposed various institutional reforms on Korea that included radical opening, financialization, and globalization in line with the Anglo-American economic systems of shareholder capitalism. As the party responsible for the 1997 crisis, the liberal–conservative coalition government lost the 1997 election to the progressives, and newly elected President Kim Dae-jung moved Korea in a slightly more progressive direction. President Kim Dae-jung was followed by President Roh Moo-hyun, who died from suicide in 2009.

Interestingly, this left-oriented government continued to support a liberal market economy approach and even initiated negotiations over free trade agreements with the United States and others. Subsequently, under two conservative administrations lasting from 2009 to 2017, a series of free trade agreements were reached, first with the United States and then with China, the European Union, and India. In 2017, President Park Geun-hye, the daughter of former president Park Chung-hee, was impeached due to her abuse of presidential power. In the subsequent election, Moon Jae-in was elected president in a landslide victory made possible by leftist and pro-gressive political groups. However, Moon failed to manage the economy, in particular, rising house prices, effectively, and thus his party lost the 2022 presidential election to Yoon Suk-yeol, the former head of the prosecutor's office, who had been appointed to the position by Moon himself.

Although the past several decades of Korean history have been turbulent, the economy has continued to enjoy consistent growth. Indeed, the country recovered quickly from several crises, including the 1979–1980 crisis following the assassination of President Park and the 1997–1998 Asian financial crisis, both of which caused negative growth rates. Korea also recovered from the 2008–2009 global financial crisis. During the late-1980s to mid-1990s, the Korean economy grew beyond the upper middle-income stage, or the so-called "middle-income trap stage," to join the OECD. Again, throughout the two crises from 1997–1998 and 2008–2009, manufacturing exports by big businesses recov-ered mainly due to the depreciation of currency values, and Korea's per capita income reached 70% of the US level by the end of the 2010s and converged with or exceeded that of Japan (Figure 2.2).

5.3   THE MYTH OF THE "KOREAN MODEL"

There are diverse views on Korea's success. In what follows, I review these opinions critically and provide my own view, arguing that such steady and resilient growth was possible due to the emergence and growth of domestically owned yet export-oriented conglomerates and their smart specialization in short-cycle technology-based sec-tors, such as IT, which are low barrier-to-entry sectors during the middle-income stage.

5.3.1   *Favorable Initial Conditions versus "Taking Care of the Basics First"*

In the context of South Korea's economic takeoff, some scholars assert that Korea enjoyed favorable initial conditions, such as a high level of human capital and physical infrastructure that was built during the colonial period. However, the Japanese colonial government did not educate Korean people beyond primary school, and even at primary schools, enrollment rates were rather low at approximately 47%. Moreover, most infrastructure was destroyed during the Korean War which broke out immediately after liberation. In fact, post-war conditions in South Korea were quite similar to many African countries, in that South Korea underwent several decades of colonial rule, several years of civil war, and a period of hunger and food shortage in the 1950s, during which Korea relied on US food aid. South Korea also suffered from an acute lack of natural resources, as all minerals were located in North Korea. Beginning in the early 1960s, Park Chung-hee launched a series of five-year economic plans. Even at this time, Korea's situation was still similar to other developing countries in that it faced continual external imbalances and persistent trade deficits until the late 1980s (Lee & Mathews, 2010; Lee, 2016, Chapter 1). Given these initial conditions, one of Korea's first tasks was solving the food shortage and enhancing the level of human capital.

5.3.1.1 Solving the Food Shortage via an Agricultural Revolution

Following the Korean War, Korea suffered a food shortage that lasted, in part, up until the 1970s. Food shortages stemmed from low agricultural productivity, which itself was due to a lack of technology, capital, and fertilizer, as well as peasants working small plots of farmland. Food shortages in South Korea were exacerbated by the influx of approximately 2.5 million refugees from North Korea (Hsiao, 1981). Following land reform in 1948 and 1950, Korean farmers became smallholder farmers, but food shortages persisted. In the 1950s, Korea experienced a 2–20% shortage of the rice and grain needed to feed the population. In particular, production satisfied only 70% of demand in 1952 and 1953 due to the Korean War.

Furthermore, the social unrest that accompanied liberation in 1945 and the Korean War in 1950 caused the production of Korean staple grains, such as rice and barley, to stagnate from 1940 to 1960.

To solve the food shortage problem, the US government started an aid program known as the Public Law 480 program in 1954, and the United States provided food grains to Korea beginning in 1956. Public Law 480 provided both foodstuffs and agricultural inputs, such as fertilizer, to increase domestic agricultural productivity (Friedmann & McMichael, 1987). Owing to the fast growth of input (fertilizer) and the increase in the area of farmland via large-scale reclamation projects by the new Park government, rice production increased rapidly in the 1960s. The overall growth in rice production in the 1960s was 29.3%, and daily rice consumption per capita increased from 289 g in 1963 to 373.7 g in 1970.

However, despite increases in agricultural output in the 1960s, Korea continued to depend on food aid from the United States because food demand increased rapidly due to population growth and income growth from industrialization. In fact, US food aid increased steadily from 669,000 metric tons in 1965 to 3.6 million tons in 1972, which constituted one-fourth of South Korean grain consumption (Hsiao, 1981). However, in 1970, the Title II Program under Public Law 480, which provided direct donations of food aid, ended (Hsiao, 1981). This placed a great burden on Korea's balance of payments. In 1971, Korean exports were just $1 billion, but imports were $2.4 billion. Rice and grain imports were $200 million. Thus, the Korean government tried to achieve self-sufficiency in rice.

President Park, who came to power in 1961, was keen to develop a new rice variety to overcome the food shortage problem and save foreign currency. After several failures, Korean scientists developed a new rice variety known as "IR667" in 1966 with the help of the International Rice Research Institute. The new variety was a hybrid of Japonica-type rice and high-yield Indica-type rice. In 1969, after the Korean Rural Development Administration made some improvements to the seeds, IR667 demonstrated an extremely high yield of about 630 kg per 10 are during tests,[2] which was 80% higher than the

---

[2] An "are" is 0.01 hectare (ha).

average yield of a Korean farm. The Korean government started supporting IR667 intensively, and IR667 was supplied nationwide. With the introduction of IR667 and its varieties, rice production reached 6 million metric tons, and in 1977, Korea became self-sufficient in rice, although it had to import other grains. In 1977, the national average yield per 10 are was 494 kg, which was greater than the previous world record set by Japan (447 kg/10 are) and 41% greater than the national average before IR667 (Moon, 2010).

Such increases in agricultural productivity were supported by increased investments in rural areas. The government quadrupled its expenditures on large-scale infrastructure projects, such as dams, reservoirs, and irrigation works (Boyer & Ahn, 1991). From 1970 to 1979, irrigation systems across 531,000 hectares, which constituted 23.8% of arable land, were improved. Farming mechanization was also pursued under the first Five-Year Plan for Agricultural Mechanization (1972–1976). During the 1970s, the number of mechanical cultivators increased from 11,884 to 289,779, and the number of tractors increased from 61 to 2,664 (Korean Economy Compilation Committee, 2010). Because of these investments, the annual growth rate of agricultural fixed capital increased from 1.69% in the 1960s to 11.86% in the 1970s (Hwang & Yoo, 2014). The growth in fixed capital offset the decrease in agricultural labor and farmland caused by urbanization and labor migration in the 1970s. Finally, in 1977, Korea achieved self-sufficiency in rice, although it had to import other grains.

Not only investments in rural infrastructure but also new pricing policies were introduced to give farmers greater production incentives. In the 1950s, the government controlled the grain market and set prices low to deal with inflation and poverty. The government purchase price for grain was very low, sometimes even below the cost of production. This disincentivized farmers from improving productivity. Beginning in 1961, the military government changed the low-price policy, and in 1968, it increased the government purchase price for grain.

Beginning in 1969, the Korean government instituted a dual price policy for grain, by which the government purchased grain at a high price from farmers and sold it to consumers at a low price. The program sought to subsidize the household expenses of both urban workers and rural farmers. Under this system, the government purchased grain from farmers at 130% of the production cost of marginal paddy land and sold the grain to consumers at 70% of the government purchase price (Ministry of Agriculture, Forestry and Fisheries of Korea, 1978). The policy was introduced because of political concerns about farmers who, in the late 1960s, were becoming increasingly dissatisfied with their economic situation, especially compared to their urban counterparts. This program provided farmers with incentives to increase productivity and introduce new rice varieties, such as IR667. The proportion of rice purchases made by the government was less than 10% of total rice purchases before 1970, but this figure surpassed 10% in 1971 and rose to 23.4% from 1977 to 1979, during which time the IR667 varieties were at their peak. However, this put a substantial financial burden on the Korean government. The government cost of purchasing and releasing grains reached KRW 209 billion, which was 4.1% of government expenditures in 1979. The program was abolished in 2005 due to international pressure from the WTO.

5.3.1.2 *Building Initial Human Capital: The 1960s and 1970s*

In 1944, one year before Korea was liberated from Japanese colonial rule, total enrollment in primary education among Korean children was only 47%. Following liberation in 1945, primary education enrollment increased rapidly, from 45% in 1945 to 82% in 1949 (Ryu, 2002). The number of elementary school students doubled during this period because, from 1945 to 1948, the provisional government under the USAMG attempted to educate every child aged six and older who wished to attend school (Kim, 1999). Furthermore, the Korean government made primary school education compulsory in June 1950. The Korean government also implemented the Compulsory Education Achievement Plan from 1954 to 1959 (McGinn et al., 1980). Total enrollment in primary education reached 91.65% in 1959.

The new government under President Park carried out the Five-Year Plan for the Expansion of Facilities of Compulsory Education from 1962 to 1966 and then again from 1967 to 1961. These plans were carried out alongside the Five-Year Economic Development Plan. As a result, 811 schools and 53,726 classrooms were built from 1962 to 1971 (Korean Economy Compilation Committee, 2010), and by the late 1960s, Korea had achieved universal primary education.

Enrollment in secondary education also increased significantly in the 1960s. As primary education became universal in the 1960s, more children completed elementary school and desired to attend secondary school (Ryu, 2002). Thus, secondary education enrollment increased further (Korean Economy Compilation Committee, 2010). In contrast, enrollment in tertiary education remained low at 6–8% throughout the 1960s.

Catch-up efforts during this period relied mostly on imported, turnkey technology, and there was a critical shortage of technical personnel who were able to operate imported equipment after receiving either on-site training or instructional manuals (Lee, 2013b). Thus, the government emphasized raising the level of human capital, and substantial improvements were made by the mid-1970s. In 1975, primary school enrollment was 106.86%, and secondary and tertiary enrollment rates were 56.35% and 6.9%, respectively.

5.3.2 Free Markets versus State-led Industrial Policies

When discussing Korean takeoff, some scholars have argued that the Korean miracle was possible because the government followed the principles of free markets and openness (Balassa, 1988). This emphasis on the role of markets is often represented by the so-called Washington Consensus (Williamson, 1990), which focused on macroeconomic stabilization, trade, and financial liberalization. However, a study by the Economic Commission for Latin America and the Caribbean on reform in Latin America found that macroeconomic stability is not a sufficient condition for ensuring long-term growth and that growth is more closely linked to the dynamics of the production structure. Furthermore, well-functioning institutions and infrastructure are essential, but these generally do not play a direct role in bringing about changes in the momentum of growth (Ocampo, 2005). A World Bank assessment of the reform decade of the 1990s conceded that growth entails more than the efficient use of resources and that growth-oriented actions meant to stimulate, for example, technological catch-up or risk-taking for faster accumulation, may be needed (World Bank, 2005).

Openness and trade liberation have generally been regarded as key policy ingredients for developing countries. Many countries have simply resorted to devaluation or standard trade liberalization, which led to export booms caused by the resulting price effects and to temporary stabilization of external balances. However, there are numerous cases of macro-oriented reform bringing immediate, yet unsustained, recovery that eventually results in another round of crises.[3] Countries tend to experience some economic growth after trade liberalization and devaluation; however, this tends to be short-lived or occur in a stop-and-go cycle. This is because countries following the principles of the Washington Consensus failed to enhance the capabilities of the private sector (Lee & Mathews, 2010).

The belief that allowing market forces to operate freely despite the inherited backwardness in the capabilities of the private sector, especially manufacturing, is not consistent with the rise of capitalism in continental Europe after England's industrialization. Russian historian Gerschenkron analyzed the industrialization

---

[3] For example, the three reform cycles in Indonesia (1983–1991, 1994–1997, and post-1998) show that rapid success with macro-reform, if not supported by microeconomic changes, tends to fade fairly soon, triggering a subsequent balance-of-payment crisis. A similar pattern is unfolding in Nepal with respect to the 1990s reforms (Lee, 2006).

of Germany and Russia and introduced the notion of "latecomers' disadvantages," asserting that in a backward country, state intervention may be necessary to compensate for its deficiencies (Gerschenkron, 1962). Specifically, he proposed the need for the formation of large banks to provide access to the capital needed for industrialization. The situation confronted by the developing world after World War II was worse than that faced by Germany or Russia because they lagged much farther behind the leading economies. Amsden (1989) was the first to attribute the successful economic catch-up in Korea to the industrial policies of the government, specifically in the form of "getting prices wrong and creating rents for targeted sectors."

Industrial policy in Korea has more or less followed the example of Japan, which has been well documented in the influential work of Johnson (1982), who attributed the Japanese miracle to the role of Japan's super ministry, the Ministry of International Trade and Investment. One of the first definitions of industrial policy was presented by Johnson (1982), who defined it as policies that aim to improve the structure of a domestic industry to enhance a country's international competitiveness. Thus, this book defines industrial policy as building the capabilities of private firms to sustain long-term economic growth rather than as picking winners or providing protection for some firms or sectors (Lee, 2013a).

In 1960s Korea, the Park regime established various institutions, including the Economic Planning Board, which formulated economic plans; the Ministry of Trade and Industry, which supported industrial policy and exports; and the Ministry of Finance, which funded economic plans (Lee, 2013b). These government agencies were important for identifying and promoting key industries and technologies, as explained below. In what follows, we present two cases of industrial policy to suggest that the Korean miracle was not simply a result of free markets or openness. The first case is the use of financial control to stimulate manufacturing, and the second is the protection of domestic markets by tariffs.

5.3.2.1 Financial Control and the Industrial Policy of Credit Allocation

In Korea, the extreme scarcity of capital resulting from weak domestic savings in the 1960s and 1970s forced firms to depend heavily on credit to raise funds beyond retained earnings. In the absence of effective capital markets, the state used its control over the banking system to channel domestic and foreign savings to selected industries and firms (Lee, 2016, Chapter 2). After taking power in 1961, Park nationalized the commercial banks, and the banks remained under state ownership until 1980, when they were privatized. In Korea, the government exercised near complete control over the private sectors through their control of credit.

For effective state activism and industrial policy, the ability of the state to control finances was critical. The critical difference between the state's financial control through credit allocation and other control instruments, such as tariffs, import quotas, tax incentives, and entry or trade licenses, is often overlooked. First, financial control implies more discretionary control. Through credit allocation, the state can not only control the financial abilities of firms but also demand firms' compliance on other matters. Second, it is important to note that the Korean state's financial control was not based on its political authority, which was the case for other instruments that were supported by legislation or regulations. Rather, the Korean state's financial control was based on its economic power, which was enabled by its ownership of banks. Third, most other controls, except licensing, were aimed at specific industries or sectors and, thus, affected firms only indirectly. In contrast, financial control was directly aimed at individual firms.

In this regard, a simple but fundamental fact should be noted: The state's financial leverage allowed it to control firms because firms had a strong motivation to improve their performances and because firms believed credit supply to be critical. In Korea, firms' motivation for success was derived from private ownership and the expectation that firms would benefit from their own good performance. Thus, even if big businesses were under so-called "soft budget constraints" due to their special connections with state agencies, this did not necessarily lead to weak motivational efficiency as it did in socialist countries. Rather, it led to exactly the opposite behavior, that is, excessive risk-taking.[4]

Korea experienced a large saving gap in the 1960s, with domestic savings at 9% of GDP and gross investment at 15% of GDP. Therefore, Korea had to borrow foreign capital to fill the gap. That is why exports were crucially important, and earning US dollars via exports was the critical binding constraint on growth for an economy at the low- and middle-income stages. Despite its low income and resulting low domestic saving, Korea maintained a high investment rate; and one of the reasons for this high investment was low interest rates, which were maintained by the government. Therefore, Korea existed in a state of financial repression. Or, to borrow the language of Hellman et al. (1997), Korea was maintaining a set of "financial restraints" in the sense that real interest rates were at least positive. Despite these suppressed interest rates, the domestic savings-to-GDP ratio in Korea continued to increase, owing to the growth of income associated with strong investment over the decades. The domestic savings rates increased from 9% in the early 1960s to approximately 30% in the mid-1980s (Cho, 1997).

In the Korean experience, the banking sector had always been intended to "serve" the real sectors by providing a stable supply of so-called "growth money" at affordable rates, and the manufacturing and production sectors had always been given priority. Of course, such practice was possible because Korea established several development banks, such as Korea Development Bank, the Export–Import Bank, and the Industrial Bank (for SMEs), and also because most of the commercial banks were under government ownership or control until they were privatized in the mid-1980s. With very minute margins

---

[4] Park (1990) mentioned risk taking in the form of excessive and duplicative investment in the heavy industry drive in Korea in the late 1970s.

between lending and deposit interest rates, the profitability of the banking sector was extremely low, which boosted the profitability of the manufacturing sector. Consequently, private investment flowed into manufacturing rather than into financial businesses.

Allocating credit to manufacturing was combined with controlling entry into specific sectors, primarily the sectors targeted for promotion. This was done on the premise that five profitable firms in a single sector are better than ten unprofitable firms. This practice of limiting the number of firms in a given sector to approximately three or fewer caused return rates to be higher than interest rates, which was advantageous for boosting private investment in manufacturing. This, in turn, generated high rates of return with longer time horizons. In this way, manufacturing firms were able to earn "rents" associated with entry control enforced by the government. Industrial policy was oriented around determining the optimal number of firms in each sector in consideration of the market size, somewhat guaranteeing admitted firms a minimum level of profits (rents) that could serve as a source of investment funds for the future. Causing the rate of return to be higher than interest rates in certain industrial sectors is another possible goal of industrial policy, especially in the context of high interest rates.

The practice of entry control has typically been an industrial policy tool in Japan. In Korea, the tradition of implementing entry controls in many sectors has been regarded as an industrial policy that was copied from Japanese practices (Johnson, 1982). Entry control has two purposes. The first is to differentiate between the "good" and "bad" producers, and the second is to ensure stable profits for the selected producers so that they will be more inclined to invest in fixed capital for business expansion.

5.3.2.2 *Enhancing Export Performance via Protective Tariffs*
One of the most conventional industrial policy tools is infant industry protection via tariffs. However, empirical studies report conflicting results on the effectiveness of tariffs. According to Beason and

Weinstein (1996), tariff protection, preferential tax rates, and subsidies did not affect the rate of capital accumulation or total factor productivity (TFP) in Japan from 1955 to 1980. Moreover, Lee (1996) found that tariffs had either no effect, or a negative effect, on TFP. Nevertheless, several studies verify the positive contributions of industrial policy, in particular, tariffs. For instance, my own work with a colleague, Shin and Lee (2012), studied the same period and sectoral data as Lee (1996), and found that tariff protection leads to the growth of export share and comparative advantages. This makes sense because the goal of such industrial policy during the early development stage (the 1960s and the 1970s) was not TFP enhancement but rather output and market share growth. Aghion et al. (2015) also found that subsidies widely distributed among Chinese firms had a positive impact on both TFP and new product innovation in highly competitive sectors. Both of these recent studies identify competition and discipline as common preconditions for effective industrial policy.

An example of success with tariffs would be the case of Hyundai Motors, which was established in 1970. Hyundai's first car brand was the Pony, which captured 44% market share in Korea in 1976. However, at this time, Hyundai Motors was protected by a tariff on imported cars, including Japanese cars, that reached 82%. While the price of the Pony in Korea was approximately $4,500, it was exported to the US market at the price of $1,850. In other words, without such dumping, Hyundai cars were unable to compete with other cars, and Hyundai Motors' continued investment was possible due to the additional profits generated by its oligopoly in the domestic market enabled by tariffs. At this time in the 1980s, Japanese and German cars of a similar automotive class were sold for $2,300 in US markets. In other words, domestic profits compensated for losses in foreign markets, and these guaranteed profits helped Hyundai survive and invest in fixed capital and R&D for expansion.

Thus, it can be argued that if Korea had opened up from the beginning without tariffs, the Korean economy would not have been as successful in promoting domestic firms and sustaining their catch-up in market share. An underlying assumption of trade liberalization is that local firms are sufficiently competitive to potentially compete against foreign companies and imported goods. This assumption is not true in many cases. Indeed, naive trade liberalization can lead to foreign companies establishing monopolies or destroying the local industrial base.

A more advisable opening strategy, as discussed by Shin and Lee (2012), is "asymmetric opening," according to which latecomer economies liberalize the import of capital goods for the production of final and consumer goods while protecting their consumer goods industries by levying high tariffs on imported goods. In fact, Korea implemented an asymmetric tariff policy for its consumer and capital goods, imposing extremely high tariffs on consumer goods (e.g., around 70% for household electrical appliances in the 1970s), which were promoted as export industries, and considerably lower tariffs on capital goods, such as machinery, which Korea had to import for domestic manufacturing, primarily consumer goods manufacturing.

Of course, one can point out that the protection of local firms by tariffs and entry controls will lead to an oligopolistic domestic market. However, a study by me and a colleague, Jung and Lee (2010), demonstrates that monopoly rents can be used to fund investments because firms are exposed to the discipline of world export markets and because their privileged protection from the government is not unconditional but linked to export performance. In other words, the combination of rent-generating protection in the domestic market and discipline by world markets was an important aspect of Korea's industrial policy during the catch-up stage, which began in the mid-1980s and lasted throughout the 1990s. Jung and Lee (2010) also confirm that such financed R&D investment led to enhanced innovation capabilities among Korean firms, which enabled them to catch up to the productivity of Japanese firms from 1985 to 2005.

5.3.3 Institutions versus Capabilities

Following the decline of the Washington Consensus, the literature on economic development began to focus on the role of institutions as a more fundamental determinant of economic growth compared to economic openness and liberalization (Acemoglu et al., 2001, 2002; Rodrik et al., 2004). These scholars assert that although the policy prescription of liberalization was correct, the policies were not effective due to bad underlying institutions, such as political inclusiveness, corruption, the rule of law, and the protection of private property and intellectual property rights. In other words, although the seed was sound, the soil was bad. Along these lines, Acemoglu and Robinson (2012) distinguish between inclusive institutions and extractive institutions.

Interestingly, this literature (Acemoglu et al., 2001, 2002) contrasts South and North Korea, claiming that the former prospered due to democratic institutions and free markets, whereas the latter failed due to extractive institutions. However, Glaeser et al. (2004) found that the human capital variable is more robust than the institution variable for explaining economic growth, and they presented the examples of South and North Korea to argue that institutions are not the sources of growth. Rather, they asserted that it is actually economic growth that gives rise to institutions such as democracy, as in the case of former authoritarian states like South Korea. In Korea, economic growth gave birth to a middle class, which continually demanded democracy, resulting in political democracy (Eichengreen et al., 2015, p. 27). Indeed, economic growth tends to have the effect of reducing the political costs of overthrowing authoritarianism (Chen & Feng, 1996).

While the case of South Korea can serve as an example for arguing against the institution-centric view of economic growth, it can also serve as a powerful case to advocate for the importance of economic policies. The two Koreas have pursued quite different growth strategies. However, if we confine ourselves to comparing the two

Koreas, it is difficult to disentangle the impact of policies from those of institutions because institutions, such as the protection of private property rights, also differ markedly between the two Koreas. The importance of policies is more visible if we look at the case of China (Qian, 2003). It is obvious that China's miraculous growth can be attributed to sudden changes in its economic policies geared toward nurturing an open, market-oriented economy. Post-1990 India is another case where major changes in the country's policy line were responsible for economic takeoff (Tendulkar & Bhavani, 2005).

While the institution supremacy view tends to ignore policies in favor of institutions, this book takes the view that both factors matter, albeit differently and at different stages of economic development. By using the number of granted US patents and the amount of R&D expenditure as an index for innovation, my own work with a colleague, Lee and Kim (2009), shows that innovation capability is more important for economic growth in countries that have advanced beyond the middle-income stage, whereas political institutions are binding constraints on economic growth in lower-middle and low-income countries. This implies that an emphasis on tertiary education and R&D expenditures can explain the "reversal of fortune" between East Asian economies and Latin American countries over the last four decades.

In fact, one factor behind South Korea and Taiwan being able to overcome the MIT and become advanced economies was high R&D investment during the mid-1980s (Lee, 2013c). South Korea's and Taiwan's R&D investment-to-GDP ratios surpassed the 1% threshold by the late 1980s, and private R&D investment surpassed public R&D investments; this was not the case in most Latin American countries (Lee & Kim, 2009). The experience of Korea and Taiwan suggests that the fundamental solution to overcoming the MIT is the capability to innovate, which enables countries to produce higher value-added products through technological innovation (Lee, 2013c).

5.3.4   Openness, Import Substitution, and Export Orientation

Other scholars writing on the economic success of Korea and East Asia tend to contrast export orientation in Asia with import substitution in Latin America. This comparison is consistent with the broader observation that contrasts Asia's openness with Latin America's relatively closed economic policies. Openness – that is, global economic integration – has long been considered an important element of policy prescription, particularly in the context of the Washington Consensus (Dollar, 1992). Global economic integration has been represented by one or a combination of several of the following three variables: trade openness (trade to GDP ratio), export diversification, and FDI. However, the actual growth effects of these variables are still under debate.

For instance, whereas some studies have found a positive correlation between economic growth and trade openness, others have found that trade openness is not robust as a factor for economic growth. Similar controversies exist over the FDI variable, as scholars are divided between pro-FDI and FDI-skeptical groups. Export diversification is another variable that is subject to debate because some scholars find this concept significant for economic growth, whereas others find export specialization to have significant effects on growth. In place of these three variables, my own work with a colleague, Ramanayake and Lee (2015), introduces export growth and sustainment as alternative variables to represent economic integration and openness. Considering exports as an important factor for economic growth is not new. In particular, economic growth in many emerging countries has taken the form of export-led growth (Krueger, 1978; Cline, 1982; Balassa, 1985).

The variable of export growth, rather than the variables of openness to trade and export-to-GDP ratio, is most consistent with the actual experience of the Korean economy. The argument that export growth (sustaining exports) is one of the strongest binding factors on economic growth in the Global South is consistent with the reasoning that developing countries must earn hard currency by exporting to pay for the imported capital goods that are required investments for sustaining economic growth. In other words, export growth promotes economic growth by generating the foreign exchange necessary for importing machinery and intermediate goods, which are needed for investment. The limits of import substitution as a growth strategy are that it has no method for generating dollars to pay for the capital or intermediate goods needed to run factories that produce consumer goods in substitution for imported consumer goods, given that the consumer goods industries in developing countries still rely on imports of capital goods to run such operations.

It is somewhat less known that Korea pursued exports of consumer goods, from textile goods during its early stage of development to consumer electronics in its later stage, while simultaneously seeking to replace imported capital and intermediate goods in export-oriented sectors with domestic production, which is a clear policy of import substitution. Such export orientation, in combination with import substitution, was desperately needed in Korea because the common mode of exporting manufactured goods tended to be accompanied by imports of expensive intermediate goods from Japan and Germany, as well as trade deficits. In fact, the Korean economy suffered from chronic trade deficits, with imports several times larger than exports in the 1960s, and these deficits persisted until the late 1980s. While the trade surplus of the late 1980s was due to the so-called "three lows" of low oil prices, low interest rates, and a low currency value (that is, a strong Japanese yen), a trade surplus emerged as Korean industry moved to high value-added goods and formerly imported capital goods were replaced by domestically produced goods.

This tendency of import substitution can also be verified by looking at the share of FVA in gross exports of Korea. FVA is one measure of a country's participation in the global value chain. As noted by Lee et al. (2018), Korea demonstrates the so-called "in-out-in again" pattern of global value chain participation. In other words,

FVA increased during the 1960s and in the 1970s, during which time Korea initiated its export-led growth strategy and began integrating into the global economy. However, FVA began to decline in the mid-1980s and throughout the 1990s as Korea replaced imported capital goods with domestically produced goods, such as car engines. However, in the 2000s, FVA again rose as Korea pursued globalization by initiating overseas investment and establishing factories abroad in Southeast Asia and China, where labor is less expensive. Some Korean firms began producing lower-cost intermediate goods abroad for export back to Korea for final assembly.

A notable case of early import substitution is the development of Time-Division Exchange (TDX), a public–private R&D consortium in the early 1980s that produced digital telephone switches (Lee et al., 2012). On the one hand, TDX and its production of telephone switches was an example of localizing imported products. On the other hand, however, it was also one of the first attempts by a Korean firm to domesticate important capital goods in the IT industry. In the 1970s and 1980s, Korea faced a telephone service bottleneck. Until the late 1970s, Korea had neither a domestic telecommunications equipment manufacturing industry nor an R&D program (Lee et al., 2012). As a result, most equipment and related technologies were imported, and Korean technicians merely installed foreign switching systems into the nation's telephone networks. To avoid purchasing imported telephone switches at monopoly prices from foreign companies, Korea decided to build its own manufacturing capability and initiated an R&D program to develop its own digital phone switching systems (Lee et al., 2012). In this project, which targeted specific products for import substitution, the Korean team faced less uncertainty and risk because the targeted technologies, namely telephone switches, were mature products that were less resistant to technology transfers and thus were appropriate targets for imitative R&D via a private and public collaboration (Lee, 2013b).

In collaboration with a national network of switching system manufacturers and distributors, the Korean consortium TDX and the Korean Electronics and Telecommunications Research Institute developed a proprietary digital switching system called the TDX series from 1981 to 1983. This indigenous product took over markets previously dominated by imports and MNCs (Lee et al., 2012). Over the following decades, Korea accumulated experience, leading to the growth of indigenous capabilities in wireless telecommunications in the 1990s. Around the turn of the millennium, a similar takeover occurred, with Samsung and LG taking over the mobile phone market from Motorola (Lee & Lim, 2001).

These cases are indicative of how Korean firms, with the support of the government and its affiliated research institutes, were able to successfully overtake markets previously dominated by MNCs and joint ventures to become exporters. The cultivation of new industries necessitates state-led efforts by a variety of agencies that offered support in the form of acquiring technology, securing financing (including credit rationing), adopting nurturing strategies (including tax concessions and R&D subsidies), controlling excessive competition to allow companies time to develop their products and markets, and opening up markets to the full force of international competition in a phased manner (Lee, 2013b). However, this state action should be phased out at later stages because, by this time, the costs of local production and the risks of entering new markets will have been reduced due to the dynamic learning effects that result from the cumulative output (Lee & Mathews, 2010).

5.3.5   In Search of a Korean Model beyond the Myths

In this section, I have discussed the diverse views on Korea's economic achievement over the last several decades. First, I suggested that such achievements happened not owing to any favorable initial conditions but rather in spite of the constraining conditions that resulted from several decades of colonial rule and several years of civil war, as well as the lack of exportable natural resources and a base for manufacturing. Second, despite these disadvantageous conditions, economic takeoff was achieved through purposeful planning and industrial policy by the government, not the magic of "letting markets do their job." Third, it is not the case that political democracy or inclusive institutions supported economic growth. Instead, capability building for economic growth developed under political authoritarianism, and the resulting economic growth at later stages brought about political democracy. Fourth, economic growth was sustained not only owing to exports but also import substitution of formerly imported capital goods, which was enabled via enhanced local capabilities in innovation.

The final question, then, is what constitutes the essential aspects of the Korean model of development. In the following two sections, the Korean model will be redefined in terms of, first, promoting locally owned big businesses and their technological capabilities at the lower middle-income stage and, second, smart specialization into low barrier-to-entry sectors based on short-cycle technologies during the upper middle-income stages.

5.4 KOREA'S FIRST DETOUR: BIG BUSINESSES FIRST, SMEs LATER

5.4.1 From Technology Imports via Licensing to In-house R&D

In the 1960s and 1970s, the technological capabilities of domestic Korean firms were very poor, and most exports in the manufacturing sector were produced through assembly-type production or the processing of imported parts and raw materials in labor-intensive sectors. The level of technology investment was extremely low: R&D expenditures in 1965 were only 0.26% of gross national product (GNP) and never exceeded 0.5% of GDP during the 1960s and 1970s. Nevertheless, domestic firms strove to overcome their technological deficiencies by investing in learning about foreign technologies from advanced countries, which consisted mainly of importation of assembling technology and packaged technologies to be applied at turnkey factories (Lee, 2013b). Further efforts concentrated mainly on learning operational technologies, namely how to operate imported capital goods and facilities.

The importation of foreign technology in the form of licensing began to increase in the mid-1970s; this period has been referred to as one of "imitative innovation" (Kim, 1997b).[5] The so-called "strategic" industries, such as iron and steel, nonferrous metals, general machinery, automobiles, shipbuilding, petrochemicals, and electronic equipment, were actively promoted via tax incentives and preferential credits, and firms in these priority industries were also allowed to import foreign technologies by utilizing foreign currency allocated by the government. The Korean government felt that this switch to capital-intensive sectors was necessary for several reasons, such as the argument that labor-intensive exports alone cannot generate sufficient dollars and trade surpluses because these labor-intensive sectors must import a considerable amount of capital goods.

In these capital-intensive sectors, the government evaluated and selected target firms based on the specific criteria of (1) the economic benefits provided to the nation, (2) the technical and financial feasibility of projects, (3) the prospects for profitability, and (4) the quality of management (Korea Development Bank, 1979). Firms demonstrating better performance were given preferential access to dollars to pay for foreign technology, whether directly through an approval system or indirectly through financial commitments made by government-controlled banks. The first entrants into these industries were either state-owned enterprises, such as POSCO, or chaebol affiliates, which had a record of successfully launching new businesses in related and unrelated fields.[6]

By 1978, the top forty-six chaebol groups' share of total output in the heavy industries reached 60%. Moreover, chaebol affiliates,

---

[5] This sub-section is based on Lee (2013b) and Lee and Kim (2010).

[6] Many SOEs were subsequently privatized once they became more competitive by international standards. Examples are SK-Telecom (top telephone service firm), POSCO (global steel firm), Korean Air (global air-carrier), and Doosan Heavy Industry (turbine producer).

along with state-owned firms that had been newly privatized (e.g., POSCO and KT), were at the center of R&D efforts in the 1980s and 1990s (Sakong, 1993, p. 249). Because R&D for new industries requires heavy and risky investments, it is likely that larger firms and chaebol affiliates required more than just government support to sustain their foreign technology acquisitions and in-house R&D. To recover the costs of prototyping, tooling, and development, firms had to produce a large volume of product, which is more feasible for larger firms, including chaebol affiliates (Amsden, 2001, pp. 194–201). Thus, firms in the government-targeted heavy industries, many of which were chaebol affiliates, had grown in size and had increased their capital intensity, innovative capabilities, and labor productivity. Some of these firms were selected again in subsequent rounds of competition and granted permission to enter new target industries. They were permitted to import foreign technology and conduct R&D efforts. Through this repeated process of selective and targeted promotion that began in the mid-1970s, big businesses emerged and grew, forming chaebols, and they gained a share of the market in capital-intensive industries (Lee, 2013b).

Many foreign technology licensing contracts in Korea, especially those made during the early stages of development, involved know-how (a form of tacit knowledge); in this way, these contracts differed from the licensing of patent rights (a form of codified or explicit knowledge) for advanced technologies. My own work with a colleague, Chung and Lee (2015), used a unique data set of 3,141 foreign technology acquisition contracts that were filed between 1970 and 1993, classifying them into three categories: know-how-only, know-how-and-patent-rights, and patent-rights-only acquisitions. Know-how-only acquisition typically consists of technical services and training that are bundled with relevant documents, whereas know-how-and-patent-rights transfers consist of technical services, training, and documents that are protected by the patent system. Patent-rights-only acquisitions consist of patent right licensing.

Our research (Chung & Lee, 2015) also shows that know-how licensing contracts dominated in the early years, whereas contracts that involved patents came to dominate later. Contracts involving know-how included not only printed information and blueprints but also technical services and training. Foreign engineers often came to Korea to ensure that the initial operation of a new facility went according to plan. Selected Korean engineers were sometimes sent abroad for overseas training, which demonstrates the importance of human capital investment. This, for example, was the case with leading firms in Korea, such as Hyundai Motors (Kim, 1998) and POSCO (Song, 2002). In contrast, technologies that were bundled with patent rights were more expensive and had a higher value than technologies that were only bundled with know-how (Korea Development Bank, 1991). Thus, patented technologies may have been adopted as a means of completing the assimilation and improving processes that were initiated via investment and know-how acquisition.

Understanding these three types of licensing contracts is quite helpful for revealing the origin of the absorptive capacity (AC) of Korean industry. AC is defined as the ability of a firm to identify, value, assimilate, and exploit knowledge from the environment, and scholars have emphasized the importance of AC in enabling Korean firms to learn and assimilate external knowledge.[7] However, it is important to consider the origin of AC and how it can be established in a firm. These questions are particularly relevant in the context of latecomer countries where firms are often hesitant to conduct their own R&D and, therefore, continue to rely on imported technology by specializing in assembly-type production.

Firms in Korea generally obtained various forms of know-how, such as operational skills and basic production technologies, while conducting their own relevant capital investment (Enos & Park,

---

[7] In two influential articles by Cohen and Levinthal (1989, 1990), AC was first proposed, and such authors as Keller (1996), Evenson and Westphal (1995), and Pack (1992), have discussed it in the Korean context.

1988; Kim, 1997b). These firms built their basic technology proficiency while building production facilities and testing operations. This allowed Korean engineers to quickly assume responsibility for their daily operations. Then, at later stages and only after they had successfully assimilated basic operational skills and basic production technologies through know-how acquisition did they advance to the acquisition of technologies that involve patent rights. Technologies that were inclusive of patent rights emerged after Korean firms improved their capacity to decipher the codified content of patents. Firms with a better capability to decipher such information gradually reduced their reliance on foreign engineers.

Subsequently, formal in-house R&D activities began after firms accumulated a certain level of experience assimilating foreign technology and conducting know-how-only acquisitions. In-house R&D became more important than foreign technology acquisition as the technological capabilities of Korean firms progressed because (1) foreign firms became increasingly reluctant to provide core technology to their potential competitors in Korea, (2) labor-cost-based competitiveness gradually disappeared, and (3) government support for private R&D increased (OECD, 1996, pp. 91–92).

Our research (Chung & Lee, 2015) has verified that those firms that acquired foreign technology through know-how licensing developed their AC and subsequently conducted in-house R&D. More specifically, we found a substituting relationship between acquisitions that involved know-how-only and patent-only licensing, because firms that licensed foreign patents may have been discouraged from conducting their own R&D to develop such technologies. In the second step of our analysis, we found that in-house R&D activities were primarily responsible for firms' capacity to generate innovations measured by either patent applications or productivity jumps, and we also identified a positive link between the acquisition of know-how or know-how and patents and the generation of patents. However, we found no such linkage between patent-only licensing and firms' generation of their own patents.

From the mid-1980s, Korean firms, realizing the limitation of licensing and embodied technology transfer, started to establish their own in-house R&D centers (OECD, 1996). In order to encourage R&D activities by private firms, the government relaxed the criteria for establishing private sector R&D institutes, resulting in the formation of many institutes (Lee, 2013b). For instance, in 1985, the required number of research personnel for an R&D lab was reduced from ten to five. When the system for registering private research institutes was first introduced in 1981, the scheme provided tax waivers for private research institutes, military service exemptions for research personnel, and tariff exemptions for research equipment (OECD, 1996). Large domestic firms eventually began to recognize the importance of in-house R&D, and the number of research institutions increased from 65 in 1980 to 183 by 1985 (Lee, 2013b). Consequently, R&D expenditures as a share of GNP continued to increase, reaching 1% in the mid-1980s (see Table 4 in Lee, 2013b).

5.4.2 The Role of Big Businesses and Business Groups

The preceding discussion suggested that a certain number of firms were preferentially selected to import foreign technologies via licensing, and these firms later came to conduct their own in-house R&D, which was also supported by the government via direct subsidies, tax exemptions, and joint R&D projects. Through this cumulative term process of "initial selection, growth, and re-selection," which is a performance-based, longer-term process that cannot be depicted simply by a phrase, like picking the winners, chaebols have established themselves in key industrial sectors in Korea.[8] Given that the clear orientation toward capability building for innovation led to the emergence of conglomerates, their rise can be understood in terms of the

---

[8] Of course, the origins of the chaebols go back further, even to the colonial period. Early on, chaebols emerged from the rent-seeking and business opportunities created by US foreign aid allocation in the 1950s (Amsden, 1989, pp. 38–40). In the absence of proprietary technology for use in related industries and in the presence of potentially high profit rates in "pre-modernized" startup industries, their initial pattern of diversification tended to be opportunistic and unrelated to technology.

Schumpeterian or Chandlerian tradition. Both economists emphasized the role of big businesses in R&D for innovation, given their
scale and resources.[9] Chandler specifically emphasized the important
role of big businesses in the United States and Germany during the
nineteenth and early twentieth centuries. Large businesses increased
their production to unprecedented levels to fully utilize their large
volume of investments and related economies of scale. In this sense,
the growth path of South Korea has replicated the conventional path
of capitalist development.

The emergence of big businesses, particularly in the form of
business groups (BGs), can also be understood in terms of transaction
cost economics and, more specifically, the concept of market failure,
especially in capital markets. Capital market failure is a particularly serious disadvantage for many latecomer economies that face
serious capital scarcity. When South Korea started industrialization
in the early 1960s, its growth potential was seriously constrained
by the extremely low amount of savings available for investment.
Given the limited size of the financial resources available, a reasonable solution was to concentrate in the hands of several large firms.
In other words, the government sought to promote a few large firms
first to expedite economic growth.

The emergence of big businesses has played an important role
in enabling Korea to sustain economic growth beyond the middle-
income stage. My own work with colleagues (Lee et al., 2013)
conducted a study of economies around the world to show that generating and maintaining a higher number of big businesses than would
be expected from the size of its economy is a prerequisite for achieving growth beyond the middle-income stage, with the examples of
South Korea and Taiwan. In contrast, a study by Beck et al. (2005)
that was sponsored by the World Bank failed to identify a robust causality between SME growth and economic growth and found only a
simple positive correlation.

[9] Their works include Schumpeter (1934, 1942) as well as Chandler (1959, 1977, 1990).

As Figure 5.1 demonstrates, the ratio of the top four and top thirty business groups' combined sales to GDP in South Korea increased sharply during the catching-up period. These ratios increased from 40% and 60%, respectively, in 1987 to close to 60% and 80% by the late 1990s. The number of Korean firms among the Fortune Global 500 increased from eight in 1994 to twelve in 1997, a period during which Korea advanced beyond the middle-income stage. Subsequently, this number reached fifteen in 2007.[10] In contrast, the number of Thai, Turkish, and Malaysian firms in the Fortune Global 500 fluctuated between one and zero for each country during the same period, which reflects their trapped situation during this period.

It is true that an increase in big businesses can lead to a concentration of economic power and can thus have negative effects on economic growth, which is also confirmed by our own analysis (Lee et al., 2013). In South Korea, the relative presence of Global Fortune 500 firms in the overall economy, proxied by the ratio of the sum of these firms' sales to GDP, increased from 31.6% in 1994 to 54.7% in 1997 and 59.2% in 2007. These ratios are indicative of an increasing concentration of economic power, although the ratios for South Korea are similar to those of Japan and Taiwan but lower than those of France and the United Kingdom. Then, what would be the net effect of having one more Fortune firm, balancing its positive contribution to growth against its negative effects associated with increasing economic concentration (namely, increasing the combined share of all of the Fortune firms in the economy)? The answer is that it is still positive, with the negative effect of increasing concentration being more than offset by the growth generation effect of the additional Fortune firm. Further, it has been shown by our analysis that an economy with more big businesses tends to display a more stable growth pattern.

Further, the presence of competitive big businesses was a key factor in Korea's quick recovery from the Asian financial crisis in 1997 and the 2008–2009 global financial crisis. These crises tended

---

[10] The source is Table 1 of Lee et al. (2013).

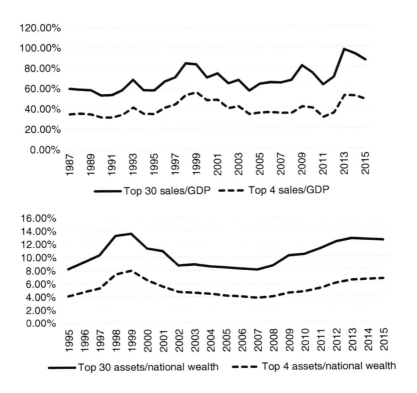

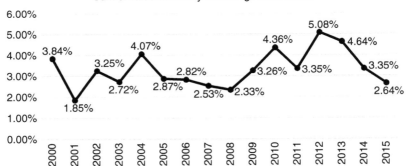

Sum of value-added by Samsung affiliates/GDP

FIGURE 5.1 Trend of economic concentration in South Korea
Notes: National wealth: the sum of tangible fixed assets, intangible
fixed assets, inventories, land assets, lumber assets, underground assets,
and durable consumer goods.
Source: Drawn using the data from Kis Value, Fair Trade Commission
(egroup.go.kr); KOSTAT (kostat.go.kr)

to cause a sharp depreciation of the Korean currency, which significantly boosted chaebol exports and thus aided the recovery of the economy. Although the 1997 financial crisis caused a negative 5% growth rate in 1998, Korea recovered quickly and continued to catch up after 1998. Korea's per capita GDP as a percentage of US per capita GDP was about 40% in the mid-1990s before the 1997 crisis, and it reached nearly 60% by the early 2010s after the global financial crisis of 2008–2009 (see Figure 2.2). Such swift catching up during these periods of crisis is comparable to the early record of catch-up during the fifteen years from the early 1980s, when Korean per capita GDP was 20% of the US level, to the mid-1990s, when it reached 40% of US levels. Finally, Korea's per capita GDP reached 70.2% of the US level in 2020, putting Korea on par with Japan, the United Kingdom, and France (see Figure 2.2).

Figure 5.1 shows that the ratios of the top four and top thirty business groups' sales to GDP increased sharply during the periods of the two crises, which indicates that the sales of these big businesses tended to recover more quickly than those of smaller companies. This is in sharp contrast to some other emerging economies, which lacked a strong manufacturing base and thus suffered longer and more frequent financial and currency crises. These countries, therefore, became caught in a MIT situation. In contrast, for mineral export countries with inelastic demand, depreciation simply meant unfavorable terms of trade without the effect of increasing demand, which translated to lower earnings in dollars.[11]

Some scholars blamed the chaebols' "excessive investments" during the early to mid-1990s as one cause of the 1997 crisis. However, my own research has found that although these investments can be regarded as overinvestment in short-term calculations, they were shown to be responsible for the growth and profitability of the post-crisis period of the 2000s.[12] In other words, these overinvestments

---

[11] This point is elaborated on in Ramanayake and Lee (2018).

[12] See Lee et al. (2010), who confirmed the positive correlation between investment during the pre-crisis period and post-crisis turnaround in performance.

were not simply waste. Some were useful for advancing know-how and building capabilities for longer-term rebounds. That is, owing to the presence of locally based big businesses with strong export competitiveness, the Korean economy was able to recover quickly from crises and maintain its pace of catch-up.

5.4.3 Large Business Groups as an Entry Device and Umbrella for SMEs

The necessity for big businesses at the middle-income stage to progress to a high-income stage can also be understood in terms of their role as vehicles for circumventing entry barriers to high-end and value-added sectors by identifying niches and mobilizing resources and competencies. If latecomer firms try to enter higher-value or more profitable sectors, they must overcome high entry barriers and beat fiercely competitive incumbents. Therefore, they tend to incur substantial losses during the initial entry settlement period. Being a BG is significantly helpful in this situation because initial losses can be "socialized" among brother and sister affiliates belonging to the same BG. In this sense, BGs are an alternative to industrial policy.

A group-level initiative to launch a new business by establishing a new firm and covering its losses during the initial period is a well-known strategy in Korea. A famous example is Samsung's memory chip business. This business is now Samsung's largest generator of profits, but it involved considerable losses over seven years during the initial period. This kind of collective catch-up strategy is especially effective when the technology involved demonstrates a substantial learning-by-doing effect proportional to the accumulation of production experience. Finance literature also reports that the so-called "socialism" in internal capital markets of BGs ensures that investment flows into loss-making or under-performing affiliates or a division inside a group or conglomerate (Shin & Park, 1999). Existing studies tend to interpret this activity as an inefficient behavior. An alternative interpretation of this finding is that it is an effective, group-level market entry strategy that makes sense in a dynamic context.

Having big businesses that are locally based is important for reaching a high-income status because big businesses tend to execute high-end and value-added activities, such as R&D and marketing, at home while locating low-end or value-added activities in the form of FDI abroad. That is, attracting FDI is not sufficient for achieving a high-income economy. Instead, an economy must be able to generate large, locally owned corporations. Of course, FDI is an important source of knowledge and know-how about foreign technologies; however, the ultimate agents of latecomer development should be locally controlled firms. While South Korea was also open to FDI, it imposed regulations preventing the share of foreign equity from exceeding 50%; this regulation remained in place until 1986.

Samsung also relied on foreign companies, mostly Japanese companies, for learning at an early stage. In the early 1970s, Samsung Electronics established two companies that would produce electronic parts: Samsung–Sanyo in December 1969, which later merged with Samsung Electronics, and Samsung–NEC in January 1970, which was owned 50% by SEC and 40% by NEC (Japan). Samsung knew that partnering with foreign firms was critically important. However, in all of the affiliates it formed with foreign partners, Samsung held at least half ownership and gradually bought out foreign equity shares, granting Samsung full control over management (Lee & He, 2009). This is consistent with the observation that in latecomer countries, firms that received FDI, especially firms controlled by foreigners, cannot be relied upon for long-term technological development, although they can serve as initial learning venues.

For growth driven by big businesses, it is important to recognize the possibility of big businesses being entrenched in their market position and dependent on government support. In fact, this issue is related to the ongoing debate over whether competitive markets or monopolistic markets stimulate additional R&D and, in turn, innovation. The view favoring competitive markets points out that without market discipline, big businesses are more inclined to be complacent given their existing success, whereas the view favoring monopolistic markets points out that only big businesses have the resources sufficient for R&D and risk-taking. The Korean experience offers insight into how to solve this dilemma. As is well known, the Korean market is much smaller than the Japanese market, and thus many sectors of the Korean economy are oligopolies. Despite this, Korean firms were mostly free from monopolistic entrenchment because they were oriented toward world markets and because privileges granted by the government were tied to export performance. In this regard, Korean industry differed from the Malaysian auto industry, which was not oriented toward world markets but rather operated in a closed, monopolistic domestic market, as discussed in Chapter 3.

My own empirical analyses that draw on firm data from the 1980s and 1990s (e.g., Jung & Lee, 2010) tend to confirm the productivity-enhancing effect of big businesses measured by the top firm dominance of sectors (a market structure variable), implying that catch-up is more likely to occur in industries with a more monopolistic market structure. Second, these studies also verify the productivity-enhancing effect of the combination of an oligopolistic market structure with world market discipline, which is measured by export orientation. Indeed, in the early phases of the Korean economy, tariffs and other protections led to export and output expansion through fixed investment; in the country's later period, R&D investment and export growth stimulated productivity growth. During both periods, the disciplinary impact of export orientation was important in the sense that such discipline pushed firms to make correct use of the rents derived from tariffs and an oligopolistic market structure for more capital or R&D investment. Another source of rent during the later period was tax exemptions for R&D investment. Clearly, government activism in South Korea has evolved from trade policy to technology policy involving diverse forms of public–private R&D.

Moreover, it is important to note that big businesses tend to generate a large number of SMEs as suppliers, and therefore, these

SMEs may also enjoy stable and less volatile growth despite not necessarily enjoying high profit rates (Kwak, 2010). Table 5.1 shows the number of suppliers each big business has across several sectors. For instance, Samsung Electronics had as many as 7,102 SME affiliate suppliers as of early 2011, whereas Hyundai and Kia Motors, together, had 6,106 SME affiliate suppliers. An estimate indicates that these supplier SMEs account for about 40% of all firms in each sector.[13] In other words, in typical manufacturing sectors, the survival of less than half of firms depends on that of big businesses, which serve as an "umbrella" for SMEs. Further, some independent SMEs have also been founded by former employees of large chaebols. Notable examples are the digital platforms Naver and Kakao, which are now among the top ten firms on the Korean stock market (see Table 5.2). Further, when considering the knowledge spillover between chaebols and non-chaebol firms (Lee et al., 2016), it is misleading to treat the relationship between big businesses and SMEs as a zero-sum game whereby the weakening of chaebols will lead to the prospering of SMEs, as some studies on the Korean economy have suggested.[14]

Given that many big businesses tend to support and generate SMEs – both directly and indirectly – one cannot say that the strong presence of big businesses will inevitably lead to the ever-increasing dominance of big businesses. In fact, the increase in economic concentration caused by the rise of big businesses has recently been

---

[13] For instance, according to Jung (2018), there were 513 firms (37.3%) distributed over the five tiers of a hierarchy, which were suppliers to Hyundai Motors and Kia Motors. In contrast, the remaining 862 firms (62.8%) were independent firms.

[14] Aghion et al.'s (2021) analysis of Korean industries found that sectors dominated by chaebols during the pre-crisis (1997) period showed an increase in productivity after post-crisis reforms. They interpret these results to mean that the post-crisis reform and collapse of some former chaebols opened up the economy, removed entry barriers, and thus helped non-chaebol firms prosper. However, if one believes in the mutual supplier relationship and knowledge spillover between chaebols and non-chaebols, the coefficient may be a reflection of such positive spillover from chaebols to non-chaebol firms. Actually, their own study found less exit of firms over the crisis period in sectors with strong chaebol dominance, which may be indicative of the role of chaebols as an umbrella for SME suppliers.

Table 5.1 *Number of supplier companies of each chaebol company: Chaebols' affiliate suppliers and non-affiliate suppliers by size*

Company Types	Electronics			Automobiles			Shipbuilding		
	Samsung Electronics	LG Electronics	SK Hynix	Hyundai Motors	Kia Motors	GM Korea	Hyundai Heavy Industries	Samsung Heavy Industries	Daewoo Shipbuilding & Marine Engineering
Chaebol Affiliates	22	21	3	20	16	0	4	0	4
Large	306	127	52	202	78	108	210	80	31
Medium	1,661	969	186	1,024	315	520	1,235	552	185
Small	5,441	3,248	417	3,943	824	1,937	4,831	2,020	493
Total	7,530	4,365	658	5,191	1,233	2,565	6,280	2,652	713

Source: Adaptation of Table 4 from Hong and Chang (2015)

Table 5.2 *List of top ten firms in Korea by market values*

	1974	1980	1990
1	KEPCO (electricity)	Samsung Electronics	KEPCO (electricity)
2	Hanil Synthetic Fiber Ind	Taihan (Cable)	POSCO (steel)
3	Taegu Textile	Lucky-Goldstar (LG)	Samsung Electronics
4	Hanil Cement Co.	Daelim E&C (construction)	Hyundai Motors
5	Daewoo	Hyundai Motors	Hyundai Engineering & Construction
6	Tong Yang Nylon Co.	Ssangyong C&E (construction)	Lucky-Goldstar (LG)
7	Korean Air	Korean Air	KIA Motors
8	Cheil Jedang	Hanwha (chemicals)	Korean Air
9	Lucky (LG)	Capro	Samyang Steel (Hyundai BNG Steel)
10	Union Steel Co., Ltd.	SK	Ssangyong C&E
Sum of values in mil. $	500.5	506.8	28,791.4
as % of GDP	2.56	0.78	10.16
Sales sum / GDP	6.34	7.32	13.93

Table 5.2 (cont.)

	2000	2010	2020
1	Samsung Electronics	Samsung Electronics	Samsung Electronics
2	SK Telecom	POSCO	SK HYNIX
3	KT (telecom service)	Hyundai Motors	Samsung Biologics
4	KEPCO	KEPCO	NAVER
5	POSCO	Hyundai Heavy Industries	LG Chemicals
6	HYNIX (semiconductor)	LG Chemicals	Celtrion
7	Samsung Electro-Mechanics	Hyundai Mobis	Hyundai Motors
8	KT&G (tabaco)	LG Electronics	Samsung SDI
9	Hyundai Motors	HYNIX	KAKAO
10	KIA Motors	LG Display	LG Health & Beauty
Sum of values in mil. $	133,117.7	291,667.4	603,015.2
as % of GDP	23.1	25.5	36.67
Sales sum/GDP	19.06	25.70	14.97

Source: Calculations using the data from KIS VALUE, ECOS (ecos.bok.or.kr); KOSTAT (kostat.go.kr); data from the Center for Economic Catch-Up

checked or even reversed, depending upon the indicators considered. Figure 5.1 shows that the top four or top thirty business groups' combined sales revenue as a percentage of GDP peaked at 80% and 60%, respectively, around the year 1998, which was the height of the financial crisis. This demonstrates their relative strength and resilience during crisis conditions. The sharp drop in these numbers since 2000 is related to the fact that some chaebol groups went bankrupt before and during the crisis and the rise of new SMEs and startups. However, these ratios increased again beginning in the mid-2000s and peaked in 2008, the year of the global financial crisis. Since then, they have entered a state of decline, which has accelerated since 2013. A similar trend can be confirmed in terms of Samsung Group's value-added as a percentage of national GDP, the top four and thirty BGs' sales as a ratio of total industry sales, and the top four and top thirty BGs' total wealth (assets) as a percentage of total national wealth (Figure 5.1). Overall, various measures of the share of big businesses have tended to fluctuate with the business cycle, and the long-term trend does not increase indefinitely but instead suggests an upper limit.

In Korea, this inverted U-shaped trend of increasing centralization among big businesses followed by gradual decentralization is consistent with the increasing concentration of the NIS during the catching-up stage, which was followed by eventual decentralization beginning in the 2010s (see Figure 2.3D), as discussed in Chapter 2. In other words, Korea's NIS displayed a tendency of increasing concentration of innovation during the 1990s and 2000s, only to reverse in the late 2000s and move toward decentralization.[15] This reversal of centralization indicates that these catching-up economies experienced an increasing concentration of innovation among a small number of large inventors and corporations during their rapid catching-up period. Subsequently, some decentralization occurred, albeit only recently after they had become mature or had entered a post-catching-up phase.

---

[15] Refer to Figure 4 in Lee and Lee (2021a).

In summary, based on the experiences of South Korea, we can conclude that the formation and growth of locally owned, export-oriented corporations and BGs can be considered an organizational device for sustaining catch-up rather than simply an organizational response to market failure.[16]

5.5 KOREA'S SECOND DETOUR: FROM SHORT- TO LONG-CYCLE SPECIALIZATION

The preceding section proposed that locally owned, export-oriented conglomerates are an essential element of the Korean model of development. Thus, while such big businesses are crucial to sustained catch-up, it is necessary to point out that their capabilities were first built and utilized according to a specific mode of sectoral specialization and structural transformation. In other words, in addition to building innovation capabilities and promoting big businesses, developing countries must also solve the question of how to choose the right sectors and activities, especially after they reach the middle-income stage. This is because capability building does not take place in a vacuum but rather in specific businesses and sectors. The nature and criteria of sectoral specialization are long-discussed issues in economics, particularly within debates over unbalanced growth theories. Moreover, it is interesting that in Korea, the final stage of structural transformation accompanied the emergence of an industrial structure centered on short-cycle technology-based sectors, such as IT, after first passing through a stage of labor-intensive sector specialization and then capital-intensive specialization.

5.5.1 Theoretical Criteria for Sector-Level Specialization at the Middle-Income Stage

The comparative advantage framework considers the natural and physical endowment of a nation, including its labor force, as the

---

[16] See Steers et al. (1989).

basic criteria for specialization[17]. Given that many developing countries initially face labor abundance, as revealed by Lewis (1954), they are advised to specialize in labor-intensive sectors. Consistent with the Hecksher–Ohlin trade theory and its variations (Kahn, 1951; Sen, 1957), the capital–labor ratio is a key variable in such criteria. Despite some criticisms, this allocation criterion is useful and workable because the structural transformation of the industrial structure from agricultural to labor-intensive and then to capital-intensive manufacturing sectors characterizes the typical process of development and structural transformation (Kuznets, 1966).

However, this investment strategy does not offer an answer to the question of what countries must do when increasingly scarce and expensive labor drives them to enter capital-intensive sectors during the middle-income stage. An exemplary country is South Korea, which started as a labor surplus economy in the 1950s and later experienced an economic boom after entering labor-intensive manufacturing sectors. In the early 1970s, South Korea reached the Lewis (1954) turning point of scarce labor, during which the rapid growth of light industries increased wage rates, thereby driving the country to enter various capital-intensive sectors (i.e., automobiles, steel, shipbuilding, and chemicals) in the mid-1970s. Given the diverse types of capital-intensive sectors, nations need to be guided as to which sector they should enter first. However, the endowment-based theory of comparative advantages neither distinguishes between capital-intensive sectors nor suggests criteria for choosing among these sectors.

5.5.1.1 Latent Comparative Advantages

As one of the first to investigate the limitations of static comparative advantage, Viner (1958) applied dynamic modifications to the concept of comparative advantage, which Lin (2012a, 2012b) further developed into the concept of latent comparative advantages. Lin argued that endowment is not necessarily given or exogenous but

---

[17] This subsection is based on Lee (2013b) and Lee (2013c).

rather can change endogenously as the country grows or accumulates capital. Therefore, developing countries must conform their present endowment structure to that of forerunning countries (or countries with a GDP per capita that is twice as high as the concerned developing country) and then target mature or leftover industries from these countries.

This theory of latent advantage is an advancement, in that it suggests a criterion for choosing from various potential capital-intensive sectors; namely, it helps a developing country choose a sector that is new to the developing country yet old to the benchmark countries ahead of it. Although this strategy can help developing countries catch up with the forerunning or incumbent economies, latecomer countries always remain behind these economies. Some aspects of the actual experience of Korea are consistent with this suggestion; however, Korea not only inherited old sectors (i.e., steel and automobile) but also leapfrogged into emerging sectors (i.e., telecommunication equipment) and directly competed with the forerunning economies in these sectors (Lee, 2013c). Therefore, although this strategy may prove useful for lower-level MICs, the same cannot be said for upper-level MICs attempting to upgrade their industrial structure to match those of emerging or close-to-frontier sectors. We still need additional theoretical criteria for the sectoral specialization of MICs.

5.5.1.2   Product Spaces and Diversification

Hausmann et al. (2007) developed the concept of "product space" to determine the sophistication of a country's trade structure. They proposed that a country can achieve gradual sophistication (and diversification) in its trade structure by moving into neighboring spaces or capturing low-hanging fruit. Therefore, the export structure of a country must be expanded to include highly sophisticated products to achieve sustained export performance and economic growth. However, such an idea has some limitations from the perspective of developing countries.

Hausmann et al. (2007) and Hidalgo et al. (2007) considered the proximity between product spaces as an important variable in determining the feasibility of diversification. However, their criterion does not disclose much information about the "directions" of diversification because there exist numerous spaces located at similar distances. In other words, they focus on the "distance" rather than the "specific directions" of diversification. The distance-based argument of diversification fails to address which sectors among the similarly distanced ones the latecomer economies must diversify in first.

The empirics of Hausmann et al. (2007) and Hidalgo et al. (2007) are based on trade data, which do not contain any information on the value added of traded products or information on how products are made. Therefore, technological (or value-added) content cannot be assessed based on such data (Sturgeon & Gereffi, 2012). Although developing countries export high-tech goods, as reflected in their trade data, the highest value-added components of these goods are often produced in a third party country or advanced economy.[18] Hausmann et al. (2007) and Hidalgo et al. (2007) also used income level as a weighting factor to calculate the degree of sophistication; that is, countries that produce the goods currently exported by high-income countries are considered highly sophisticated. This method makes such a measure tautological. In other words, a country can become rich by producing goods currently made by rich countries.

Further, this strategy does not consider the ability of a country to compete in the international market. Specifically, the strategy informs latecomer countries that they must try to produce products being made by incumbents but does not inform them about how to compete with these incumbents in identical or similar sectors. Instead of avoiding direct confrontation with incumbent countries, latecomer countries must find a niche within which they can survive and compete effectively in the market.

In summary, Hausmann et al. (2007) and Hidalgo et al. (2007) failed to propose an effective method for MICs to reach the core

---

[18] For example, only $4 out of the $299 retail price of an Apple iPod goes to China (Linden et al., 2009).

structure. Instead, they merely argued that countries can reach the core only by traversing "empirically infrequent" (meaning long) distances, which is a very difficult task to achieve. However, Hausmann et al. (2007) and Hidalgo et al. (2007) do not discuss how these countries can traverse long distances to reach the core space. This observation may help us understand why poor countries have trouble developing more competitive exports and fail to match the income levels of rich countries.

5.5.2   A Detour from the Short-Cycle to Long-Cycle Technology-based Sectors

The above discussion gives latecomer firms and economies, particularly those at the middle stage of development, some ideas on what to look for regarding viable specialization criteria. Given their weak capabilities, latecomers need to establish their niche in the international division of labor and participate in sectors where they can achieve better growth prospects and survive by competing effectively with incumbents. In this case, "the possibility for entry/survival with some growth prospects" represents a viable criterion.

I have proposed in my earlier book (Lee, 2013c) that for middle-income countries, CTT presents a viable criterion for technological specialization. The cycle time of technologies measures how fast technologies change or become obsolete over time.[19] Additionally, short CTT means that "creative destruction" (Schumpeter, 1942, p. 73) occurs more frequently and therefore the knowledge base of existing technologies is more quickly destroyed or made obsolete.[20]

---

[19] Jaffe and Trajtenberg (2002) defined the cycle time of technologies as the time difference between the application or grant year of the *citing* patent with that of the *cited* patents. Park and Lee (2006) applied this concept in the context of industrial catch-up in South Korea and Taiwan.

[20] Aghion and Howitt (1992) developed an endogenous growth model, focusing on the intertemporal implications of expectation of creative destruction, in which the prospect of future research associated with creative destruction discourages current research by threatening to destroy the rents created by current research. In the context of my book, I focus on the entry barrier implication of creative destruction.

Thus, Lee (2013c) argues that qualified latecomers can achieve considerable advantages by targeting and specializing in technological sectors with a short cycle time because in short CTT-based sectors, the dominance of incumbents is often disrupted by new innovations and the continuous emergence of new technologies can generate opportunities. Minimal reliance on existing technologies represents both lower barriers to entry and profitability, which are associated with few collisions with the technologies of advanced countries, fewer royalty payments, first- and fast-mover advantages, and product differentiation (Lee, 2013c). In other words, a sector that is based on technologies with a short cycle time satisfies the two criteria for viability, namely, entry possibility and growth prospects. This is because short-cycle technology-based sectors have minimal reliance on existing technologies and can leverage the opportunities resulting from the emergence of new technologies. For example, information technologies have a shorter cycle than pharmaceuticals in the sense that new innovations in information technology tend to rely less on existing or stock knowledge.[21]

The advantage of specializing in short-cycle technologies is consistent with the leapfrogging concept, according to which the emerging generations of technologies allow catching-up countries to obtain a head start.[22] When competing under a new techno-economic paradigm, both incumbents and latecomers begin from the same starting line, and incumbents often adhere to the existing technologies from which they derive their supremacy. Leapfrogging is similar to the "long jumps" (Hidalgo et al., 2007) that economies must

---

[21] For this reason, not all emerging technologies are considered short cycle because even new products in the pharmaceutical industry tend to rely heavily on existing or stock knowledge, depending on the nature of such innovations (i.e., disruptive or competence-enhancing). Therefore, information technology is more prone to disruptive innovations than long-cycle sectors.

[22] Replacing analog technologies with digital ones provides a window of opportunity for some latecomers, especially South Korea. The digitalization of products and the production processes entails fewer disadvantages for latecomers because the functions and quality of these products are determined by electronic chips rather than by the skills of engineers, who are more critical for analog products.

perform to pivot into product spaces that are located far from their current position and achieve subsequent structural transformation.

5.5.2.1   The Korean Experience: From Short to Long Cycles

The technological development of South Korea over the last three decades of its catch-up period (Lee, 2013c) has witnessed the increasing specialization of South Korean firms in short-cycle technologies. South Korea began by specializing in labor-intensive (low value-added, long-cycle technology) industries, such as the apparel and shoe industries, in the 1960s. The economy then entered the medium-cycle sectors of low-end consumer electronics and automobile assembly in the 1970s and 1980s; the shorter-cycle sectors of telecommunication equipment (telephone switches) in the late 1980s; and then memory chips, cellphones, and digital televisions in the 1990s.

I consider the mid-1980s as an important turning point, because this was when South Korea achieved sustained catch-up beyond the middle-income stage. Korea reached the middle-income level during this period, and its GDP per capita reached 25% of that of the United States. Since then, South Korea has continued to increase its R&D expenditures, and the country's R&D-to-GDP ratio eventually surpassed the 1% level. Along with this upgrading of technological capabilities, the country has pursued various short-cycle technology-based sectors, such as the information technology sector.[23]

Specializing in short-cycle technologies does not entail a fixed list of technologies (Lee, 2013c). Instead, in sectors with short-cycle technologies, new technologies always emerge to replace existing ones. In other words, the criterion for technological specialization

---

[23] One intriguing question is whether policymakers in South Korea were aware of such criteria as short-cycle time when they planned their economic development. While the answer is "no," they were, in fact, continually asking themselves, "What's next?" They closely observed which industries and businesses were likely to emerge in the immediate future and thought carefully about how to enter emerging industries (Lee, 2013c). New or emerging industries and businesses are often the ones with short-cycle technologies because they rely less on existing technologies. Therefore, in effect, the policy makers were always chasing short-cycle industries.

is less about the cycle length itself and more about entry barriers. In this sense, latecomers should choose technological sectors that are less reliant on existing technologies dominated by incumbents. Additionally, continuous technological emergence suggests that new entrants have fresh windows of opportunity available to them that are not confined to the old, dominant technologies. This concept stands in stark opposition to the product life cycle theory of Vernon (1966), according to which latecomers merely inherit old or mature industries (or segments thereof) from incumbent economies (Lee, 2013c). In fact, South Korean firms continually sought to enter newly emerging, shorter-cycle technologies and, in the end, achieved technological diversification.

That is, in contrast to Hausmann et al. (2007), who suggested that developing countries should seek to emulate rich countries as quickly as possible, we propose that the transition strategy of a developing country must involve entering sectors that are based on short-cycle technologies instead of those that are dominated by rich countries, such as long-cycle technologies. However, as countries reach technological maturity and achieve a somewhat high level of capabilities (as South Korea did in the early 2000s), they are driven to adopt long-cycle technologies, such as biomedical or pharmaceutical industries, which is what Samsung has been trying to achieve recently.

Figure 5.2 illustrates the trend of normalized CTT as calculated from US patents for selected economies (South Korea, Taiwan, China, Brazil, and Germany). Now, considering that all the average CTTs have tended to increase across all fields since the early 2000s, I present the series of normalized (or relative) CTT by dividing the absolute CTT values by the average of all patents registered each year. Thus, in Figure 5.2, the values lower than 1 refer to relatively short CTTs, whereas the larger values refer to relatively long CTTs. These figures are based on a three-year moving average of CTTs to show a smooth transition, with the average relative CTT of Germany highly stable at approximately 1.1 for most of the period beginning in the 2000s.

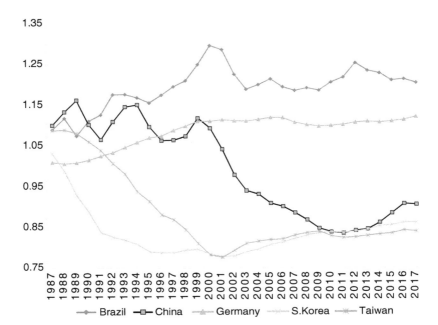

FIGURE 5.2 Trend of relative (normalized) cycle time in selected economies
Notes: The numbers refer to the three-year moving average of cycle time of technologies of patents filed by each economy.
Sources: Drawn using the United States Patent and Trademark Office bulk patent documents.

Most importantly, South Korea and Taiwan have experienced a decrease in CTTs from approximately 1.05 in the mid-1980s to approximately 0.78 at the end of the 1990s or 2000, which encompasses the period of their rapid catch-up in economic growth. Since the 2000s, these two economies have shown a reversal of the CTT trend into an increasing trend. Such reversals indicate that these economies have passed the short-to-long turning point, realizing a new gradual specialization into long-CTT sectors. This new pattern of specialization also means that their NIS are transitioning from catch-up to mature conditions. China has followed the path of South Korea and Taiwan with an approximate ten-year lag, and it experienced

Table 5.3 *Top ten classes and number of patents registered by South Korea, 2000–2003 and 2013–2017*

		2000–2003					2013–2017		
	Class	Patent count	Class Name	Rel. CTT		Class	Patent count	Class Name	Rel. CTT
1	438	1750	Semiconductor device manufacturing: process	0.78	1	438	5106	Semiconductor device manufacturing: process	0.78
2	365	809	Static information storage and retrieval	0.70	2	726	4489	Information security	0.80
3	257	737	Active solid-state devices (e.g., transistor)	0.79	3	714	4176	Error detection/correction and fault detection/recovery	0.80
4	349	437	Liquid crystal cells, elements, and systems	0.76	4	455	3519	Telecommunications	0.77
5	345	326	Computer graphics processing & display systems	0.80	5	257	3472	Active solid-state devices (e.g., transistor)	0.79
6	327	324	Miscellaneous electrical nonlinear devices & systems	0.83	6	73	3206	Measuring and testing	1.08
7	370	323	Multiplex communications	0.68	7	370	3013	Multiplex communications	0.68
8	313	318	Electric lamp and discharge devices	0.95	8	725	2695	Interactive video distribution systems	0.87
9	348	300	Television	0.82	9	345	2599	Computer graphics processing & display systems	0.80
10	375	290	Pulse or digital communications	0.78	10	429	2088	Chemistry: electrical current producing apparatus, product, and process	0.99
			Weighted mean	0.78				Weighted mean	0.82

Notes: Rel. CTT means the relative (normalized) cycle time of technologies
Source: Adaptation of Table 2 in Lee and Lee (2021a)

the same decrease in the average CTT from the mid-1990s to the end of the 2000s, which is consistent with its rapid catching-up in economic growth. By contrast, Brazil has recorded very high values, which is interpreted as an undesirable pattern of specialization. Long CTT corresponds to high barrier-to-entry technologies that present difficulties for latecomers seeking to realize commercial success (Lee, 2013c, Chapters 3 and 6).

Table 5.3 reveals further details of US patenting by South Korea; in particular, it provides information on the top ten patent classes, where the largest number of patents were filed for the two periods of 2000–2003 and 2013–2017. During the former period, the average CTTs of Korea reached the lowest points in Figure 5.2, whereas the latter period represents a dramatic change in the top ten classes. For instance, in Korea in the early 2000s, the top three classes were all fields related to integrated circuit chips, and other classes also correspond to those with relatively short CTT, mainly those below 0.8. By contrast, in the mid-2010s, six new classes emerged in the top ten, with most having a CTT above 0.8. Class number 73 (measurement and testing) features a long CTT of 1.08 and ranks in the top six, besides the class of chemistry. Thus, the weighted average CTT of Korea increased from 0.78 during the early 2000s to 0.82 during the mid-2010s.

The above graph and table of CTTs are suggestive of the changing nature of NIS in South Korea and Taiwan during the post-catch-up stage that began in the 2000s. These two economies are moving away from sectors based on short-cycle technologies and pursuing sectors based on long-cycle technologies. Thus, their NIS are approaching the levels of countries with advanced or mature NIS, and regression analysis by me and a colleague (Lee & Lee, 2021a), has confirmed the contribution of long-CTT specialization since the 2000s to economic growth. In this way, the so-called "detour" hypothesis, which posits that a successful catching-up economy follows a technological detour of initially specializing in short CTT sectors and later turning to long-CTT-based and thus high-entry-barrier sectors, has been confirmed. Firm-level data also shows that Korean firms are no longer simply oriented toward short-CTT technologies, as they have diversified into non-short-CTT technologies, which is also discussed in Chapter 4 (Section 5.5), relying on a previous work of mine with a colleague (Im & Lee, 2021).

Further, Table 5.2 displays lists of the top ten firms in terms of their values in the stock market from 1974 to 2020. In the past, the top ten firms were in either the IT or auto and steel sectors. In the most recent year of 2020, three bio and health firms were in the top ten, including Celtrion, Samsung Biologics, and LG Health, some of which produce so-called biosimilars and COVID-19 vaccines and medicines. Additionally, the top ten list includes two digital platform firms, Naver (Korean counterpart to Google) and Kakao (Korean counterpart to Facebook). In sum, half of the top ten firms are new firms. This phenomenon reflects the trend of increasing diversification into non-short-cycle fields and the rise of new, non-chaebol firms.

One may doubt the necessity of entering industries with long CTT, which is usually difficult for latecomers to achieve because of the high entry barriers and long gestation periods. Instead, one might suggest that South Korea should continue specializing in sectors with short CTT (e.g., IT), where they currently excel. However, the problem is that other next-tier latecomer countries, such as China, can also quickly and easily catch up with South Korea in such industries in a short time span. In fact, China is rapidly catching up in sectors with short CTT, such as cell phones; however, it has been relatively slow with regard to medium- and long-cycle technology-based industries, such as producing parts and source materials for automobiles and machinery (Lee et al., 2017). In other words, although the old catching-up NIS enabled Korea to catch up with high-income economies in the 1980s and the 1990s, a transition to post-catch-up NIS is currently necessary, and this includes moving into long-cycle technologies.

Since the 2000s, the South Korean government has been promoting certain industries, including biotechnology. Moreover, big businesses, such as Samsung, LG, and SK Group, have all entered these new industries. At the same time, the further advancement of short-CTT activities is increasingly carried out by new ventures and startups, including the creative industries of music, film, and other entertainment sectors. These new ventures in services, which are outside the manufacturing industry, are an example of exploring the low entry barriers of short-CTT activities via the power of digital technologies that enable various new channels of marketing and business-to-consumer approaches.

5.6   THE KOREAN MODEL AS A DETOUR TO MANAGE THE GLOBAL–LOCAL INTERFACES

The discussion in Sections 5.4 and 5.5 underscores the two essential detours of the Korean model for catch-up, which have been somewhat ignored in the literature. The first detour involves initially promoting large domestically owned and export-oriented big businesses, often in the form of business groups, and subsequently promoting SMEs. The second detour involves first specializing in short CTT- and later long-CTT-based sectors. By combining these two detours, we arrive at a definition of the Korean model as "short-CTT sector specialization led by domestically owned, export-oriented conglomerates." Some discussion of this model follows.

First, it is important to note the necessity of combining local ownership and short-CTT specialization in this model. This is because, without local ownership, short-CTT specialization may be inadequate to achieve sufficiently fast localization of knowledge creation and diffusion. As addressed in Section 3.4 of Chapter 3 in the discussion of the three regions of Shenzhen, Penang, and Taipei, the same specialization in short-CTT sectors in the IT industry led to divergent outcomes regarding innovation and economic growth. The difference between the fast catch-up in Shenzhen and the slow catch-up in Penang lies in the contrast between the rapid and strong emergence, growth, and eventual dominance of domestically owned firms in Shenzhen and Penang's continued reliance on MNCs. MNCs tend to rely on their home countries for important R&D and thus

are less interested in enhancing local R&D activities and local innovation. Thus, as Shenzhen did, latecomer economies should start
by learning from FDI and MNCs but should also pursue the eventual creation of domestically owned firms. In particular, if a country
reaches the upper middle-income stage or approaches the frontier,
it cannot expect to benefit from technology transfers and licensing
from incumbent firms and countries; rather, it must conduct its own
indigenous R&D.

This transition from foreign learning to local innovation is an
essential aspect of all successful catching-up stories in East Asia. As
discussed above, the affiliates of Samsung Electronics shared ownership with their Japanese partners to facilitate learning. Moreover,
Samsung also bought back these former shares from their Japanese
partners, securing domestic ownership. Similarly, Hyundai Motors
shared ownership with Japanese Mitsubishi to facilitate technology
transfers, and it too later bought out its Japanese partners. In contrast, Daewoo Motors, another automaker in South Korea, entered a
joint venture with GM. However, as GM held a controlling stake in
the joint venture, it was apprehensive about using its Korean affiliate
to conduct R&D, and therefore, it did not feel the need to conduct
R&D in Korea. Only after separating from GM did Daewoo return to
conducting R&D.

South Korea maintained a policy of limiting foreign ownership
of Korean companies in strategic industries to less than 50% until
1986, when this practice was abolished. A similar cap had existed
in China, too, although it was only for a very limited number of
industries, including automobiles. Consumer goods and other labor-
intensive industries, however, had no such regulations. The net costs
and benefits of such restrictions on foreign ownership are debatable,
and it is often difficult to maintain such a policy for a long period.
Thailand had also imposed similar restrictions in several industries,
including automobiles. However, it had to abolish these restrictions pursuant to the demands of the WTO. Since then, Thailand
has adopted a policy of promoting the automobile sector by relying

fully on foreign-owned car manufacturers, such as Japanese manufacturers. This approach has achieved mixed results, as its level of domestic value-added as a share of its gross exports remains limited (Lee, Qu & Mao, 2021).

The case of Proton, the now defunct, nationally owned automaker in Malaysia discussed in Section 3.3 of Chapter 3, illustrates that local ownership should be subject to market discipline from either export or domestic markets, or, even better, both. Otherwise, local ownership might degenerate into an entrenchment. Thus, the effective model for latecomer development should include export orientation. Export orientation is, of course, needed because all latecomers must have enough dollars or convertible currencies to pay for their imports of capital goods and technologies (licensing fees and royalties), without which growth cannot be sustained.

The above discussion also indicates the importance of strategically managing local–global interfaces. Given the lack of indigenous bases for knowledge and capital, all latecomers must learn from foreign countries and firms. Eventually, however, they must seek to generate domestically owned firms. This detour process is difficult because the transition from foreign to local firms often involves competition with incumbents or separation and independence from former partners. That is why many latecomers fail to realize the transition and become stuck in the MIT. As discussed above, the need to specialize in short-CTT sectors arises because latecomers must identify sectors that have low barriers to entry and are frequently subject to creative destruction. Entry into such sectors allows latecomers to avoid a direct collision with incumbents. Likewise, latecomers also require big businesses to enter into competition with incumbents. SMEs, in contrast, are insufficient for outcompeting large incumbents. With a business group structure, a latecomer can concentrate all its resources in new sectors and ventures so that it can endure initial loss-making or otherwise difficult periods, taking advantage of internal capital markets and resources. When these are insufficient, latecomers should seek help from the public sector or government in terms of asymmetric industrial and innovation policy, which has been observed in the Korean experience.

It is also important to note that the Korean model discussed above involves a detour from big business dominance to decentralization by SMEs, combined with a transition from short- to long-CTT sectors. The detour reflects the actual experience of South Korea, where the dominance of big businesses was checked by the tendency toward decentralization that began in the 2000s, which was the post-catch-up stage.

Given that these two aspects of decentralization and diversification are typical attributes of advanced Western economies, this long-term detour can also be discussed in the context of the possible convergence of the Korean model. The point is that such convergence has been possible only through a detour that has gone in the opposite direction from that of the advanced economies. Such a detour has also been observed in terms of the fact that the Korean economy used to be mostly closed or protected by high tariffs and asymmetric support for domestic companies. However, Korea is now a mostly open economy with free trade agreements with the United States, the EU, China, India, and more. Therefore, this detour has taken Korea from a closed to an open economy. This convergence via divergence (or detour) constitutes the so-called "catch-up paradox" (Lee, 2019, p. xxi) that can be summarized in the following sentences: "You cannot catch up if you just keep catching up." "To be open, you have to be closed for a while." And, "A detour can be faster than a straight road."

In this context, the Korean model can be redefined as a "detour from short- to long-CTT specialization led by export-oriented, indigenous conglomerates." Of course, it was also a detour to political democracy via a transitory phase of political authoritarianism. This political transition or democratization was realized by mass demonstrations in 1987 and the subsequent beginning of a new civilian government in 1993. During this period, South Korea was reaching the end of its upper middle-income stage and was entering a high-income stage, which was marked by its entrance into the OECD. In other words, South Korea finished the process of democratization before it became a high-income economy. The middle class, which arose alongside economic growth and prosperity, demanded democratization. The activism of citizens was mostly peaceful and compromising and thus did not disrupt economic growth before South Korea was able to join the OECD. Although the mismanagement of financial liberalization led to the 1997 crisis, the recovery was quick and prompt, again owing to the strength of large domestic firms.

However, the crisis ended in IMF reform, which accelerated Korea's transition to financialization, increasing sociopolitical cleavages and path-dependent convergence in terms of slow growth and rising inequality. Specifically, the share of foreign owners of Korean stocks jumped from less than 5% before the crisis to about 40% in the post-crisis period of the early 2000s, becoming one of the highest rates in the world. These foreign shareholders have been contributing to the reform of corporate governance in Korean firms, causing them to align with Anglo-American style governance in the name of global standards. Additionally, they have tended to demand greater dividends rather than profit reinvestment, which has translated into lower investment and firm growth, and as a consequence, has possibly eliminated domestic jobs and increased inequality.[24] My colleague and I (Im & Lee, 2021), have conducted a firm-level analysis to show that Korean firms no longer borrow heavily or invest aggressively, which is also discussed in section 4.5 of the Chapter 4. Instead, they pursue high profitability.

The country now faces the serious challenges of growth slowdown, rapid aging, and rising income inequality between rich and poor, which are similar to the issues of advanced or mature economies. If these challenges become permanent features of South Korea,

---

[24] A firm-level analysis by Kim and Cho (2008) confirms this negative linkage from more foreign share to less investment. Shin and Lee (2019) confirm the positive linkages from more dividends payment to more inequality measured by the income share of the top 10% richest.

this will signal the end of East Asian capitalism, which is characterized by high growth and low inequality, and the convergence toward Anglo-American capitalism, which is characterized by low growth and high inequality. Taking the perspective of the literature on the varieties of capitalism, an empirical analysis done by my colleague and me (Lee & Shin, 2021) classifies Korea and Japan since the 2000s as liberal market economies – that is, Anglo-American-type capitalist countries – in terms of the three criteria of GDP growth, employment rates, and the income share of the richest top 10% of citizens.

5.7 SUMMARY AND CONCLUDING REMARKS

This chapter attempted to redefine the Korean model of catch-up development by identifying new elements that have seldom been discussed in the literature. In doing so, Section 5.2 provides an evaluation of the existing theories of the Korean model of development. I then suggested that the "Korean miracle" happened not owing to any favorable initial conditions but rather in spite of several disadvantageous conditions. Moreover, overcoming these obstacles required government initiatives, including various forms of industrial policy. We also noted that inclusive institutions did not precede economic growth. Rather, capability building for economic growth proceeded under political authoritarianism, and the resulting economic growth at a later stage brought about political democracy.

Next, Sections 5.3 and 5.4 underscore the two essential factors of the Korean model that have been largely overlooked in the literature. They are, first, domestically owned and export-oriented conglomerates, often in the form of business groups, and second, specialization in short-CTT-based sectors, such as IT. By combining these two factors, we can say that the driving forces of the Korean miracle were short-CTT sector specialization led by domestically owned and export-oriented conglomerates. This understanding of the Korean miracle indicates the importance of strategically navigating global–local interfaces, thereby promoting the emergence of large domestically owned corporations and a period of increasing concentration. However, the longer-term evolution of Korea's economic development has involved detours in two senses. First, it has been a detour from dominance by big businesses to decentralization alongside the emergence of SMEs. And second, it is a transition from short- to long-CTT sectors. In this sense, the Korean experience is an exemplary case of an innovation–development detour that can be summarized as a detour from short- to long-CTT specialization led initially by export-oriented, indigenous conglomerates, followed later by SMEs.

In the typical context of latecomer economies, asymmetric promotion of a few firms is necessary due to the limited tangible and intangible resources at the initial stage. Thus, certain firms are selected first, and then these firms tend to grow further through a system of positive reinforcing mechanisms that reward high-performing firms by selecting them for a second round of resource mobilization and concentration. Further, BGs and conglomerate structures facilitate business diversification into new and high-end sectors and activities, thereby expanding the selected corporations. Short-cycle specialization is necessary because realizing catch-up growth during the upper middle-income stage cannot be achieved simply by diversifying into areas closely related to the existing businesses. Instead, it often involves venturing into promising but low barrier-to-entry activities largely unrelated to the existing activities.

6 The Roles of Government in Development Detours

6.1 INTRODUCTION

Over the past decade, a new trend toward de-globalization has emerged that has been triggered by a series of events, including the 2008 global financial crisis, the rise in US–China tensions since 2019, the COVID-19 pandemic, and the Russia–Ukraine War. Moreover, this trend is now being accompanied by the increasing and changing role of national governments, not only in developing but also in developed economies. In particular, industrial policy, which was once taboo in mainstream economics, has continued to evolve, producing diverse variations, such as innovation policy (Edler & Fagerberg, 2017; Soete, 2007), industrial innovation policy (Nelson & Langlois, 1983), and mission-oriented innovation policy (Mazzucato, 2018). Recently, it has finally reemerged as a major topic of discussion in economics. In academia, this revival has been most prominently dealt with in the works of Stiglitz et al. (2013), Mazzucato (2011), and Chang and Andreoni (2020). Such a revival is unsurprising given that although there have been many cases where industrial policy has failed, no latecomer economy has achieved sustained catch-up without relying on some form of industrial policy or public intervention. Classical works, such as that by Johnson (1982), defined industrial policy as any policy that improves the structure of a domestic industry in order to enhance a country's international competitiveness. In recent decades, however, its meaning has changed and evolved to deal with the pressing concerns of the twenty-first century, including environmental degradation and sustainable development (Radosevic et al., 2017; Larrue, 2021).

The neo-Schumpeterian approach to industrial and innovation policy tends to focus on capability building and improving innovation systems (Lee, 2013a, 2013b, 2013c). This approach emphasizes that industrial policy must not only correct market failures but also overcome capability failures in emerging economies and system failures in advanced economies. The market failure approach tends to assume that firms are already capable of innovation and thus need to be provided with more monetary incentives. However, firms in developing countries are poorly equipped to conduct in-house R&D. Correcting such failures requires more than the simple provision of R&D subsidies; rather, various methods for cultivating R&D capability are necessary. In comparison, system failure can occur when missing or weak connections (and synergies) between actors constituting innovation systems result in poor performance in innovation.[1] The concept of system failure is consistent with the concept of coordination failure, in that its correction requires coordinated action among relevant actors, which can be facilitated by public agencies as intermediaries.

In their article on policy matrixes for inclusive growth, Rodrik and Stantcheva (2021) argue that governments should intervene during the production stage using various means, including industrial policy. In contrast, the conventional view has been to intervene during either the pre-production or post-production stages using such means as education or welfare schemes. Proponents of this approach argue that if a government fails to intervene during the production stage and successfully promotes the international competitiveness of its domestic industries, its firms may fail and workers will lose their jobs, placing a burden on welfare systems.

Beginning with a discussion on the three types of failure (capability, market, and system failure) that considers the wider context

---

[1] An early discussion of this concept can be found in Bergek et al. (2008) and Dodgson et al. (2011). System failure arises due to cognitive distance (Nooteboom, 2009) among actors, which is associated with the tacitness of knowledge resulting in cognition failure. Policy interventions often pursue transitioning toward a new system.

of government intervention, this chapter advances the discussion on the role of government while also focusing on the emerging economy context. It develops the concept of "detour" by elaborating on the government's role in managing global–local interfaces to promote the growth of domestically owned big businesses and their coevolution with SMEs and startups.

The preceding chapters have proposed and elaborated on the idea of multiple or nonlinear development pathways (detours) for latecomers at the national and firm levels. More specifically, in the preceding chapters, this book has presented the theory of innovation–development detours, focusing on building technological capabilities in big businesses while managing global–local interfaces. However, previous chapters have not been explicit in their discussion of the role of government in innovation–development detours. Thus, this chapter concludes the book by discussing the role of government and specific policies in achieving detour. One of the initial focuses is the question of whether the idea of detour or nonlinearity is applicable to the role of government.

Section 6.2 discusses the provocative idea that the level of government intervention should not decrease in a linear fashion during the development process; rather, I assert that the role of government must increase as the country approaches the upper middle-income stage and then decrease as it reaches the high-income stage, forming an inverted U-shaped curve. The theory of comparative advantages holds that during the low-income stage, economic growth does not necessitate direct government intervention in the affairs of firms. However, for a country to enter high value-added sectors and catch up with leading countries already in the upper middle-income stage, governments may need to undertake more direct forms of intervention, such as pursuing public–private R&D initiatives.

Section 6.3 addresses the role of government in global–local interfaces. This section elaborates on two modes of government involvement – that is, a slow and fast mode of catch-up – for overcoming the challenge of strategically managing global–local interfaces. In the slow but steady mode of catch-up, public intervention primarily focuses on re-skilling and up-skilling local labor forces so that FDI and MNCs remain in the same localities and pursue high-valued activities and hire local workers. The fast, aggressive mode of catch-up, in contrast, involves asymmetrical intervention to nurture domestically owned firms and their R&D instead of prioritizing MNCs and foreign-owned firms. Section 6.4 focuses on the role of government in fostering big businesses and their coevolution with startups and SMEs, and Section 6.5 discusses how countries can make a successful transition from short- to long-CTT sectors. The final section provides a summary and concluding remarks.

6.2   A DETOUR IN THE ROLE OF GOVERNMENT: THE INVERTED U-SHAPE OR "LESS, MORE, AND LESS"

This section explores whether the concepts of detour and nonlinearity are also applicable to the role of government. The conventional view holds that the role of government should decrease as a country's development progresses and that government intervention should be phased out as an economy matures into a high-income economy. Such statements about the decreasing role of government intervention over time are a reflection of the fact that in advanced economies, the role of government tends to be limited to the provision of basic civil services. Although it is undeniable that the role of government decreases in the high-income stage, I suggest that this decrease may not be linear. Instead, I hypothesize that during the middle-income stage, the role of government must temporarily increase rather than steadily decrease. That is, the necessary degree of government intervention may not be a linear or downward slope but rather an inverted U-shape. In short, government intervention may need to increase before it eventually decreases.

This hypothesis can be rationalized as follows. For countries at the low-income stage, a typical development policy is to attract FDI in order to capitalize on the comparative advantages related to a country's respective resource endowment. Growth achieved through such comparative advantages does not necessitate direct or vertical intervention by the government, and any government intervention is often restricted to providing tax exemptions or other financial incentives to attract FDI, as well as various indirect and horizontal interventions meant to improve investment climates associated with legal structures and physical infrastructure.

However, as an economy reaches the middle-income stage and strives to enter high value-added or high-end sectors and activities, it may find that there is little room for entry and that technology transfers are difficult and expensive, as incumbents are concerned with possible boomerang effects and a rise in new competitors from the Global South. Simply put, incumbents often do not want latecomers to advance along value chains; they want them to adhere to low-value-added activities. Incumbents may even try to establish entry barriers by initiating IPR disputes and accusing latecomer countries of copying or stealing the IPR of certain products and technologies. Incumbents may also attempt price dumping or lower the price of their product to drive out new entrants. I have elaborated on these barriers to catch-up in Chapter 3 of this book and in previous studies (Lee, 2019).

In order to strategically manage the global–local interfaces first discussed in Chapter 3, countries must generate a critical mass of local firms after learning from foreign firms. The necessary knowledge for this process may require not less but more intervention and support on the part of the government. The need for national governmental intervention arises primarily due to power asymmetries between latecomers and incumbents in GVC governance. Additionally, given that market structures are typically oligopolistic or nearly entirely monopolized by a few incumbents at high-end segments, public intervention can be justified in terms of correcting market failures to ensure higher economic efficiency by reforming oligopolistic markets to be more competitive. I will illustrate the above point regarding the need for more government involvement at the upper middle-income stage by using the example of Samsung and drawing on previous research conducted with a colleague (Lee & Lim, 2001).

In the 1970s, several Korean firms began wafer fabrication for semiconductor manufacturing by absorbing low-level technologies. These Korean firms were original equipment manufacturers, and their facilities were imported from foreign firms. These firms received no systematic government assistance. Without government help, Samsung began producing 64-kilobit DRAM chips in the early 1980s. Samsung was able to buy 64-kilobit DRAM design technology from Microelectronic Technology, a small American venture company, and it purchased the necessary manufacturing technology from the Japanese company Sharp. A few years after producing DRAM using borrowed manufacturing technology, Samsung began to develop their own circuit design technology, first developing and producing 256-kilobit memory chips in the mid-1980s. Samsung chose to develop its own design technology for 256-kilobit or higher DRAM, as it was not easy or cheap to buy the design for these chips (Kim, 1997a). Therefore, Samsung decided to develop its own designs rather than pay high prices (Kim, 1997b). It was only after Samsung independently developed a 256-kilobit DRAM chip that some foreign companies were willing to sell their 1-mega DRAM design technology to Samsung. Additionally, it was around this time, in January 1986, that Texas Instruments brought a patent infringement lawsuit against Samsung.[2]

It was only in 1986, when the target size of chips to be developed reached a larger capacity (namely 4-mega bit or higher), that the government initiated the formation of a semiconductor R&D consortium with private firms, including Samsung. This public–private consortium was necessary, as the amount of R&D expenditure and the involved risk of developing high-capacity chips was much larger than during past generations of smaller capacity chip production. The final product of this public–private enterprise was the world's first

---

[2] The United States International Trade Commission placed a ban on Samsung's exports to the United States. After extensive litigation, Samsung settled with Texas Instruments by entering into a new patent licensing agreement worth more than $1 billion. See Lee and Kim (2010) for details.

256-megabit chip. Since then, Korean firms have become world leaders in memory chip manufacturing, and the role of public research institutes was phased out as private firms were able to be self-reliant. This history of Samsung's memory chip manufacturing is a clear demonstration of the inverted U-shaped path of public intervention; that is, the public sector became more directly involved during the later stage of the industry's development in the form of public–private R&D.

The story of the digital TV and display industry in South Korea is quite similar to that of memory chips in terms of the nonlinear, inverted U-shaped pattern of public intervention. In the 1970s, Korean firms began producing black-and-white TVs using technology licensed from Japan. In the 1970s and 1980s, the government intervened to ensure general market protection, enforcing very high tariffs (as high as 80%) on imported TVs. It was only in the 1990s that the Korean government began intervening more directly to create public–private R&D consortiums, as around this time, the government had decided not to follow Japan into analog-based high-definition TV production and instead leapfrog into digital TV development ahead of Japan. This consortium included the participation of the Ministry of Industry and Resources, the Ministry of Information and Communication, and the Ministry of Science and Technology, as well as seventeen institutions, including private firms, government research institutes, and universities. This consortium set out on a five-year project (June 1990–July 1994) to develop high-definition TVs. This public–private coalition encouraged private firms to commit to a risky R&D project by channeling R&D funds and forming a knowledge-sharing network connecting researchers from various firms, universities, and governmental research institutes. The consortium's success in developing and producing the world's first digital TV was the turning point that enabled South Korea to overtake Japan in the display market, as Japan fell into the incumbent trap of trying to develop analog-based high-definition TVs.

One can observe a similar story of an increasing degree of government intervention in Taiwan. Up until the 1980s, the key product of the Taiwanese electronics industry was the compact electronic calculator (Amsden & Chu, 2003, pp. 28–32). Without government help, young and educated Taiwanese engineers contributed to the rise of the industry beginning in the 1970s by taking existing designs and modifying them slightly. However, upgrading from compact calculators in the 1980s to PC laptops in the 1990s could not be accomplished by small- and medium-sized enterprises (SMEs) alone, and therefore this process required more direct invention by public-sector institutions, primarily government research institutes like the ITRI. The government initiated an ITRI-led, public–private R&D initiative that lasted for a year and a half from 1990 to 1991 (Mathews, 2002b). This consortium developed a "common machine architecture" as a prototype that could easily be translated into a series of standardized components, which SMEs then mass produced. In the context of several previous failures, the consortium represented a watershed moment, indicating the potential of R&D consortiums to help establish new "fast follower" industries (Mathews, 2002b).

In terms of per capita income relative to US levels, the upper middle-income stage corresponds to 20–40% of US levels. South Korean per capita income reached 30% of the US level by the late 1980s and 40% by the mid-1990s (Figure 2.2). Indeed, it is during this period from the late-1980s to mid-1990s that the Korean government began intervening more directly to facilitate public–private R&D initiatives. In the 1960s, 1970s, and early 1980s, industrial policy mainly took indirect forms, including import tariffs and loans from state-controlled banks. In other words, government intervention shifted from indirect intervention in the low or lower middle-income stage to direct intervention at the upper middle-income stage.

Until the early 1980s, private R&D constituted less than half of the total R&D in South Korea. Beginning in the mid-1980s, the government began encouraging private firms to establish in-house R&D centers by granting tax exemptions for R&D expenditures and by initiating public–private joint R&D. As a result of these initiatives, the share of private R&D surpassed half of total R&D in the late 1980s and reached 70% by the mid-1990s. In this sense, the rise of private R&D was not simply a result of private-sector actions but also government initiatives. Public-sector involvement in the form of public–private joint R&D did not crowd out private R&D; rather, the private and public sectors evolved together in a relationship of beneficial mutual feedback.

Such government intervention into private R&D did not occur in Southeast Asia until later. For example, in the Malaysian semiconductor sector, such intervention did not occur until the late 1990s, more than a decade after South Korea. South Korea's per capita GDP started to surpass that of Malaysia beginning in the mid-1980s (Figure 2.2). The lesson from this discussion may be that it is not the degree of government intervention that is important but rather the nature of the changing role played by the government during different stages of development. Nevertheless, public–private joint R&D is more of a direct form of involvement than financial incentives and horizontal market protection via tariffs, which are indirect.

6.3 THE ROLE OF GOVERNMENT IN GLOBAL–LOCAL INTERFACES

Given latecomers' lack of capital, skills, and technologies, they must rely on foreign resources and capabilities. This presents the eventual challenge of how to create innovation systems that support the local creation of value-added and knowledge to thereby generate a critical mass of domestically owned enterprises. That is, as discussed in Chapter 3, the challenge is how to strategically manage global–local interfaces to strengthen a domestic base for innovation and entrepreneurship. Such a need for domestically owned firms and corresponding innovation systems arises for two reasons. First, because any successful economic growth that relies on foreign sources tends to cause wage rates to rise accordingly, FDI firms and MNCs tend to look for cheaper labor costs in "next-tier down" countries that may displace the concerned country's position in GVCs. Second, as latecomers achieve successful catch-up and approach a technological frontier, they find it increasingly difficult to receive technology transfers from incumbents.

Facing this challenge, latecomers find themselves having to choose between two possible responses; these two responses can be generalized as a slower and faster mode of catch-up. The slow and hopefully steady mode of catch-up largely corresponds to the history of the IT cluster in Penang, Malaysia, and the auto sector in Thailand, which were discussed in Chapter 3. Within this mode, the main focus of public intervention is not on generating domestically owned firms but rather on re-skilling and up-skilling the local labor force to prevent FDI firms and MNCs from relocating and, in turn, to encourage them to engage in high-value activities and continue hiring local workers at higher wage rates. The faster catch-up mode, in contrast, closely corresponds to the situation of Shenzhen, China, and the Chinese auto sector, which are discussed in Chapter 3. In this mode, the focus of public intervention is on creating domestically owned firms as opposed to foreign-owned firms. Next, I elaborate on these two different modes of catching up.

6.3.1 A Slow but Steady Mode of Catch-Up

As discussed in Section 3.4 of Chapter 3, Penang, Malaysia, has long been recognized as a productive cluster capable of hosting MNCs that produce electronic parts and components. MNCs began operating in Penang in 1972 following the establishment of a free trade zone in that year. In the 1970s, MNCs were attracted to Penang because it was one of the few locations that offered attractive incentives, such as cheap labor costs and low taxes. Although Penang has not been as successful as Shenzhen at generating domestically owned firms, it does not represent a failed attempt at catch-up; rather, Penang is a decent case of steady catch-up. Penang's per capita income level is much higher than the average level in Malaysia. Due to rising wage rates, some MNCs in Penang have downsized their manufacturing operation, moving low value-added operations to lower wage countries. However, many MNCs have maintained operations in Penang, as they benefit from privileged access to strong supply chains enabling them to produce and provide cutting-edge technology products and services. Further, a new cycle of firms emerged and performed high value-added activities, including high-value engineering tasks, such as prototyping and services. For instance, Motorola oversees a full cycle of engineering operations for its telecommunication business, from R&D to prototyping, production, and engineering services (Lee et al., 2020).

In summary, Penang has evolved from a labor-intensive manufacturing center into a cluster that provides software, engineering design, R&D, and industrial system-based services. Consequently, low value-added manufacturing has largely disappeared from Penang. Notably, a new cycle of development is emerging, and Penang has diversified into high value-added servicing activities and industries, such as medical tourism, education, shared service centers, and R&D (Penang Institute, 2015, pp. 10–15). Next, I will discuss the key local institutions that have facilitated such value chain upgrades at MNCs.

Policy intervention in Penang aimed at upgrading social capital and state-of-the-art skills useful in GVCs. The key vehicle for this upgrading was the Penang Skill Development Centre (PSDC), a public agency established to cultivate production-related skills among the blue-collar workforce, as explained in detail in Lee et al. (2020). Established in 1969, the Penang Development Centre (PDC) was a state agency that supported the development of industrial parks in Penang and employment creation. The PDC also cooperated with MNCs, such as HP, Intel, and Motorola. Together, they founded the PSDC in 1989, a nonprofit institution that provided technical knowledge and training programs to technicians and engineers within the industrial park. The center has an established network of industry partners and a robust knowledge base, and it can teach specialized knowledge useful for advanced industrial operations. Approximately 200 company members of the PSDC contribute to its technical knowledge base and enjoy access to a stable supply of labor power. The PSDC also hosts several laboratories that provide shared services to members. In 2016, the PSDC trained and certified 7,048 individuals as skilled workers in the industrial park, a ratio of 35 workers per company in Penang. The PSDC also runs training programs to develop the necessary human competencies for Industry 4.0.[3]

6.3.2 A Faster Mode of Catching Up

Although both Penang and Shenzhen began as FDI-led growth economies at their initial stages, Shenzhen came to adopt a faster mode of catch-up. The discussion in Section 3.4 of Chapter 3 demonstrates that one important source of the different speeds of catch-up between Penang and Shenzhen has been the emergence of domestically owned and globally successful firms in Shenzhen. Therefore, the important question is to determine how this was possible in Shenzhen and other regions of China. The answer is a strategy that combines firm-level R&D efforts with supportive industrial and innovation policies by the government, including public–private collaborations (Lee et al., 2021; Yang, 2015). This strategy can be further demonstrated by several cases of catch-up in China, in particular, the case of Huawei in Shenzhen.

Huawei was established in 1987 by Ren Zhengfei, a former communications officer for the People's Liberation Army, and five of his fellow PLA members with a starting capital of Renminbi 20,000 (about $3,000).[4] Huawei began from nothing in the city of Shenzhen. The firm began as a telecommunication equipment distributor operating out of a barn on a farm in Shenzhen that was used as an office. From here, the founders sold telephone switches imported from Hong Kong. In 1990, Huawei decided to attempt to transform itself

[3] The titles of offered programs include I4.0: The Idea, Architecture, Demand, and Approach; Embedded Systems for IoT; Cloud Architectures & Technologies; Cybersecurity Fundamentals for Industry 4.0; Big Data: Methods and Solutions; and The Robot Operating System. All of this information relies on the author's work (Lee et al., 2020).

[4] Information about Huawei is mostly from Mu and Lee (2005).

into a telecommunication equipment manufacturer by relying on in-house research and development rather than forming a joint venture with a multinational firm, which was the typical strategy of most Chinese manufacturers at that time. This constituted a significant risk, as Huawei had neither the relevant knowledge nor sufficient money to develop the capacity to manufacture telecommunications equipment. Despite this, Huawei evolved to become a global player in both telecom systems and cell phones. What were the sources of the stunning growth of this private startup company?

A subsequent driver of growth of this company had been the spillover and diffusion of knowledge; knowledge began by spilling over from the FDI firm Shanghai Bell to a public–private R&D consortium and then finally to Huawei (Mu & Lee, 2005). In the 1980s, the telecom equipment market in China, particularly fixed-line telephone switch manufacturing, experienced an unmet demand surge following the opening and growth of the Chinese economy. In response, the Chinese government invited several foreign firms to form joint ventures with Chinese partners to produce and sell goods in the Chinese market. Shanghai Bell was one such joint venture, with the Chinese holding a majority stake of shares at 60%. This joint venture was an exemplar case of the Chinese strategy of "trading market for technology" (Mu & Lee, 2005), with the Chinese government leveraging its ability to grant access to the massive Chinese market as a bargaining tool to induce foreign firms to transfer important technology and know-how to their Chinese partners.

The Chinese government did not stop at facilitating joint ventures. Soon after, they initiated a public–private R&D consortium designed to take advantage of knowledge spillover from joint ventures. This consortium eventually developed a large-capacity digital telephone switch (model HJD-04) in 1991, which was first installed in rural markets in 1992. This indigenously developed digital switch technology was transferred to four local manufacturers, including three state-owned enterprises (SOEs) and one private firm (Huawei). As we now know, Huawei was the ultimate winner in the market among these four companies, and its success was due to its aggressive corporate culture and commitment to in-house R&D. Huawei also continued building up its technological capabilities by recruiting engineers with experience and knowledge of the development of the HJD-04 system. Huawei rapidly increased its market share by spearheading an aggressive marketing campaign and taking advantage of the Chinese government's support, as exemplified by its "buy local" policy and preferential loans.[5] In 1998, Huawei became the largest digital switch supplier in China (Mu & Lee, 2005).

The above history of Huawei demonstrates that there would have been no Huawei today if the Chinese government had not taken the initiative to establish a public–private R&D consortium for the development of domestic telephone switch manufacturing. Government policies supporting local manufacturers were also crucial to this success. As these cases show, inviting FDI is not the end but just the beginning of the long-term process of economic development. However, the type of government intervention that is most effective is dependent on contextual factors, such as time and place. For instance, in the case of Tencent, another pioneering firm that is also based in Shenzhen, the primary assistance provided by the local government came in the form of guaranteeing funding by attracting venture capital (with public capital involvement) and other financial investors during the initial growth stage (Breznitz & Murphree, 2011, pp. 175–178; Yang, 2015). There has been an impressive rise in local innovators in Shenzhen, which is reflected in the list of the top ten patent assignees in the region. In 2002, foreign firms dominated the list. However, by 2015, all of the top ten assignees were Chinese firms, including Huawei, ZTE, Tencent, and BYD.

The basic role of the public sector in China's telecom sector and in Shenzhen was similar to that of FCh in the Chilean salmon

---

[5] The Chinese Government started to impose tariffs on imported telecommunications equipment, and extended Huawei CNY 3.9 billion in buyer's credit from the China Construction Bank. It also provided CNY 3.5 billion of revolving credit from the Bank of China and Industrial and Commercial Bank of China.

sector, as discussed in Section 3.2 of Chapter 3. FCh, however, is not a public–private consortium but a nonprofit organization. Salmon is not native to Chile and thus Chile has no comparative advantage in the salmon business. However, FCh was dedicated to fostering the salmon business and its growth, and it was instrumental in importing Norwegian technology and experimenting with farming various species under different conditions, eventually proving that cultivating salmon was commercially viable. Salmones Antártica, a salmon production and processing company created by FCh, successfully demonstrated the economic potential of salmon cultivation as an industry, and subsequently, more entrepreneurs have entered the salmon business.

6.3.3 Transitioning from Slow to Fast Catch-Up: The Auto Sector in China

The Chinese auto sector is a typical example of shifting from a slow mode of catch-up that relies on FDI or joint ventures to an eventually faster mode of catch-up that relies on domestically based firms[6]. China initiated economic reforms and an open-door policy in the late 1980s, and subsequently, it sought to establish its own automotive industry. In the initial stages, this industry was to rely on foreign joint ventures. The Chinese government anticipated benefiting from technology transfers by forming joint ventures and pursuing a policy strategy of leveraging the "market for technology." This approach was also applied to other industries, such as telecommunication equipment (Mu & Lee, 2005).

One of the first joint ventures was the Beijing Jeep Company formed in 1983, followed by a joint venture between Shanghai Auto Industry Corporation (SAIC) and Volkswagen in 1984 and Guangzhou-Peugeot in 1985. More joint ventures followed in the 1990s (Chu, 2011). In these joint ventures, foreign ownership was capped at 50% (Liu et al., 2014), and foreign joint ventures were required to

---

[6] This section utilizes information from a previous publication of colleagues and mine (Lee, Qu & Mao, 2021).

establish R&D centers (Yu et al., 2008). However, this strategy of relying on FDI and joint ventures did not yield the anticipated benefits in terms of technology transfer and the eventual enhancement of the technological capabilities of Chinese automakers (Chu, 2011). In the early stages of the industry, the size of China did not constitute a considerable advantage; rather, it was a source of information and coordination failure due to the complex politics involving the central and local governments, which made it difficult to conduct Japan–Korea-style centralized industrial policy (Lee et al., 2021).

Although the central government attempted to achieve economies of scale by limiting the number of firms in the auto industry to three major and three minor automakers, provincial governments often circumvented such regulations and allowed entries by local firms and foreign joint ventures. Consequently, China ended up with over 110 automobile assembly plants, with nearly half being foreign joint ventures (Chu, 2011). The problems of the Chinese auto sector have been summarized as "outdated products, high prices, and no R&D capabilities," as well as "too many production sites, indiscreet project approval, redundant investment, and slow localization" (Chu, 2011). Joint venture firms tended to adopt old, mid-market designs from foreign partners and concentrated on fulfilling government-mandated localization requirements rather than developing their own engines or undertaking R&D (Thun, 2018). Guangzhou-Peugeot Automobile Company, which closed in March 1997, is a representative example of a joint venture that failed in China (Lassere & Zeng, 2002). Peugeot was unwilling to promote local value chains and instead continued to rely on foreign imported parts, which ultimately raised the final cost of products (Harwit, 1994). Thus, the Chinese partner believed that Peugeot was focusing on obtaining short-term profits from quickly selling knock-down kits without facilitating localization.

It is domestically owned companies that secured the success of the contemporary Chinese auto sector, and these domestic firms only entered the market after China joined the WTO in 2001. Before 2000, joint ventures dominated the Chinese market. Beginning in 2001, domestically owned manufacturers, such as Great Wall, Chery, and Geely, began emerging rapidly, and they continued to increase their market share, reaching 30% in 2009 (Tian et al., 2010). These new companies pursued slightly different strategies from those of foreign joint ventures in building their technological capabilities and acquiring foreign technology. They conducted in-house R&D activities, filed more patents than foreign joint ventures,[7] and relied on active licensing and international M&As. For example, Chery bought a used assembly line from SEAT, a Volkswagen subsidiary in Spain, and an engine factory from a Ford plant in England in 1997 (Lee et al., 2009). After importing this assembly line, they recruited engineers from foreign joint ventures. For example, Chery CEO Tongyao Yin was a former manager at FAW-Volkswagen, and over 100 engineers of FAW-Volkswagen also left to join Chery. Moreover, thirteen key engineers moved to Chery from Dongfeng-Nissan. They joined the development team for the famous QQ model, the success of which resulted in the rapid growth of Chery (Lee et al., 2007).

Given the strong motivation for success associated with private or nonstate ownership and the pressures of tough market competition, indigenous firms, including Chinese conglomerate BYD, invested aggressively in new facilities and technologies to build their technological capabilities.[8] Chery acquired Jaguar Land Rover to enhance its brand reputation and technological capabilities. In 2007, Geely established an overseas factory and bought a stake in the UK cab firm Manganese Bronze Holdings. In 2009, Geely acquired the Australian company Drivetrain Systems International, the world's second-largest gearbox manufacturer, and Geely further improved its technological capabilities through an acquisition of Volvo. The

[7] According to previous research I conducted with colleagues (Lee, Qu & Mao, 2021) in 2007, both Shanghai-GM and Volkswagen filed fewer than 10 patents each, whereas Chery filed 107. The number of utility model patents (petty patents) filed by these joint ventures between 1998 and 2007 was only 24 for Shanghai-Volkswagen and 31 for Shanghai-GM. In contrast, Chery filed 254, and Geely filed 128.

[8] Information in this paragraph relies on Lee et al. (2009).

rise of indigenous firms also created more competition between local firms and joint ventures, which further contributed to the deepening and widening of local supply chains in China, which was also facilitated by the local contents requirement policy.

While one may emphasize the unique Chinese advantage of large market size, the story of the auto sector in China suggests that market size can only be utilized as such when government has an effective plan and the will to promote local industry. Thus, the so-called "trading market for technology" strategy was effectively utilized in the case of telecommunication switch development in China. However, this was not the case in the auto sector because the government, during the industry's early stages, failed to implement a similar strategic vision and did not begin providing effective coordination for the promotion of a part–supplier network until the 2000s (Chu, 2011).

Furthermore, there were several policy measures that contributed to the successful rise of domestically owned firms in China. In addition to the local contents requirement policy, which was eventually canceled in accordance with WTO demands, there were three other policy initiatives: import restrictions, entry controls, and market discrimination. First, since the promulgation of the Automotive Industry Policy Law in 1994, import quota licenses have been used to regulate the import of auto parts and assembled cars. Even the types of cars allowed for import are regulated in accordance with nationwide policies meant to promote the automotive sector. Therefore, the importation of both used cars and parts for car assembly is forbidden, which implies that automotive manufacturers are not allowed to import semi-knock-down kits to produce cars (Chen & Han, 2007). Second, foreign enterprises are not allowed to establish more than two joint ventures producing the same type of car in China. For investment projects related to completely built units and engines, foreign automotive manufacturers are required to collaborate with domestic manufacturers (Nan, 2005). Third, foreign cars face higher registration fees and taxes in the market than domestic cars (Chen & Han, 2007).

6.3.4   *The Key Takeaways*

The takeaway of this chapter is not that the same measures should be applied to all contexts and countries but rather that latecomers require some forms of tailored asymmetric support, as they are unable to compete against incumbent foreign firms. Without such asymmetric support, latecomer economies and industries will continue to be dominated by foreign firms and FDI firms, and given the existing asymmetry in power and technologies, domestically owned firms will fail to emerge. For domestic firms, there is no such thing as a peaceful rise to prominence; their emergence always entails some form of rivalry and tension with incumbent firms. This is because any effort to establish and strengthen domestic firms is often met with hostile reactions or counterattacks by incumbents and existing joint venture partners. In such cases, public intervention is justified to correct market imperfections and inefficiency because incumbents often abuse their market power and the market structure to maintain their monopolistic power. Power and technology asymmetries in GVCs are the source of latecomers' failure to upgrade. I will now elaborate on this point while providing several examples.

The three modes of original equipment manufacturer (OEM), original design manufacturer (ODM), and original brand manufacturer (OBM) are examples of GVC participation where flagship firms from advanced economies, such as Nike, sit at the top of value chains due to their brand power (or power as OBMs), while latecomer firms serve brand owners by producing for them as OEMs and ODMs. Although OEMs and ODMs strive to become OBMs and capture a larger share of global profit, upgrading from one mode to the next is neither automatic nor easy. Transitioning into an OBM involves several risks, including weathering counterattacks from incumbents and flagship firms in existing GVCs. This finding was noted in a previous essay of mine discussing how Korean SMEs try to become OBMs (Lee et al., 2015), as well as in another case study on the footwear and furniture sectors in Brazil (Navas-Alemán, 2011). The aversion of former buyer firms toward suppliers that are trying to transform into OBMs was also documented in earlier studies on Latin America (Giuliani et al., 2005; Navas-Alemán, 2011). Thus, this transition can be prolonged by a slowdown, which may even lead to a decline in sales or market shares for latecomer firms trying to upgrade. And eventually, this can cause a possible crisis for such firms. For instance, as I noted in an earlier essay (Lee, 2019, Chapter 4), in the consumer goods sector, former vendor companies (brand owners) often cease their patronage of OEMs that begin to sell their competing brands in order to destroy the former OEM firms. In the case of capital goods, when an incumbent realizes that a latecomer firm has become successful in developing products that can compete with the incumbent, they often begin charging predatory prices in the market.

The pervasiveness of such interference tactics by leading incumbent firms in GVCs implies that functionally upgrading to an OBM requires a latecomer to fight with leading firms for their independence in GVCs. To some extent, this argument contradicts several studies in the GVC literature that tend to emphasize collaborations between flagship firms in the Global North and firms in the Global South (e.g., Ernst & Kim, 2002; Sturgeon & Lester, 2004). Latecomer firms in the South have the option of choosing "no fight and no associated risk"; however, they can also choose to remain dependent on one or several MNC vendor firms, or a single client firm. This strategy of dependent or path-following catch-up is not always detrimental because it may lead to temporary growth during the low or lower middle-income stages. However, in the long term, it is not certain that this strategy can guarantee long-term survival, as new late-entrant firms will emerge from the next tier of catch-up countries and offer lower wages and costs.[9] The footwear sector in

---

[9] The limitations of these dependent catch-up strategies have been demonstrated in the cases of other countries reported in previous studies, such as Van Dijk and Bell (2007) and Rasiah (2006).

southern Brazil is an example of a cluster that was once prosperous but subsequently declined after the rise of China as an alternative site of production (Lee et al., 2018).

6.4 THE ROLE OF GOVERNMENT IN THE DETOUR FROM BIG BUSINESSES TO SMEs

The preceding chapters, in particular Chapter 5, emphasized the role of big businesses in fostering growth beyond the middle-income stage. The next issue to tackle is how to first generate big businesses, and then SMEs and startups at a later stage. In what follows, I first discuss how to promote big businesses and then how to grow SMEs and startups.

6.4.1 How to Generate Big Businesses

In a country like the United States, which has a large market size and a higher degree of market efficiency, there is no need for intervention via public policies to promote big businesses. Many startups in the United States tend to grow quickly into "unicorns" within a short period of time.[10] Therefore, it is important to ask why other countries fail to generate such unicorns.

One answer could be that a typical emerging or developing country faces a high degree of market failure while also having to overcome its smaller market size. In such situations, productive ideas by individuals or startups tend not to be financed either by venture capital or bank loans. When making a loan, banks typically require some form of collateral, regardless of expected return on investment projects. The literature on business groups and conglomerates in emerging economies tends to identify market failures as a factor influencing the rise of conglomerates (Lee, 2019, Chapter 4). That is, business groups and family-owned conglomerates are understood as entities that emerge to fill institutional voids or to correct market failures by utilizing internal capital markets and labor markets.

---

[10] A unicorn company is a privately held startup company that is valued at more than $1 billion.

When business groups and family-owned conglomerates have started new businesses or entered new sectors, they have tended to secure initial capital not via regular capital markets but through funds received from sister companies within the business group. The government or public agencies often participate in this process by issuing debt guarantees when the private firms try to obtain loans from domestic or foreign banks.

In advanced economies, market failures tend to refer to entire sectors becoming oligopolies or monopolies. In contrast, in developing economies, market failures are more fundamental in nature, as they involve the very absence of a market or the thinness and smallness of markets, which can give rise to an inability to finance large or long-term projects. This, in turn, results in an inability to generate big businesses. In such cases, an alternative method for growing big businesses is for the government to create them directly. In many cases in the Global South, governments are directly involved in creating SOEs. Governments can grow SOEs quickly by mobilizing all domestically available resources and competencies, allowing the enterprises to go public via an initial public offering (IPO), and finally pursuing gradual privatization. There are various examples of governments building SOEs to eventually be converted into big businesses.

One example is POSCO in South Korea, which is one of the top five steel companies in the world. As Korea lacked any private capitalists who could take on such a project, only the government was positioned to create the beginnings of a Korean steel-making industry. From 1958 to 1968, the Korean government tried six times to construct an integrated steel mill but failed each time. The World Bank and the United States Agency of International Development refused to provide loans for the project over doubts that Korea could repay them; they also doubted the necessity of a large-capacity steel mill in a small developing economy (D'Costa, 1994, p. 64; Song, 2002, p. 57). Instead, these agencies suggested that Korea develop steel-consuming industries, such as machinery, automobiles, and shipbuilding (Song, 2002, p. 57). However, the Korean government insisted that the construction of steel-consuming industries was not a prerequisite for the successful development of the Korean steel industry and that the steel industry should first expand and supply quality steel at competitive prices, after which steel-consuming industries would follow (Song, 2002, p. 58).

Former President Park Chung-Hee made this steel project a top priority of the second Five-Year Economic Development Plan (1967–1971). The Korean government established POSCO as an SOE in 1968. The government held 56.2% of the company's shares, and the remaining 43.8% were held by the state-run Korea Tungsten Co. In retrospect, the plan to construct a steel mill before the development of steel-consuming industries turned out to be valid, as evidenced by the subsequent strong growth of steel-consuming industries in Korea since the 1970s, such as the automotive and shipbuilding industries. Since the 2000s, POSCO gradually become privatized, and the government distributed a portion of its shares to all Korean citizens free of charge.

Another example is TSMC, the world's largest semiconductor foundry. As discussed in Section 4.4 of Chapter 4, TSMC was created in 1986 as a spin-off of a government research institute known as ITRI and started as a joint venture with Philips, as well as other fabless firms. Further, the rise of the semiconductor industry in Taiwan was not simply a natural process; rather, it was the product of a policy of targeted industry promotion. With a clear and calculated vision, the government in Taiwan first allocated robust resources to ITRI and two other research institutes in Hsinchu to develop the capabilities needed for the foundry businesses, in particular fabrication services (Yeung, 2016, p. 138). TSMC's rise to global prominence occurred ten to fifteen years after its spin-off from the ITRI, which could be attributed to firm-specific innovation efforts undertaken after the initial government promotion of the industry in the 1980s (Yeung, 2016, p. 140).

Chapter 3 discussed several resource-based sectors in Malaysia that served as a growth engine for the country past the middle-income stage. The oil and gas company Petronas is the only Malaysian company that ranks in the Fortune Global 500. This SOE has gradually developed its capabilities and upgraded into higher-value activities, and it is now a fully integrated international oil and gas company that operates in over thirty countries. The public sector also played a critical role in the early stages of the Malaysian rubber and palm oil sector. Malaysia nationalized several domestic firms to consolidate them into a larger firm, and in 1981, it also executed a hostile takeover of three British palm oil and rubber plantation conglomerates listed on the London Stock Exchange (Lebdioui et al., 2021). Such initiatives were important for the growth of these resource-based sectors.

SOEs are not necessarily inefficient as long as they are subject to global market discipline and are run by competent managers. There are multiple examples of successful SOEs, such as Singapore Airlines, Aramco, and Ethiopian Air. For instance, Saudi Arabian Oil Company, or Aramco, has overtaken Apple as the world's most valuable company, worth about $2.43 trillion compared to Apple's $2.37 trillion as of May 2022.[11] Some SOEs have also proven to be extremely innovative, such as the State Grid Corporation of China, which was thoroughly analyzed by Rikap (2022). The State Grid Corporation of China is a leading firm in artificial intelligence applications for the energy sector, and it became an innovator by relying on China's national innovation system, particularly its public research organizations, public funding, and innovation and energy policies. It is unique for not having relied on technology transfers from global leaders, unlike other large firms from developing or emerging countries.

It is no surprise that many of the Fortune Global 500 firms located in emerging economies tend to be SOEs, such as POSCO in South Korea and many SOEs in China. This contrasts sharply with the case of advanced economies, where most Fortune Global

---

[11] https://edition.cnn.com/2022/05/12/investing/saudi-aramco-becomes-most-valuable-company-intl-hnk/index.html (retrieved on 2023-10-20).

500 firms are not SOEs. A similar contrast can be observed when looking at related sectors; for example, the French energy and petroleum company Total Energies and the US company Shell are private corporations, whereas the Saudi Arabian company Aramco and the Malaysian company Petronas are SOEs. Such a contrast has to do with the different origins of these firms. There exists a high degree of market failure in emerging economies, and therefore, big businesses tend to be either SOEs or business groups, like Korean chaebols. It takes time for them to become privatized or for a new generation of private firms to emerge. China provides a typical example. The Chinese firms on the Fortune Global 500 list were at one time mostly SOEs. Currently, however, many of the Chinese companies on the list are not SOEs. Even though China is a state-led economy, it has been able to generate dynamic non-SOEs, like Huawei, Alibaba, Baidu, and Tencent, some of which are listed on US stock exchanges.

In general, policymakers in emerging economies face two alternatives. They can adopt a slow mode and continue to deploy their resources to a large number of SMEs and startups with the objective of growing them into big businesses, or they can adopt a fast mode, concentrating their resources in a few big businesses to achieve rapid growth. A practical compromise between these two approaches would be to start with a certain number of firms and then focus on a few among them. The Korean experience, as discussed in Chapter 5, is consistent with such a compromise, in that all present-day big businesses in Korea used to be small companies, particularly when judged by international standards. However, they grew into large corporations through a cumulative process that involved screening candidates for privileged support, evaluating firms based on performance, and then selecting the best-performing firms for new projects.

6.4.2 Transitioning from Big Businesses to SMEs and Startups

Once a country achieves success in generating a critical mass of big businesses, these big businesses tend to serve as an umbrella and generator of startups and SMEs in diverse ways, including enabling spin-offs, providing venture capital, and purchasing the products of SMEs. In other words, in emerging economies, it is big businesses that tend to facilitate the growth of startups and SMEs, whereas in an environment absent of big businesses, SMEs and startups take more time and have more difficulty growing into big businesses. In China, large tech giants, such as Alibaba and Tencent, served as vital sources of venture capital for many startups. For instance, Tencent is reported to have invested in over 730 startups from 2006 to 2022, including seven in 2012, forty-two in 2015, ninety-seven in 2018, and ninety-six in 2021.[12] It is well known that in Shenzhen, China's most innovative city, the role of public–private collaborative venture capital has played a central role in fostering many startups. In South Korea, the tech giants Naver and Kakao, which are the Korean equivalents to Google and Facebook, respectively, were founded by former employees of Samsung. Startups and SMEs tend to grow into big businesses only when the public sector offers critical assistance in correcting market, capability, or system failures.

In fact, one study on entrepreneurship sponsored by the Asian Development Bank found that while the presence of big businesses in a low- or middle-income economy tends not to harm the emergence of startups with any statistical significance, it tends to lead to more startups in high-income economies.[13] Such results can be explained by the fact that big businesses tend to have both negative and positive effects on startups. That is, they have a negative effect on startups by discouraging them from offering job opportunities to talented young individuals and possible entrepreneurs while

---

[12] www.crunchbase.com/search/funding_rounds/field/organizations/num_investments/ tencent (retrieved on 2022-12-15).

[13] Several papers were produced as a result of this project, and they are available at www .adb.org/documents/asian-development-outlook-2022-update-background-papers; retrieved on 2023-10-20. The specific paper focusing on the linkage between big businesses and entrepreneurship is by Xin and Lee (2022); it can be found at the following link: The Role of Big Businesses in Entrepreneurship: A Cross-Country Panel Analysis using the GEM Data (adb.org).

also positively affecting them by serving as sources of funds and producing employees who, after leaving the corporation, start their own businesses. These opposing effects offset each other in low- and middle-income economies; in contrast, the net effect is positive in high-income economies. In a low- or middle-income economy with a higher degree of market failure, especially in capital markets, the risk of starting a new business is higher, and therefore, people tend to prefer being hired by a big business. In contrast, in a high-income economy with a lower degree of market failure, the risk associated with startups is lower than in low- or middle-income economies. In this context, it makes sense to promote the growth of big businesses in low- or middle-income economies with the anticipation that such big businesses will generate more startups at later stages of development.

However, these linkages between big businesses and SMEs are not automatic and, therefore, may require policy intervention. South Korea, like other countries, has tried many policies to promote SMEs and startups; many of them, however, were unsuccessful. Nevertheless, there are several policy initiatives that have proven to be effective. As is explained below, their common success factor is that they have all tried to mobilize synergies and spillover between SMEs and large firms to correct various failures in markets, systems, and capabilities.

In South Korea, one such successful intervention was the so-called AMC (advance market commitment) R&D program, which involved supporting the R&D programs of SMEs so that SMEs could develop parts and supplies on the advance commitment by big businesses and state-owned enterprises to use and purchase them once they are developed successfully.[14] The nature of the program is similar to the AMC used to develop vaccines.[15] Such a program is advantageous, as it is designed to overcome coordination and system

---

[14] Information about this program is based on Korea-ITEP (2009), Shin (2016) and Shim and Seo (2015).

[15] Please refer to the information about AMC available at https://fiftrustee.worldbank.org/en/about/unit/dfi/fiftrustee/fund-detail/amc (retrieved on 2023-10-20).

failures. The nature of coordination failure is as follows. On the one hand, SMEs do not want to take the risk of launching R&D projects to develop parts and supplies without a guarantee that large assembly companies will purchase their products. On the other hand, large assembly companies tend to purchase high-tech parts and components from foreign suppliers because they are uncertain about the quality of comparable products made by domestic SMEs. Given the South Korean government's mandate to promote local value chains and domesticate the production of formerly imported parts and components to save dollars, the government intervened between supplier SMEs and large client firms and devised a scheme to overcome this coordination failure by mobilizing public R&D.

According to South Korea's AMC R&D program, products to be developed are first proposed by either large user firms or supplier SMEs; subsequently, a government agency evaluates the request and decides whether to support it. Once approved, the SME receives an R&D subsidy for two to three years, which covers 55% to 75% of the total R&D expenses. Once an SME is able to generate revenue, it must pay back up to 20% of the received subsidy as a royalty. This program began in 2002 on an experimental basis. Support was provided to thirteen SMEs, with an average subsidy amount of 70 million won. Since then, it was expanded in scale and scope. In 2005, eighty-seven SMEs received an average subsidy of 110 million won (about $110,000) each. In 2010, this had expanded to 214 SMEs receiving an average annual subsidy of 280 million won, involving 177 large user firms. As of 2022, this program is still in operation, indicating its success relative to other programs that were suspended due to ineffectiveness. This initiative was successful because it was designed not only to correct coordination failures but also to promote R&D collaborations between large user firms and supplier SMEs, thereby enhancing the know-how and capabilities of SMEs.

The second policy initiative designed to promote SMEs in South Korea was the opening of a secondary stock market to handle market failures facing new firms in financing their investment in capital market. On this secondary stock market, the requirements for a startup or SME to be listed for an initial public offering were less strict than those for the primary stock markets. This secondary market established by the South Korean government is known as the KOSDAQ (Korean Securities Dealers Automated Quotations) and it is equivalent to the NASDAQ (National Association of Securities Dealers Automated Quotation) in the United States.[16] Since opening in 1996, the KOSDAQ has grown rapidly. At the end of 1997, there were 359 firms listed in the market, and by February 2000, there were 469 firms listed. The market value of the KOSDAQ has grown from 7 billion won (about $6 million) at end of 1997 to 105 trillion won (about $100 billion) by February 2000. If we compare the KOSDAQ with the Korean Stock Exchange (KSE), the number of the listed firms is not small, since there are only 725 firms listed in the KSE in 2000. In terms of market value, the aggregate market value of KOSDAQ firms is currently below that of the KSE; however, when KOSDAQ reached its peak in 2001, its market value approached that of the KSE, with as many as 153 new firms listed in 2002.

The KOSDAQ market mainly targeted so-called "venture companies," which are technology-oriented startups that spend more than 5% of their sales on R&D and receive venture capital investment. Out of the 469 firms listed on the KOSDAQ in 2000, 150 were officially classified as venture companies. These companies were specifically promoted via a law enacted in 1997 to promote startup and venture companies. It is also notable that beginning in December of 1997, South Korea suffered a financial crisis and bankruptcies of some chaebol firms, which led to the IMF bailout. Many of the entrepreneurs who founded these companies were former employees of big businesses and chaebols, where they had built up their experiences, skills, and technological know-how. Moreover, the 1997 crisis was an important trigger factor, as one-third of the top thirty chaebols

---

[16] Information about KOSDAQ and the related startups is all from Lee and Kim (2000) unless noted otherwise.

declared bankruptcy and had to fire many employees. Subsequently, in 1999, venture companies experienced their first boom, which coincided with the post-crisis turnaround of the Korean economy, which witnessed 9% real growth.

This growth was not simply natural; rather, it should be partly attributed to the policy commitments made by the new Kim Dae-jung government, which promised to transition from a "chaebol-led" to a "venture-led" economy. In 1998, the Korean government promulgated the Five-Year Plan for the Vitalization of Venture Companies. Being labeled a "venture" company benefited South Korean firms, as it guaranteed firms substantial tax benefits and exempted them from the strict requirement for being listed in the KOSDAQ. According to the Office of the SME, the number of venture companies grew from a mere 304 in May 1998 to 6,004 in March 2000. The value of the products of these venture companies accounted for about 4.8% of GDP in 1999, and these companies hired a cumulative total of 180,000 workers.

The KOSDAQ experienced a phenomenon similar to overheating in 2001 due to many individual investors rushing to purchase stocks in expectation of quick capital gains. In the early 2000s, even big businesses expressed concern as they witnessed many of their former employees quit their jobs to create startups. Furthermore, in July 2013, the Korean government created a third stock market called the Korea New Exchange (KONEX), which was to offer public listing opportunities for less qualified firms than those on the KOSDAQ. As of 2022, there are about 130 firms listed on the KONEX.

China has also created two secondary stock markets. The ChiNext, which was formed in 2009, is a NASDAQ-style subsidiary of the Shenzhen Stock Exchange. The Shanghai Stock Exchange Science and Technology Innovation Board (SSE STAR Market) was formed in July 2019. It was launched with an ambition to rival the NASDAQ, and by July 2020, it was ranked second globally for capital raised via IPOs. As of October 2022, it

Table 6.1 *Platform companies' year of establishment and stock market listing: The United States, China, and South Korea*

Company	Founded	Listed	Origin	Exchange market	Years taken for listing
Google	09-04-98	08-19-2004	USA	NASDAQ	6.0 years
Amazon	06-05-94	05-15-1997	USA	NASDAQ	2.9 years
Facebook	02-04-04	05-18-2012	USA	NASDAQ	8.3 years
Baidu	01-01-00	08-05-2005	China	NASDAQ	5.6 years
Alibaba	06-28-99	09-19-2014	China	NYSE	15.2 years
Tencent	11-11-98	06-16-2004	China	HKEX (Hong Kong)	5.6 years
Naver	06-02-99	10-29-2002	Korea	KOSDAQ	3.4 years
Kakao	02-16-95	11-11-1999	Korea	KOSDAQ	4.7 years

Source: Announced documents of each stock exchange market (USA, China, Hong Kong, and Korea)

had 480 listed firms, including some multi-listed firms, such as SMIC, China's fast growing semiconductor foundry.[17] Although the amount raised via IPOs on Chinese stock markets (approx. $35 billion) was more than double that raised on Wall Street (approx. $16 billion) as of June 2022, much of the fundraising occurred on the Star Market and ChiNext Market, with the majority raised by companies in the fields of renewables, semiconductors, and other high-end manufacturing sectors.[18]

These secondary stock markets have served as a key vehicle for startups to grow into big business and have enabled venture capital to quickly recoup their investments. Table 6.1 shows the number of years it took several startups to be listed on various stock markets, such as NASDAQ in the United States, KOSDAQ in South Korea,

[17] http://star.sse.com.cn/star/en/infodisclosure/newsrelease/c/c_20221103_5711260 .shtml (retrieved on 2022-12-17).

[18] "China IPO fundraising doubles US total to top global ranks." *Financial Times*, 2022-06-20. www.ft.com/content/752f69f2-393e-4f32-ad15-798b9a6e8b0a (retrieved on 2022-06-20).

Table 6.2 *Cumulative numbers of unicorns created by country, 2012–2021*

Country	2012	2013	2014	2015	2016	2017	2018	2019	2020	2021
USA	11	19	52	102	129	169	240	324	415	728
China	1	1	7	39	66	98	143	173	189	217
India	1	2	3	5	7	8	15	24	40	88
UK	0	0	0	3	7	13	22	29	36	58
Germany	0	1	2	4	5	6	11	16	17	35
Israel	0	1	1	2	2	2	6	12	19	34
France	0	0	0	1	1	1	1	4	8	20
Korea	0	0	3	4	5	8	10	14	15	19
Brazil	0	0	0	0	0	0	2	5	7	19
Singapore	0	0	2	2	2	2	4	7	9	18
Canada	0	1	2	2	2	3	4	5	7	17
Australia	0	0	1	1	1	1	3	3	6	10

Source: Author's tabulation using CB insights and Tracxn data; www .cbinsights.com/research-unicorn-companies/; https://tracxn.com/d/ unicorn-corner/home

and the Hong Kong Stock Exchange. It took 3 years for Amazon to be listed, 6 years for Google, and 8.3 years for Facebook. Therefore, it is interesting to note that the years taken for comparable platform firms in Korea are not that different from US platforms. Indeed, it took Naver, the Korean equivalent of Google, 3.4 years to be listed on the KOSDAQ, and it took 4.7 years for Kakao, the Korean equivalent of Facebook, to be listed. Similarly, Baidu, the Chinese equivalent of Google, took 5.6 years, compared to Google's 6 years, to be listed on the NASDAQ. Tencent, the Chinese equivalent of Facebook, took 5.6 years to be listed on the Hong Kong Stock Exchange, whereas it took Facebook 8.3 years to be listed on the Nasdaq.

Further, Table 6.2 presents the number of "unicorns" generated by each country from 2012 to 2021. Not surprisingly, as of the end of 2021, the United States has generated the largest number at 728. China and South Korea have demonstrated comparable performances, generating 217 and 19 unicorns, respectively; Germany and France have generated 35 and 20, respectively.

The third example of successful policy intervention by the Korean government is the so-called "creative economy innovation center" program, which was instituted in 2014 to promote SMEs and startups.[19] Interestingly, this program was designed not only to handle market failures in financing but also to solve capability failures by SMEs by assigning a top business group to the respective innovation center in each of South Korea's seventeen provinces. Of course, not every province has achieved success, as success has been dependent on the commitment of the individual business groups. The most successful cases were Samsung in Gyongbuk Province and GS Group in Jeonnam Province. As of April 2021, this program had generated 9,854 startups. In 2016, the base year, 1,221 startups were created. In 2018, the program created 1,796, and in 2020, it created 3,432. These startups worked in partnership with 458 different facilitators, including universities, angel investors, venture capital, and public agencies, generating 25,508 jobs. In many cases, the initial commitment or investment by each assigned big business motivated other entities to join as investors or partners.

For the Gyongbuk Center, Samsung contributes 4 billion won (about $3 million) per year for equity investment into startups.[20] Samsung runs this center in conjunction with its Creative-Lab (C-Lab) Outside program, which is a Samsung program designed to support independent startups. In contrast, Samsung's Creative-Lab Inside program supports intra-Samsung ventures. Samsung's C-Lab program first began in 2012 to promote intra-Samsung ventures; it was expanded in 2015 to include a spin-off program. Finally, in 2018, the C-Lab Outside program was created to promote independent

---

[19] This information comes from the Ministry of SMEs and Startups website (www.mss .go.kr/), as well as www.korea.kr/special/policyCurationView.do?newsId=148865474 (retrieved on 2022-12-17).

[20] This information about C-Lab was retrieved on December 17, 2022, from: www .ftoday.co.kr/news/articleView.html?idxno=246484 (in Korean), and from www .ftoday.co.kr/news/articleView.html?idxno=246484 (in English).

startups outside of Samsung. The C-Lab Outside program provides selected startups with cash grants of up to 100 million won (approx. $80,000), office space, mentoring, and consultation services. The C-Lab Inside program offers current employees one year to pursue independent business ideas that may later evolve into a C-Lab spin-off. C-Lap spin-off founders are offered monetary grants and the option to return as an employee within five years.

Over the ten years from 2012 to 2022, a total of 846 start-ups were generated, including 385 inside Samsung and 460 outside Samsung, and many of them were awarded the Innovation Prize at the CES Convention. For instance, twenty-nine startups won this award in 2023. These startups have attracted equity investments of about 1.34 trillion won (approx. $1.34 billion) and have created about 8,700 jobs. Competition to be selected as a C-Lab startup is high, with approximately only 1 in 38 startups being selected.

This policy intervention designed to nurture startup hubs in the Creative Economy Center was more successful when it was insti-gated alongside another startup program called TIPS, or Technology Incubator Programs for Startups, which also started in 2013.[21]

6.5 THE ROLE OF GOVERNMENT IN THE DETOUR FROM SHORT- TO LONG-CYCLE TECHNOLOGIES

One important component of the innovation–development detour is the detour from short- to long-CTT sectors. This detour presents an intriguing question: Did policymakers in successful catch-up econo-mies in Asia consciously prioritize short-cycle technologies when they developed their industrial development strategies? The answer to this question is "no"; however, they did constantly ask themselves, "What's next?" They keenly observed which industries and businesses were most likely to emerge in the near future and concentrated on develop-ing strategies to enter them. New or emerging industries and businesses are often in short-cycle technologies because such sectors rely less on

---

[21] Information about TIPS came mostly from its website. Source: www.jointips.or.kr/global/.

existing technologies. Therefore, without any specific planning, policy-makers were, in effect, always pursuing short-cycle industries.

In the past, latecomer economies tended to enter new industries at later or mature stages. However, by replicating this practice of constantly seeking entry into new industries, emerging economies have begun entering new industries at increasingly earlier stages. In other words, the emerging economies discussed here evolved from being late latecomers to simply latecomers. And eventually, they are no longer latecomers at all, but rather competitors trying to become first movers in emerging industries. Another term for this process of latecomers achieving increasingly earlier entry compared to incumbents is leapfrogging (Lee, 2021b).

Moreover, with the accumulation of a high level and wide scope of technological capabilities, latecomers may try to enter long-CTT sectors during the post-catch-up stage, which follows the short-CTT specialization catch-up stage. In South Korea, the government has overseen the targeted promotion of biotechnology since the 1990s; this strategy is part of the shift from short- to long-CTT sectors in South Korea. Rather early on in 1994, the Korean government promulgated the Basic Plan to Promote Biotechnology. This plan was initially implemented from 1994 to 2007 under the name "Bio-Tech 2000," and it was based on the Law on Promotion of Bio-Technology.[22] In December 2001, the National Science and Technology Council approved the Basic Plan for the Third Stage for the Promotion of Biotechnology (2002–2007), which included public R&D investment worth 5 trillion won (approx. $5 billion) during the six-year period. The proportion of biotechnology investment to total government R&D was planned to increase from 8% in 2001 to 14% in 2005 and 20% in 2010. This plan was mostly realized. Public R&D investment reached 3.3 trillion in 2016, or 18.8% of total government R&D, and 3.5 trillion won in 2018, or 19.2%.[23]

---

[22] Information on this initial promotion of biotechnologies relies on Choi and Jung (2002).

[23] Based on Joint Task Forces for Innovative Growth, the Government of Korea (2020).

This promotion of biotechnology can also be understood as an example of always looking for "what is next" as a part of industry promotion and targeted specialization. In the 1990s, the Korean government funded R&D initiatives in an effort to attract participation from the private sector, and by the 2000s, just a decade later, an estimated 500 large enterprises and SMEs had entered the industry. In August 2003, the Korean government designated biotechnologies as one of "ten future growth strategy sectors."[24] However, although Korea started to file an increasing number of patents in this long-cycle sector as early as the early 2000s, the commercial success of these biotech initiatives did not become apparent until the 2010s. Additionally, in 2008, Samsung selected biotechnology as its one of the top five future business areas; however, it did not achieve meaningful success in this field until the end of the 2010s. This slow progress is not surprising, given the long cycle time and high barriers to entry typical of biotechnologies.

Therefore, there were two important windows of opportunity that enabled the growth of the biotechnology industry in South Korea by building on the initial efforts of the government. The first window was the arrival of new recombinant DNA technology, which enabled an innovation known as "biosimilar" (also known as "follow-on biologic" or "subsequent entry biologic"). Biosimilar is an almost identical copy of an existing product, the patents of which have expired. This theoretical knowledge and technology had been discovered earlier by researchers in advanced economies. However, the Korean firm Celtrion, which was established in 2000, was the first to develop the technology and commercialize it into an antibody biosimilar. The first biosimilar product was a medicine which was marketed under the brand name Remsima as a drug for autoimmune diseases. This world-first biosimilar was approved by the European Medicine Authority in May 2013, and from 2020 to 2022, it captured

---

[24] On this designation, refer to the information accessible at www.korea.kr/news/policyNewsView.do?newsId=20003234 and https://m.dongascience.com/news.php?idx=-49130 (retrieved on 2023-10-20).

60% of market share in the European market. Samsung Group had also entered the biotech field by establishing two subsidiaries. In 2011, it created Samsung Biologics, a contract manufacturing organization (CMO), and in 2012, it founded Samsung Bioepis. Samsung Biologics has already become a top global CMO firm with a total capacity of 364,000 liters among its three factories.

The second window of opportunity was the COVID-19 pandemic, which swept across the planet in 2020. The pandemic suddenly lowered entry barriers to biotechnology, medicine, and medical devices. Indeed, these sectors had long been high barrier-to-entry sectors subject to long clinical trial times and strict safety regulations. Taking advantage of this window, Korean firms made some progress as new contract suppliers of COVID-19 vaccines and medications, as well as various medical devices, including COVID-19 testing kits.

Witnessing these successes, eight of the ten top Korean chaebols entered the biotech and pharmaceutical sectors. Therefore, these sectors are expected to emerge as the next growth engines of the Korean economy following the IT sector. It is important to note that if there had been no initial public promotion of biotechnologies in the form of R&D initiatives, these two windows of opportunity might not have been taken advantage of by Korean firms.

6.6 SUMMARY AND CONCLUDING REMARKS

This chapter addressed the question of whether the concepts of detour and nonlinearity are applicable to the role of government. It presented the argument that the role of government should not decrease in a linear fashion during the development process but rather must increase at the upper middle-income stage, with the level of government intervention forming an inverted U-shaped curve.

Economic growth at the low-income stage is based on a country's comparative advantages and, therefore, does not require considerable direct government intervention in the affairs of firms. However, upgrading to enter high value-added sectors and catching up with the frontier during the upper middle-income stage may require more direct intervention by the government, such as intervention to foster public–private R&D consortiums. Such intervention becomes necessary and is justifiable because firms at this stage face increased difficulty in terms of entry barriers, IPR disputes, and technology transfers. Normally, at this stage, the target markets tend to be oligopolistic, as incumbents enjoy near-total monopolistic domination in these markets.

To overcome the challenge of strategically managing global–local interfaces, two modes of government involvement, described here as slower and faster modes of catch-up, are possible. The slow but steady mode of catch-up corresponds to the case of the IT cluster in Penang, Malaysia, and the auto industry in Thailand, where the main focus of the public intervention was on re-skilling and up-skilling local labor forces so that FDI firms and MNCs would choose to stay put and engage in high value-added activities and hire local workers. The faster mode of catch-up more closely corresponds to the situation of Shenzhen and the Chinese auto sector. In both cases, asymmetric intervention was mobilized to foster domestically owned firms, as opposed to foreign-owned firms, and promote their R&D activities. The automobile sector in China also demonstrates that it is possible for a country to switch dynamically from the first mode, which is slower and prioritizes FDI firms, to the second mode, which is faster and prioritizes nurturing domestically owned firms while enhancing capabilities over time.

A final question addressed by this chapter was how to generate big businesses as an engine for growth beyond the middle-income stage, as well as how to promote the coevolution of big businesses and SMEs. This is a serious challenge for latecomers, given their high degree of market failure and the thinness and smallness of markets. Under such conditions, it is not surprising to see the emergence of business groups and conglomerates, which often accompanies public support in the form of debt guarantees for their loans from banks. Another alternative is to create and nurture state-owned enterprises by mobilizing all domestically available resources and competencies, and subsequently allowing these enterprises to go public through

IPOs. Then, at a later stage, these state-owned enterprises can be gradually privatized.

Finally, the coevolution of large and smaller firms may also require diverse forms of public intervention to overcome failures in markets, systems, and capabilities. Thus, this chapter has discussed useful examples of how to promote SMEs and startups. The policy interventions mentioned included establishing secondary stock markets to handle market failures, implementing AMC R&D programs to handle system failures, and operating startup incubating programs to solve capability failures via three-party commitments involving angel investors, subsidy-granting public agencies, and large firms.

7   Summary and Concluding Remarks

Emerging and latecomer economies continue to face difficulties in sustaining economic development, and these difficulties have been exacerbated by the COVID-19 pandemic, resulting in an increasing divergence between rich and poor countries. East Asian countries that have experienced successful catch-up, however, are an exception. For latecomer countries, one crucial decision is whether to follow the path of economic development traveled by rich countries or to seek out new trajectories (Lee, 2019). Despite the fundamental importance of this question, scholars who have offered mainstream prescriptions regarding latecomer development have not sufficiently explored this issue.

This book began with the recognition that latecomers do not always follow advanced countries' paths of technological development; rather, they sometimes skip certain stages and even create their own paths by taking detours and pursuing a leapfrogging strategy. The need for latecomers to take detours or attempt leapfrogging is due to the entry barriers to high-end segments that countries face in the middle-income stage. These barriers include intellectual property rights restrictions, protectionist measures instituted by incumbent countries, and the limiting of policy spaces by international economic bodies, such as the WTO. This book proposes an effective alternative to prevailing development thinking by focusing on non-linearity and the multiplicity of pathways for latecomers.

First, in the context of the classical debate on balanced versus imbalanced paths of economic development, this book discusses the use of balanced versus imbalanced NIS by latecomers to achieve sustained economic catch-up. I examine how the success or failure of catch-up can be explained in terms of the catch-up NIS and trapped NIS. NIS in mature and advanced economies tend to be well balanced and score high for all the five variables of NIS. In other words, their innovations tend to be highly dispersed over a large number of firms, and they tend to specialize in long-CTT sectors where barriers to entry and profitability are high. A balanced catch-up NIS for a latecomer may refer to a latecomer improving in a linear and balanced manner in terms of the five NIS variables, such as in the case of Spain and Ireland and, more recently, Russia and India. In contrast, an imbalanced catch-up NIS pathway may refer to countries in East Asia that have nurtured a few big businesses specializing in short-CTT technologies while also continually improving their technological diversity and localization. This concept of the imbalanced catch-up NIS is consistent with the nonlinear catch-up model, in the sense that latecomers do not follow the same path as incumbents – that is, long-CTT and decentralized NIS – but instead seek out their own niches.

Such nonlinearity is a rational response to the high barriers to entry in long-CTT sectors; it also reflects the need for latecomers to concentrate their resources among a few big businesses to facilitate entry into low barrier-to-entry (short-CTT) sectors and technologies. Short-CTT sectors have lower barriers to entry because existing technologies owned by incumbents tend to become quickly obsolete or disrupted by frequent "creative destruction." Late latecomers facing higher barriers to entry in high-end and value-added segments and sectors may seek diverse entry points not necessarily in hard manufacturing but in knowledge-intensive IT services or resource-based sectors by pursuing detours or leapfrogging. Such strategies are also consistent with the concept of the multiplicity and nonlinearity of development paths.

Second, for latecomers, successfully managing global–local interfaces is crucial to building up technological capabilities and sustaining economic development. Although all latecomer economies have welcomed FDI, they have found it difficult to utilize FDI to nurture local production and innovation capacity. If a latecomer economy fails to properly manage this dimension of the global–local interfaces, it often falls into a liberalization trap, whereby local capabilities fail to grow while MNCs come to dominate the local economy. The worst consequence of this trap is premature de-industrialization and stagnation in the MIT. Local ownership becomes important during the middle-income stage and later because FDI firms tend to become increasingly reluctant to transfer or sell technology and are prepared to relocate to other production sites offering lower wages. These observations are consistent with the so-called "in-out-in again" hypothesis (Lee et al., 2018), which asserts that although latecomers should be open to GVCs by inviting FDI and MNCs during the early stages of development, they must eventually develop domestic production and innovation capabilities to increase domestic value-added and reduce the backward linkage to GVCs (share of foreign value-added in gross exports). Subsequently, as a final step, they must leverage their enhanced local capabilities to engage again with more GVCs.

However, it is crucial that local ownership and knowledge also be subject to global market discipline. The auto sector in Malaysia lacked global market discipline, and it failed to evolve into a globally competitive firm. Ultimately, the determining factor for success was whether domestically owned firms grew to be successful exporters in global markets. The emergence and growth of domestically owned firms do not occur spontaneously; rather, this process must be assisted by effective policy interventions that promote local capabilities. Moreover, such successes are possible not only in manufacturing but also in resource-based and IT service sectors.

Third, by focusing on the interactions between corporate innovation systems with sectoral, regional, and national innovation systems, this book emphasizes the importance of firms, particularly big businesses, as the ultimate drivers of catch-up growth in the latecomer context. This leading role of big businesses is consistent with the nonlinear pattern of latecomers increasing rather than decreasing the degree of concentration of innovation during the catch-up stage. These growth-leading big businesses do not emerge spontaneously. Rather, they are the result of domestically owned firms building their capabilities with the assistance of various industrial and innovation policies. TSMC is an example of this, as it began as a spin-off from a public research organization. Any policy design must consider the coevolving nature of surrounding institutions and firms because private firms cannot prosper without sound institutions, and simultaneously, institutional development is useless unless there are private, domestically owned firms that can benefit from this institutional development.

7.2   KOREA'S INNOVATION–DEVELOPMENT DETOURS AND THE ROLE OF GOVERNMENT

This book has reinterpreted South Korea's growth miracle as a case study that demonstrates that multiple catch-up pathways are possible for latecomers and that latecomers do not necessarily follow the trajectories of incumbent advanced economies in a linear manner. This book redefines the Korean experience as an exemplary case of a country that took a detour from short-CTT to long-CTT sectors and from big business dominance to SME emergence. These two elements constitute a detour because advanced economies tend to be dominant in long-CTT, high barrier-to-entry sectors with innovations dispersed among both SMEs and big businesses. In this way, this book departs from conventional views in debates over the source of the Korean success, such as the influence of (un)favorable initial conditions, markets versus the government, inclusive versus exclusive institutions, and import substitution versus export promotion. The Korean experience demonstrates that successful economic catch-up involves strategically navigating global–local interfaces to promote the emergence of big domestic businesses. In other words, no successful catch-up has occurred without generating a certain number of big businesses, which are needed not only to overcome latecomers' disadvantages regarding entry barriers but also to ensure a certain degree of resiliency against crises. This observation differs from the existing development literature, which asserts that no country has successfully achieved a high-income economy without growing its manufacturing sector.

The Korean case is also consistent with the detour view on the role of government, which asserts that government should not decrease its intervention in a linear manner over the stage of development but rather may need to increase it at the upper middle-income stage. In this scenario, the scope of government intervention forms an inverted U-shaped curve. For a country to enter high value-added sectors and catch up with leading countries, governments may need to undertake more direct forms of intervention, such as initiating public–private R&D initiatives. Such interventions may be necessary because firms at this stage face increased difficulty in terms of entry barriers and intellectual property rights disputes. Moreover, technology transfer becomes more difficult as a country approaches frontier technologies, and high-end sectors in the global market tend to be oligopolistic or monopolistic in nature.

Therefore, there are two possible modes of government involvement: a slow and a fast mode of catching up. In the slow yet steady mode of catching up, the main focus of public intervention is on re-skilling and up-skilling the local labor forces so that MNCs do not move to other locations but rather stay in the same location and engage in high-value activities while hiring local workers. The other, faster catch-up mode resembles the situation in Shenzhen and the auto sector in China, where asymmetric intervention has been mobilized to foster domestically owned firms and their R&D activities rather than foreign-owned firms. Regarding the need to switch to a more decentralized mode of innovation and growth, a slow mode of catching up relies on spinoffs and positive externalities from MNCs, whereas a faster mode involves active utilization of public venture capital and the creation of secondary stock markets for IPOs by startups.

7.3   CONTRIBUTIONS, LIMITATIONS, AND THE FUTURE

This book counters prevailing views on economic development and offers a unique contribution to the literature on economic catch-up. Whereas the traditional linear view of development has taken a "more is better" approach, this book advocates that latecomers should pursue detours or leapfrogging, which conforms with a "less is better" approach. Instead of the conventional prioritization of manufacturing, this book proposes prioritizing domestic ownership and knowledge in specific sectors and regions, and asserts that no country has successfully developed a high-income economy without generating a certain number of globally competitive big businesses. Instead of placing priority on free markets, as the Washington Consensus does, this book argues that economic catch-up is only possible with active and planned government interventions, which are needed to overcome latecomers' disadvantages regarding barriers to entry at the middle-income stage.

The book is not free from certain limitations, and it leaves several questions to be addressed by future research. First, while this book proses a theory of how governments can facilitate development detours, it does not elaborate on the detailed rules and modus operandi of governments and relevant agencies. While the key underlying concept in the book is innovation systems, the book has not fully engaged with what can be called the varieties of government systems. The roles and types of government may exceed the simple dichotomy of democratic versus authoritarian governments, and the roles of these two governance systems may also change over the stages of development. Whereas this book tends to give more weight to vertical rather than horizontal industrial policy, the effectiveness of any policy intervention critically depends on the capacity and autonomy of government and its agencies, which are somewhat taken as a priori conditions in this book. When capacity and autonomy (free from vested interests) are weak, pursuing active intervention is risky. Broadly speaking, interaction and coevolution between innovation systems and government systems may exist, and this dynamic should be analyzed in future studies.

Second, the impact of any policy intervention is constrained by initial conditions, including historical legacies and political conditions. In latecomer economies, one of the most important conditions is colonial experiences and their legacies, which include, most importantly, land ownership and land reforms. One of the historically important conditions that differentiates East Asia from Latin America is land reform. Land reform is important because it gives peasants some ownership of land, which can be utilized for newer forms of commercial venturing or can be sold to pay to educate their children, resulting in human capital creation. Land reform and its impacts on the traditional ruling class also affect and determine the political landscapes of post-colonial economies and subsequent economic policy trajectories.

Third, the political and economic power balance between global institutions and national actors determines the nature and dynamics of global–local interfaces, which is one of the core topics of this book. Former colonial forces tend to influence latecomer economies and policymaking by forming alliances with the new ruling parties and classes. Consequently, any economic policy which tries to build local economic entities in defiance of foreign-aligned entities is affected. For instance, in Brazil, the Lula government (2003–2011) tried to revive industrial policy, whereas the Bolsonaro government tried to abolish any institutional vehicle involving industrial policy. Most recently, changing geopolitics involving the US–China confrontation has emerged as an important factor that may affect economic policymaking and global–local interfaces for latecomer economies in the Third World. The entirety of global governance, including the WTO regime, faces great changes that will substantially affect economic policies and the fortunes of economies around the world. Each country will be forced to formulate new strategies for achieving growth and sustainable development. This topic should be explored in future studies.

Finally, this book does not engage with the issue of sustainable development and net-zero or negative carbon emissions. Indeed, this is too important a topic to be dealt with as a side topic in this book, which has a different focus. Broadly speaking, seeking alternative economic development strategies that produce fewer carbon emissions is consistent with the idea of nonlinearity and the multiplicity of developmental trajectories, which are the key concepts of this book. With this issue as well, the positions and strategies of latecomers should be different from those of the advanced and incumbent economies. While the concept of leapfrogging is still appealing (Lee, 2019, Chapter 7), it must be further elaborated on and tailored to the context of sustainability. This is an important issue to be explored in future research. A recent work by Lundvall (2022) provides an effective framework about how to utilize the concept of innovation systems to deal with this issue of sustainable development including climate change.

References

Abramovitz, M. (1986). Catching up, forging ahead, and falling behind. *The Journal of Economic History, 46*(2), 385–406.

Acemoglu, D., & Robinson, J. A. (2012). *Why nations fail: The origins of power, prosperity, and poverty.* New York: Crown.

Acemoglu, D., Johnson, S., & Robinson, J. A. (2001). The colonial origins of comparative development: An empirical investigation. *American Economic Review, 91*(5), 1369–1401.

Acemoglu, D., Johnson, S., & Robinson, J. A. (2002). Reversal of fortune: Geography and institutions in the making of the modern world income distribution. *The Quarterly Journal of Economics, 117*(4), 1231–1294.

Aghion, P., & Howitt, P. (1992). A model of growth through creative destruction. *Econometrica, 60*(2), 323–351.

Aghion, P., Cai, J., Dewatripont, M., Du, L., Harrison, A., & Legros, P. (2015). Industrial policy and competition. *American Economic Journal: Macroeconomics, 7*(4), 1–32.

Aghion, P., Guriev, S., & Jo, K. (2021). Chaebols and firm dynamics in Korea. *Economic Policy, 36*(108), 593–626.

Agosin, M. R., Larraín, C., & Grau, N. (2010). *Industrial policy in Chile. Department of Research and Chief Economist. IDB-WP-170.* IDB Working Paper Series. Inter-American Development Bank.

Amsden, A. H. (1989). *Asia's next giant: South Korea and late industrialization.* New York: Oxford University Press.

Amsden, A. H. (2001). *The rise of "the rest": Challenges to the west from late-industrializing economies.* Oxford: Oxford University Press.

Amsden, A. H., & Chu, W. W. (2003). *Beyond late development: Taiwan's upgrading policies.* Cambridge, MA: MIT Press.

Amsden, A. H., & Hikino, T. (1994). Project execution capability, organizational know-how and conglomerate corporate growth in late industrialization. *Industrial and Corporate Change, 3*(1), 111–147.

Ariffin, N., & Figueiredo, P. N. (2004). Internationalization of innovative capabilities: Counter-evidence from the electronics industry in Malaysia and Brazil. *Oxford Development Studies, 32*(4), 559–583.

Asheim, B. T., Isaksen, A., & Trippl, M. (2019). *Advanced introduction to regional innovation systems*. Cheltenham: Edward Elgar Publishing.

Athukorala, P. C. (2014). Industrialisation through state-MNC partnership: Lessons from Malaysia's national car project. *Malaysian Journal of Economic Studies, 51*, 113–126.

Auty, R. M. (1994). Sectoral targeting: Auto manufacture in Korea and Taiwan. *Journal of International Development, 6*(5), 609–625.

Bai, C. E., Lu, J., & Tao, Z. (2009). How does privatization work in China? *Journal of Comparative Economics, 37*(3), 453–470.

Balassa, B. (1985). Exports, policy choices, and economic growth in developing countries after the 1973 oil shock. *Journal of Development Economics, 18*(1), 23–35.

Balassa, B. (1988). The lessons of East Asian development: An overview. *Economic Development and Cultural Change, 36*(S3), S273–S290.

Baldwin, R. (2016). *The great convergence*. Cambridge, MA: Harvard University Press.

Banga, R. (2013). *Measuring value in global value chains*. Background Paper RVC-8. Geneva: UNCTAD.

Beason, R., & Weinstein, D. E. (1996). Growth, economies of scale, and targeting in Japan (1955–1990). *The Review of Economics and Statistics, 78*(2), 286–295.

Beck, T., Demirguc-Kunt, A., & Levine, R. (2005). SMEs, growth, and poverty: Cross-country evidence. *Journal of Economic Growth, 10*(3), 199–229.

Bergek, A., Jacobsson, S., Carlsson, B., Lindmark, S., & Rickne, A. (2008). Analyzing the functional dynamics of technological innovation systems: A scheme of analysis. *Research Policy, 37*(3), 407–429.

Bernardes, A. T., & Albuquerque, E. D. M. E. (2003). Cross-over, thresholds, and interactions between science and technology: Lessons for less-developed countries. *Research Policy, 32*(5), 865–885.

Billmeier, A. & Nannicini, T. (2013). Assessing economic liberalization episodes: A synthetic control approach. *Review of Economics and Statistics, 95*(3), 983–1001.

Binz, C., & Truffer, B. (2017). Global innovation systems – A conceptual framework for innovation dynamics in transnational contexts. *Research Policy, 46*(7), 1284–1298.

Björk, I. (2005). Spillover effects of FDI in the manufacturing sector in Chile. Doctoral dissertation, Lund University.

Borregaard, N., Dufey, A., & Winchester, L. (2008). *Effects of foreign investment versus domestic investment on the forestry sector in Latin America (Chile and Brazil)-Demystifying FDI effects related to the Environment*. Discussion Paper Number 15. Working Group on Development and Environment in the Americas.

Boyer, W. W., & Ahn, B. M. (1991). *Rural development in South Korea: A sociopolitical analysis*. Newark: University of Delaware Press.

Brandt, L., & Thun, E. (2010). The fight for the middle: Upgrading, competition, and industrial development in China. *World Development, 38*(11), 1555–1574.

Bravo Ortega, C., & Eterovic, N. (2015). *A historical perspective of a hundred years of industrialization. From vertical to horizontal policies in Chile*. Working Papers wp399, University of Chile, Department of Economics.

Bravo-Ortega, C., & Muñoz, L. (2015). *Knowledge intensive mining services in Chile*. Working paper IDBDP 418. Inter-American Development Bank. DOI: 10.18235/0000187.

Brenton, P., Saborowski, C., & Von Uexkull, E. (2010). What explains the low survival rate of developing country export flows?. *The World Bank Economic Review, 24*(3), 474–499.

Bresser-Pereira, L. C., Araújo, E. C., & Peres, S. C. (2020). An alternative to the middle-income trap. *Structural Change and Economic Dynamics, 52*, 294–312.

Breznitz, D. (2012). Ideas, structure, state action and economic growth: Rethinking the Irish miracle. *Review. of International. Political. Economy, 19*(1), 87–113.

Breznitz, D., & Murphree, M. (2011). *Run of the red queen: Government, innovation, globalization, and economic growth in China*. New Haven: Yale University Press.

Busser, R. (2008). 'Detroit of the east'? Industrial upgrading, Japanese car producers and the development of the automotive industry in Thailand. *Asia Pacific Business Review, 14*(1), 29–45.

Cantwell, J. (2009). Location and the multinational enterprise. *Journal of International Business Studies, 40*(1), 35–41.

Chan, C. M., Makino, S., & Isobe, T. (2010). Does subnational region matter? Foreign affiliate performance in the United States and China. *Strategic Management Journal, 31*(11), 1226–1243.

Chandler, A. D. (1959). The beginnings of "big business" in American industry. *Business History Review, 33*(1), 1–31.

Chandler, A. D. (1977). *The visible hand: The managerial revolution in American business*. Cambridge, MA: Belknap Press of Harvard University Press.

Chandler, A. D. (1990). *Scale and scope: The dynamics of industrial capitalism*. Cambridge, MA: Harvard University Press.

Chang, H. J. & Andreoni, A. (2020). Industrial policy in the 21st century. *Development and Change, 51*(2), 324–351.

Chen, B., & Feng, Y. (1996). Economic development, political cost, and democratic transition: Theory, statistical testing and a case study. *Journal of Economic Development, 21*, 185–220.

Chen, K., & Kenney, M. (2007). Universities/research institutes and regional innovation systems: The cases of Beijing and Shenzhen. *World Development, 35*(6), 1056–1074.

Chen, X., & Han, B. (2007). Analysis of the effect of government strategic trade policy on the development of Chinese automobile industry [in Chinese]. *Jianghai Academic Journal, 1*, 69–75.

Cherif, R., & Hasanov, F. (2015). *The leap of the tiger: How Malaysia can escape the middle-income trap.* Washington, D.C.: International Monetary Fund.

Cho, Y. J. (1997). Government intervention, rent distribution, and economic development in Korea, in M. Aoki, H. Kim, Ma. Okuno-Fujiwara (Eds.), *The Role of Government in East Asian Economic Development: Comparative Institutional Analysis*, 208–232.

Choi, R. (2020, June 10). Samsung Electronics as a troubleshooter for Covid-19 testing kits ... Solgent experiences 73% jump in its productivity [in Korean]. *ChosunBiz.* https://biz.chosun.com/site/data/html_dir/2020/06/10/2020061001891.html

Choi, Y., & Jung, E. M. (2002). Policy measures to promote Post-Genome Period Innovation in bio industry in Korea [in Korean]. KIET (Korea Institute for Industrial Economy and Trade).

Chou, T. L. (2005). The transformation of spatial structure: From a monocentric to a polycentric city, in R. Kwok (Ed.), *Globalizing Taipei: The Political Economy of Spatial Development.* New York: Routledge Press, 55–77.

Chu, W. W. (2011). How the Chinese government promoted a global automobile industry. *Industrial and Corporate Change, 20*(5), 1235–1276.

Chung, M. Y., & Lee, K. (2015). How absorptive capacity is formed in a latecomer economy: Different roles of foreign patent and know-how licensing in Korea. *World Development, 66*, 678–694.

Cirera, X., & Maloney, W. F. (2017). *The innovation paradox: Developing-country capabilities and the unrealized promise of technological catch-up.* Washington, D.C.: World Bank Publications.

Cline, W. R. (1982). Can the East Asian model of development be generalized?. *World Development, 10*(2), 81–90.

Cohen, W. M., & Levinthal, D. A. (1989). Innovation and learning: The two faces of R & D. *The Economic Journal, 99*(397), 569–596.

Cohen, W. M., & Levinthal, D. A. (1990). Absorptive capacity: A new perspective on learning and innovation. *Administrative Science Quarterly, 35*(1),128–152.

Cooke, P., Uranga, M. G., & Etxebarria, G. (1998). Regional systems of innovation: An evolutionary perspective. *Environment and Planning A, 30*(9), 1563–1584.

Cuervo, A., & Villalonga, B. (2000). Explaining the variance in the performance effects of privatization. *Academy of Management Review, 25*(3), 581–590.

Cunningham, J. A., Collins, P., & Giblin, M. (2020). Evolution of Ireland's industrial, science and technology policy. *Annals of Science and Technology Policy, 4*(2), 80–210.

D'Costa, A. P. (1994). State, steel and strength: Structural competitiveness and development in South Korea. *The Journal of Development Studies, 31*(1), 44–81.

Davies, R. B., & Ellis, C. J. (2007). Competition in taxes and performance requirements for foreign direct investment. *European Economic Review, 51*(6), 1423–1442.

Diez, J., & Kiese, M. (2006). Scaling innovation in South East Asia: Empirical evidence from Singapore, Penang (Malaysia) and Bangkok. *Regional Studies, 40*(9), 1005–1023.

Dodgson, M., Hughes, A., Foster, J., & Metcalfe, S. (2011). Systems thinking, market failure, and the development of innovation policy: The case of Australia. *Research Policy, 40*(9), 1145–1156.

Dollar, D. (1992). Outward-oriented developing economies really do grow more rapidly: Evidence from 95 LDCs, 1976–1985. *Economic Development and Cultural Change, 40*(3), 523–544.

Dollar, D., Hallward-Driemeier, M., & Mengistae, T. (2005). Investment climate and firm performance in developing economies. *Economic Development and Cultural Change, 54*(1), 1–31.

Driffield, N., Munday, M., & Roberts, A. (2002). Foreign direct investment, transactions linkages, and the performance of the domestic sector. *International Journal of the Economics of Business, 9*(3), 335–351.

Dunning, J. H. (1998). Location and the multinational enterprise: A neglected factor? *Journal of International Business Studies, 29*(1), 45–66.

Edler, J., & Fagerberg, J. (2017). Innovation policy: What, why, and how. *Oxford Review of Economic Policy, 33*(1), 2–23.

Eichengreen, B., Lim, W., Park, Y. C., & Perkins, D. H. (2015). *The Korean economy from a miraculous past to a sustainable future.* Cambridge, MA: Harvard University Asia Center.

Eichengreen, B., Park, D., & Shin, K. (2012). When fast-growing economies slow down: International evidence and implications for China. *Asian Economic Papers, 11*(1), 42–87.

Eichengreen, B., Park, D., & Shin, K. (2013). *Growth slowdowns redux: New evidence on the middle-income trap* (No. w18673). Cambridge, MA: National Bureau of Economic Research.

Enos, J. L., & Park, W. H. (1988). *The adoption and diffusion of imported technology: The case of Korea*. New York: Croom Helm.

Ernst, D., & Kim, L. (2002). Global production networks, information technology and knowledge diffusion. *Industry and Innovation, 9*(3), 147–153.

Evenson, R. E., & Westphal, L. E. (1995). Technological change and technology strategy. *Handbook of Development Economics, 3*, 2209–2299.

Fagerberg, J., & Verspagen, B. (1999). 'Modern Capitalism' in the 1970s and 1980s, in M. Setterfield (Ed.), *Growth, employment and inflation: Essays in honour of John Cornwall*, London: Palgrave Macmillan, 113–126.

Fan, G., Wang, X., & Zhu, H. (2011). *NERI Index of marketization of China's provinces 2011 report, Economics Science Press* [in Chinese].

Felipe, J., Kumar, U., & Galope, R. (2017). Middle-income transitions: Trap or myth?. *Journal of the Asia Pacific Economy, 22*(3), 429–453

Friedmann, H., & McMichael, P. (1987). Agriculture and the state system: The rise and fall of national agricultures, 1870 to the present. *Sociologia Ruralis, 29*(2), 93–117.

Fu, X., Pietrobelli, C., & Soete, L. (2011). The role of foreign technology and indigenous innovation in the emerging economies: Technological change and catching-up. *World Development, 39*(7), 1204–1212.

Fujita, M. (1998). Industrial policies and trade liberalization: The automotive industry in Thailand and Malaysia. In K. Omura (Ed.), *The deepening economic interdependence in the APEC region*, Singapore: APEC Study Centre, Institute of Developing Economies, 149–187.

Fuller, D. B. (2005). The changing limits and the limits of change: The state, private firms, international industry and China in the evolution of Taiwan's electronics industry. *Journal of Contemporary China, 14*(44), 483–506.

Garcia Calvo, A. (2014). Industrial upgrading in mixed market economies: The Spanish case. *LEQS Paper* (73).

Garcia Calvo, A. (2016). Institutional development and bank competitive transformation in late industrializing economies: The Spanish case. *Business and Politics, 18*(1), 27–62.

Gerschenkron, A. (1962). *Economic backwardness in historical perspective: A book of essays* (Vol. 584). Cambridge, MA: Belknap Press of Harvard University Press.

Gill, I. S., Kharas, H. J., & Bhattasali, D. (2007). *An East Asian renaissance: Ideas for economic growth*. Washington, D.C.: World Bank Publications.

Giuliani, E., Morrison, A., & Rabellotti, R. (Eds.). (2011). *Innovation and technological catch-up: The changing geography of wine production*. Cheltenham: Edward Elgar Publishing.

Giuliani, E., Pietrobelli, C., & Rabellotti, R. (2005). Upgrading in global value chains: Lessons from Latin American clusters. *World Development, 33*(4), 549–573.

Glaeser, E. L., La Porta, R., Lopez-de-Silanes, F., & Shleifer, A. (2004). Do institutions cause growth? *Journal of Economic Growth, 9*(3), 271–303.

Goldthorpe, C. C. (2015). *Rubber manufacturing in Malaysia: Resource-based industrialization in practice.* Singapore: NUS Press.

Gopal, J. (2001). The development of Malaysia's palm oil refining industry: obstacles, policy and performance. Doctoral dissertation, University of London.

Graham, E. M., & Wada, E. (2001). Foreign direct investment in China: Effects on growth and economic performance. Working Paper 01-3, Peterson Institute for International Economics, Washington, D.C.

Granstrand, O. (2000). *Corporate innovation systems. A comparative study of multi-technology corporations in Japan, Sweden and the USA.* Chalmers University of Technology.

Greenaway, D. (1992). Trade related investment measures and development strategy. *Kyklos, 45*(2), 139–159.

Guo, B., Li, Q., & Chen, X. (2017). The rise to market leadership of a Chinese automotive firm: The case of Geely. In Malerba, F., Mani, S., & Adams, P. (Eds.), *The rise to market leadership.* Cheltenham: Edward Elgar Publishing, 20–40.

Hall, P. A., & Soskice, D. W. (2001). *Varieties of capitalism: The institutional foundations of comparative advantage.* Oxford, New York: Oxford University Press.

Han, J., & Lee, K. (2022). Heterogeneous technology and specialization for economic growth beyond the middle-income stage. *Economic Modelling, 112,* 105853.

Hao, M., Mackenzie, M., Pomerant, A., & Strachran, K. (2010). *Local content requirements in British Columbia's wind power industry.* Victoria: Pacific Institute for Climate Solutions, University of Victoria.

Haraguchi, N., Cheng, C. F. C., & Smeets, E. (2017). The importance of manufacturing in economic development: Has this changed?. *World Development, 93,* 293–315.

Harwit, E. (1994). *China's automobile industry: Policies, problems and prospects.* New York: ME Sharpe.

Hassink, R. (2001). Towards regionally embedded innovation support systems in South Korea? Case studies from Kyongbuk-Taegu and Kyonggi. *Urban Studies, 38*(8), 1373–1395.

Hausmann, R., Hidalgo, C. A., Bustos, S., Coscia, M., & Simoes, A. (2014). *The atlas of economic complexity: Mapping paths to prosperity.* Cambridge, MA: MIT Press.

Hausmann, R., Hwang, J., & Rodrik, D. (2007). What you export matters. *Journal of Economic Growth, 12*(1), 1–25.

He, C. (2003). Location of foreign manufacturers in China: Agglomeration economies and country of origin effects. *Papers in Regional Science, 82*(3), 351–372.

Hellmann, T., Murdock, K., & Stiglitz, J. (1997). Financial restraint: Toward a new paradigm. *The Role of Government in East Asian Economic Development: Comparative iInstitutional Analysis*, 163–207.

Hidalgo, C. A., Klinger, B., Barabási, A. L., & Hausmann, R. (2007). The product space conditions the development of nations. *Science, 317*(5837), 482–487.

Hirschman, A. O. (1958). *The strategy of economic development*. Yale: Yale University Press.

Hobday, M. (1995a). East Asian latecomer firms: Learning the technology of electronics. *World Development, 23*(7): 1171–1193.

Hobday, M. (1995b). *Innovation in East Asia*. Cheltenham: Edward Elgar Publishing.

Hong, J. & Chang, J. (2015). Trickle down effects of big business growth on the domestic production and employment growth in Korea. *Journal of Korean Economic Development, 21*(2), 33–26.

Hosono, A. (2010). *Nambei Chili wo sake yushutsu taikoku ni kaeta Nihonjintachi* [The Japanese who transformed Chile into a major salmon exporter]. Daiyamondo-sha, Tokyo, Japan.

Hosono, A. (2016). Genesis of Chilean salmon farming. In A. Hosono, M. Iizuka, and J. Katz (Eds.), *Chile's Salmon industry*. Tokyo: Springer, 21–44.

Hou, C. & Gee, S. (1993). National systems supporting technical advance in industry: The case of Taiwan, in R. Nelson (Ed.), *National Innovation Systems: A Comparative Analysis*. New York: Oxford University Press, 384–413.

Hsiao, H. M. (1981). *Government agricultural strategies in Taiwan and South Korea: A macro sociological assessment*. Institute of Ethnology. Taipei: Academia Sinica.

Hsu, J. (2005). The evolution of economic base: From industrial city, post-industrial city to interface city. In Kwok, R. (Ed.), *Globalizing Taipei: The political economy of spatial development*. New York: Routledge Press, 30–48.

Hu, M. C. (2011). Evolution of knowledge creation and diffusion: The revisit of Taiwan's Hsinchu Science Park. *Scientometrics, 88*(3), 949–977.

Hu, P. (2009). Formation model and cultivation path of China's independent brand auto industry [in Chinese]. *Journal of China University of Geosciences (Social Science Edition), 4*, 68–79.

Huang, L. L. (2008). Taipei: Post industrial globalization. In G. Jones and M. Douglass (Eds.), *Mega-urban regions in Pacific Asia*. Singapore: National Singapore University Press, 214–250.

Huang, Y. (2002). Between two coordination failures: Automotive industrial policy in China with a comparison to Korea. *Review of International Political Economy, 9*(3), 538–573.

Hwang, S. C., & Yoo, L. N. (2014). Measurement of total factor productivity in Korean agriculture 1955~ 2012. *Korean Journal of Agricultural Management and Policy, 41*(4), 701–721.

Iizuka, M., & Gebreeyesus, M. (2012). *A systemic perspective in understanding the successful emergence of non-traditional exports: Two cases from Africa and Latin America*. UNU-MERIT Working Papers 052, United Nations University, Maastricht.

Iizuka, M., & Gebreeyesus, M. (2017). Using functions of innovation systems to understand the successful emergence of non-traditional agricultural export industries in developing countries: Cases from Ethiopia and Chile. *The European Journal of Development Research, 29*(2), 384–403.

Im, B., & Lee, K. (2021). From catching up to convergence of the latecomer firms: Comparing behavior and innovation systems of firms in Korea and the US. *Journal of Open Innovation: Technology, Market, and Complexity, 7*(3), 191.

Intarakumnerd, P., & Charoenporn, P. (2015). Impact of stronger patent regimes on technology transfer: The case study of Thai automotive industry. *Research Policy, 44*(7), 1314–1326.

Intarakumnerd, P., & Gerdsri, N. (2014). Implications of technology management and policy on the development of a sectoral innovation system: Lessons learned through the evolution of Thai automotive sector. *International Journal of Innovation and Technology Management, 11*(03), 1440009.

Intarakumnerd, P., & Techakanont, K. (2016). Intra-industry trade, product fragmentation and technological capability development in Thai automotive industry. *Asia Pacific Business Review, 22*(1), 65–85.

Jaffe, A. B., & Trajtenberg, M. (2002). *Patents, citations, and innovations: A window on the knowledge economy*. Cambridge, MAMIT pPress.

Jaffe, A. B., Trajtenberg, M., & Henderson, R. (1993). Geographic localization of knowledge spillovers as evidenced by patent citations. *The Quarterly Journal of Economics, 108*(3), 577–598.

Javorcik, B. S. (2004). The composition of foreign direct investment and protection of intellectual property rights: Evidence from transition economies. *European Economic Review, 48*(1), 39–62.

Johnson, C. (1982). *MITI and the Japanese miracle: The growth of industrial policy, 1925–1975*. Palo Alto: Stanford University Press.

Joint Task Forces for Innovative Growth, the Government of Korea. (2020). *Bio industry innovation: Policy directions and key projects* [in Korean].

Jomo, K. S., & Rock, M. (1998). *Economic diversification and primary commodity processing in the second-tier South-East Asian newly industrializing countries*. Geneva: UNCTAD.

Joo, S. H., & Lee, K. (2010). Samsung's catch-up with Sony: An analysis using US patent data. *Journal of the Asia Pacific Economy, 15*(3), 271–287.

Joo, S. H., Oh, C., & Lee, K. (2016). Catch-up strategy of an emerging firm in an emerging country: Analysing the case of Huawei vs. Ericsson with patent data. *International Journal of Technology Management, 72*(1/2/3), 19.

Jung, J. (2018). The study on the dynamics in the automobile business ecosystem: Focused on the Hyundai and Korean GM [in Korean]. *Study on Industrial Economy, 31*(5), 1801–1830.

Jung, M., & Lee, K. (2010). Sectoral systems of innovation and productivity catch-up: Determinants of the productivity gap between Korean and Japanese firms. *Industrial and Corporate Change, 19*(4), 1037–1069.

Kahn, A. E. (1951). Investment criteria in development programs. *The Quarterly Journal of Economics, 65*(1), 38–61.

Katz, J. (2001). Structural reforms and technological behavior: The sources and nature of technological change in Latin America in the 1990s. *Research Policy, 30*(1): 1–19.

Keller, W. (1996). Absorptive capacity: On the creation and acquisition of technology in development. *Journal of Development Economics, 49*(1), 199–227.

Khanna, T., & Palepu, K. (1997). Why focused strategies may be wrong for emerging markets. *Harvard Business Review, 75*(4), 41–54.

Kim, A. R., & Cho, M. H. (2008). Types of foreign investors, dividend and investment policy: An empirical study of Korean firms. *Journal of Strategic Management, 11*(1), 25–42.

Kim, J., & Lee, K. (2022). Local–global interface as a key factor in the catching up of regional innovation systems: Fast versus slow catching up among Taipei, Shenzhen, and Penang in Asia. *Technological Forecasting and Social Change, 174*, 121271.

Kim, L. (1980). Stages of development of industrial technology in a developing country: A model. *Research Policy, 9*(3), 254–277.

Kim, L. (1993). National system of industrial innovation: Dynamics of capability building in Korea, in R. Nelson (Ed.), *National innovation systems: A comparative analysis*. New York: Oxford University Press, 357–383.

Kim, L. (1997a). The dynamics of Samsung's technological learning in semiconductors. *California Management Review, 39*(3), 86–100.

Kim, L. (1997b). *Imitation to innovation: The dynamics of Korea's technological learning*. Cambridge, MA: Harvard Business School Press.

Kim, L. (1998). Crisis construction and organizational learning: Capability building in catching-up at Hyundai Motor. *Organization Science, 9*(4), 506–521.

Kim, Y. W. (1999). *History of Korean primary education* [in Korean]. Seoul: Korean Society for History of Education.

Koopman, R., Wang, Z., & Wei, S. J. (2014). Tracing value-added and double counting in gross exports. *American Economic Review, 104*(2), 459–494.

Korea-ITEP (Korea Institute for Industrial Technology Evaluation and Planning). (2009). *A report on evaluating the outcomes of the program to support R&D by SMEs* [in Korean].

Korea Development Bank. (1979). *Annual report.* Seoul: Korea Development Bank.

Korea Development Bank. (1991). *Analysis of effects of technology acquisition* [in Korean]. Seoul: Korea Development Bank.

Korean Economy Compilation Committee. (2010). *The Korean economy: Six decades of growth and development* [in Korean], Vol. 2. Seoul: The Korean Government.

Korzeniewicz, R. P., Goldfrank, W., & Korzeniewicz, M. E. (1995). Vines and wines in the world-economy. In *Food and Agrarian orders in the world-economy.* Westport, CT: Greenwood Publishing Group, 113–138.

Krueger, A. O. (1978). *Foreign trade regimes and economic development: Liberalization attempts and consequences.* Cambridge: NBER Books.

Kunc, M. H. (2007). A survey of managerial practices in the small to medium Chilean wineries. *Journal of Wine Research, 18*(2), 113–119.

Kunc, M. H., & Bas, T. G. (2009). *Innovation in the Chilean wine industry: The impact of foreign direct investments and entrepreneurship on competitiveness.* New York: American Association of Wine Economists.

Kuznets, S. S. (1966). *Modern economic growth.* New Haven: Yale University Press.

Kwak, J. (2010). How subcontracting practices impact business performance of SMEs [in Korean]. PhD thesis, Seoul National University.

Lahiri, S., & Ono, Y. (1998). Foreign direct investment, local content requirement, and profit taxation. *The Economic Journal, 108*(447), 444–457.

Lall, S. (2000). The Technological structure and performance of developing country manufactured exports, 1985–98. *Oxford Development Studies, 28*(3), 337–369.

Larrue, P. (2021). *The design and implementation of mission-oriented innovation policies: A new systemic policy approach to address societal challenge.* OECD Science, Technology and Industry Policy Papers, No. 100. Paris: OECD

Lassere, P., & Zeng, M. (2002). *Guangzhou Honda Automobile Co., Ltd: Honda's entry into the China car market.* INSEAD Case Study. https://citeseerx.ist.psu.edu/document?repid=rep1&type=pdf&doi=c00c8266b53fdd54ca129488b3ac0c43e1be548e

Lavopa, A., & Szirmai, A. (2018). Structural modernisation and development traps. An empirical approach. *World Development, 112*, 59–73.

Lebdioui, A. A. (2019a). Chile's export diversification since 1960: A free market miracle or mirage? *Development and Change, 50*(6), 1624–1663.

Lebdioui, A. A. (2019b). Economic diversification and development in resource-dependent economies: Lessons from Chile and Malaysia. Doctoral dissertation, University of Cambridge.

Lebdioui, A. A. (2020). Local content in extractive industries: Evidence and lessons from Chile's copper sector and Malaysia's petroleum sector. *The Extractive Industries and Society, 7*(2), 341–352.

Lebdioui, A., Lee, K., & Pietrobelli, C. (2021). Local-foreign technology interface, resource-based development, and industrial policy: How Chile and Malaysia are escaping the middle-income trap. *The Journal of Technology Transfer, 46*, 660–685.

Lee, B. H. (2011). The political economics of industrial development in the Korean automotive sector. *International Journal of Automotive Technology and Management, 11*(2), 137–151.

Lee, C., Fujimoto, T., & Chen, J. (2007). The product development by Chinese automakers: The dilemma of imitation and innovation. Working paper for IMVP. Cambridge, MA: MIT.

Lee, H., & Lee, K. (2022). Institutions matter differently depending on the ownership types of firms: Interacting effects on firm productivity in China. *The Singapore Economic Review, 67*(04), 1185–1208.

Lee, J., & Lee, K. (2021a). Catching-up national innovations systems (NIS) in China and post-catching-up NIS in Korea and Taiwan: Verifying the detour hypothesis and policy implications. *Innovation and Development, 11*(2–3), 387–411.

Lee, J., & Lee, K. (2021b). Is the fourth industrial revolution a continuation of the third industrial revolution or something new under the sun? Analyzing technological regimes using US patent data. *Industrial and Corporate Change, 30*(1), 137–159.

Lee, J. D., Lee, K., Meissner, D., Radosevic, S., & Vonortas, N. S. (2021). Local capacity, innovative entrepreneurial places and global connections: An overview. *The Journal of Technology Transfer, 46*(3), 563–573.

Lee, J. W. (1996). Government interventions and productivity growth. *Journal of Economic Growth, 1*(3), 391–414.

Lee, K. (2006). The Washington Consensus and East Asian sequencing: understanding reform in East and South Asia. In J. Fanelli and G. McMahon (Eds.), *Understanding market reforms*. London: Palgrave Macmillan, 99–140.

Lee, K. (2013a). Capability failure and industrial policy to move beyond the middle-income trap: From trade-based to technology-based specialization. In J. Lin and J. Stiglitz (Eds.), *The industrial policy revolution I: The role of government beyond ideology*, London: Palgrave Macmillan, 244–272.

Lee, K. (2013b). How can Korea be a role model for catch-up development? A 'capability-based' view. In Fosu, A. K. (Ed.), *Achieving development success: Strategies and lessons from the developing World*. Oxford: Oxford University Press, 24–49.

Lee, K. (2013c). *Schumpeterian analysis of economic catch-up: Knowledge, path-creation, and the middle-income trap*. Cambridge: Cambridge University Press.

Lee, K. (2016). *Economic catch-up and technological leapfrogging: The path to development and macroeconomic stability in Korea*. Cheltenham: Edward Elgar Publishing.

Lee, K. (2019). *The art of economic catch-up: Barriers, detours and leapfrogging in innovation systems*. Cambridge: Cambridge University Press.

Lee, K. (2021a), *China's technological leapfrogging and economic catch-up: A Schumpeterian perspective*. Oxford: Oxford University Press.

Lee, K. (2021b). Economics of technological leapfrogging. In Lee, J. D., Lee, K., Radosevic, S., & Vonortas, N. (Eds.), *Challenge of technology and economic catch-up in emerging economies*. Oxford: Oxford University Press, 123–159.

Lee, K., & He, X. (2009). The capability of the Samsung group in project execution and vertical integration: Created in Korea, replicated in China. *Asian Business & Management*, 8(3), 277–299.

Lee, K., & Kim, B. Y. (2009). Both institutions and policies matter but differently for different income groups of countries: Determinants of long-run economic growth revisited. *World Development*, 37(3), 533–549.

Lee, K., & Kim, S. (2000). Characteristics and economic efficiency of the venture companies in Korea: Comparison with the chaebols and other traditional firms. *Seoul Journal of Economics*, 13(3), 335.

Lee, K., & Kim, Y. K. (2010). IPR and technological catch-up in Korea. In H. Odagiri (Ed.), *Intellectual property rights, development and catch-up: An international comparative study*. Oxford: Oxford University Press, 133–167.

Lee, K. & Lee, J. (2019). National innovation systems, economic complexity, and economic growth. *Journal of Evolutionary Economics*, DOI: 10.1007/s00191-019-00612-3

Lee, K., & Lim, C. (2001). Technological regimes, catching-up and leapfrogging: Findings from the Korean industries. *Research Policy*, 30(3), 459–483.

Lee, K., & Mathews, J. A. (2010). From Washington consensus to BeST consensus for world development. *Asian-Pacific Economic Literature, 24*(1), 86–103.

Lee, K., & Shin, H. (2021). Varieties of capitalism and East Asia: Long-term evolution, structural change, and the end of East Asian capitalism. *Structural Change and Economic Dynamics, 56*, 431–437.

Lee, K., & Temesgen, T. (2009). What makes firms grow in developing countries? An extension of the resource-based theory of firm growth and empirical analysis. *International Journal of Technological Learning, Innovation and Development, 2*(3), 139–172.

Lee, K., & Yoon, M. (2010). International, intra-national and inter-firm knowledge diffusion and technological catch-up: The USA, Japan, Korea and Taiwan in the memory chip industry. *Technology Analysis & Strategic Management, 22*(5), 553–570.

Lee, K., Cho, S., & Jin, J. (2009). Dynamics of catch-up in China's automobile and mobile phone industries. *China Economic Journal, 2*(1), 25–53.

Lee, K., Choo, K., & Yoon, M. (2016). Comparing the productivity impacts of knowledge spillovers from network and arm's length industries: Findings from business groups in Korea. *Industrial and Corporate Change, 25*(3), 407–427.

Lee, K., Gao, X., & Li, X. (2017). Industrial catch-up in China: A sectoral systems of innovation perspective. *Cambridge Journal of Regions, Economy and Society, 10*(1), 59–76.

Lee, K., Kim, B. Y., Park, Y. Y., & Sanidas, E. (2013). Big businesses and economic growth: Identifying a binding constraint for growth with country panel analysis. *Journal of Comparative Economics, 41*(2), 561–582.

Lee, K., Kim, J. Y., & Lee, O. (2010). Long-term evolution of the firm value and behavior of business groups: Korean chaebols between weak premium, strong discount, and strong premium. *Journal of the Japanese and International Economies, 24*(3), 412–440.

Lee, K., Lee, J., & Lee, J. (2021). Variety of national innovation systems (NIS) and alternative pathways to growth beyond the middle-income stage: Balanced, imbalanced, catching-up, and trapped NIS. *World Development, 144*, 105472.

Lee, K., Mani, S., & Mu, Q. (2012). Divergent stories of catchup in telecom: China, India, Brazil, & Korea. In Malerba, F., & Nelson, R. R. (Eds.), *Economic development as a learning process.* Cheltenham: Edward Elgar Publishing, 21–71.

Lee, K., Park, T. Y., & Krishnan, R. T. (2014). Catching-up or leapfrogging in the Indian IT service sector: Windows of opportunity, path-creating, and moving up the value chain. *Development Policy Review, 32*(4), 495–518.

Lee, K., Qu, D., & Mao, Z. (2021). Global value chains, industrial policy, and industrial upgrading: Automotive sectors in Malaysia, Thailand, and China in comparison with Korea. *The European Journal of Development Research, 33*, 275–303.

Lee, K., Song, J., & Kwak, J. (2015). An exploratory study on the transition from OEM to OBM: Case studies of SMEs in Korea. *Industry and Innovation, 22*(5), 423–442.

Lee, K., Szapiro, M., & Mao, Z. (2018). From global value chains (GVC) to innovation systems for local value chains and knowledge creation. *The European Journal of Development Research, 30*, 424–441.

Lee, K., Wong, C. Y., Intarakumnerd, P., & Limapornvanich, C. (2020). Is the fourth industrial revolution a window of opportunity for upgrading or reinforcing the middle-income trap? Asian model of development in Southeast Asia. *Journal of Economic Policy Reform, 23*(4), 408–425.

Lewis, W. A. (1954). Economic development with unlimited supplies of labour.

Li, J., Liu, X., Liu, J., & Li, W. (2016). City profile: Taipei. *Cities, 55*, 1–8.

Li, K., Yue, H., & Zhao, L. (2009). Ownership, institutions, and capital structure: Evidence from China. *Journal of Comparative Economics, 37*(3), 471–490.

Lin, J. Y. (2012a). *New structural economics: A framework for rethinking development and policy.* Washington, D.C.: World Bank Publications.

Lin, J. Y. (2012b). *The quest for prosperity: How developing economies can take off.* Princeton: Princeton University Press.

Linden, G., Kraemer, K. L., & Dedrick, J. (2009). Who captures value in a global innovation network? The case of Apple's iPod. *Communications of the ACM, 52*(3), 140–144.

Liu, H., Xin, Y., & Lu, Z. (2014). Analysis on the control of Chinese and foreign automobile joint ventures [in Chinese]. *Finance and Accounting (Financial Edition), 2*.

Lundvall, B. A. (1992). *National systems of innovation: Towards a theory of innovation and interactive learning.* London: Pinter Publishers.

Lundvall, B. A. (2022). Transformative innovation policy – lessons from the innovation system literature. *Innovation and Development*, 1–18.

Ma, X., & Delios, A. (2010). Host country headquarters and an MNE's subsequent within-country diversifications. *Journal of International Business Studies, 41*(3), 517–525.

Ma, X., Tong, T. W., & Fitza, M. (2013). How much does subnational region matter to foreign subsidiary performance? Evidence from Fortune Global 500 Corporations' investment in China. *Journal of International Business Studies, 44*(1), 66–87.

Malerba, F., & Orsenigo, L. (1996). Schumpeterian patterns of innovation are technology-specific. *Research Policy, 25*(3), 451–478.

Marin, A., & Bell, M. (2006). Technology spillovers from foreign direct investment (FDI): The active role of MNC subsidiaries in Argentina in the 1990s. *The Journal of Development Studies, 42*(4), 678–697.

Markusen, A. (1996). Sticky places in slippery space: A typology of industrial districts. *Economic Geography, 72*(3), 293–313.

Markusen, A. (2003). Fuzzy concepts, scanty evidence, policy distance: The case for rigour and policy relevance in critical regional studies. *Regional Studies, 37*(6–7), 701–717.

Mathews, J. A. (2002a). Competitive advantages of the latecomer firm: A resource-based account of industrial catch-up strategies. *Asia Pacific Journal of Management, 19*(4), 467–488.

Mathews, J. A. (2002b). The origins and dynamics of Taiwan's R&D consortia. *Research Policy, 31*(4), 633–651.

Mathews, J. A., & Cho, D. S. (2000). *Tiger technology: The creation of a semiconductor industry in East Asia* (Vol. 389). Cambridge: Cambridge University Press.

Mazzoleni, R., & Nelson, R. R. (2007). Public research institutions and economic catch-up. *Research Policy, 36*(10), 1512–1528.

Mazzucato, M. (2011). The entrepreneurial state. *Soundings, 49*(49), 131–142.

Mazzucato, M. (2018). Mission-oriented innovation policies: Challenges and opportunities. *Industrial and Corporate Change, 27*(5), 803–815.

McGinn, N. F., Snodgrass, D. R., Kim, Y. B., Kim, S. B., & Kim, Q. Y. (1980). Education and the development of Korea. In N. F. McGinn, et al. (Eds.), *Education and development in Korea.* Cambridge, MA: Harvard University Asia Center, 218–241.

Meyer, K. E., & Nguyen, H. V. (2005). Foreign investment strategies and sub-national institutions in emerging markets: Evidence from Vietnam. *Journal of Management Studies, 42*(1), 63–93.

Milligan, G. W., & Cooper, M. C. (1985). An examination of procedures for determining the number of clusters in a data set. *Psychometrika, 50*, 159–179.

Ministry of Agriculture, Forestry and Fisheries of Korea. (1978). *Korean History of Food Policy,* Seoul: The Korean Government.

Moon, M. (2010). The dual green revolution in South Korea: Reforestation and agricultural revolution under the authoritarian regime. *Jeollabuk Journal of History [in Korean], 36*, 155–184.

Mu, Q., & Lee, K. (2005). Knowledge diffusion, market segmentation and technological catch-up: The case of the telecommunication industry in China. *Research Policy, 34*(6), 759–783.

Nachum L. (2000). Economic geography and the location of TNCs: Financial and professional service FDI to the USA. *Journal of International Business Studies, 31*(3), 367–385.

Nan, X. (2005). Analysis and prospect of China automotive industry policy [in Chinese]. *Journal of Dalian Nationalities University, 7(6),* 80–83.

Natsuda, K., & Thoburn, J. (2013). Industrial policy and the development of the automotive industry in Thailand. *Journal of the Asia Pacific Economy, 18*(3), 413–437.

Navas-Alemán, L. (2011). The impact of operating in multiple value chains for upgrading: The case of the Brazilian furniture and footwear industries. *World Development, 39*(8): 1386–1397.

Nelson, R. R. (1991). Why do firms differ, and how does it matter? *Strategic Management Journal, 12*(S2), 61–74.

Nelson, R. R. (Ed.). (1993). *National innovation systems: A comparative analysis.* Oxford: Oxford University Press on Demand.

Nelson, R. R. (2008a). Economic development from the perspective of evolutionary economic theory. *Oxford Development Studies, 36*(1), 9–21.

Nelson, R. R. (2008b). What enables rapid economic progress: What are the needed institutions? *Research Policy, 37*(1), 1–11.

Nelson, R. R., & Langlois, R. N. (1983). Industrial innovation policy: Lessons from American history. *Science, 219*(4586), 814–818.

Nizamuddin, A. M. (2008). Declining risk, market liberalization and state-multinational bargaining: Japanese automobile investments in India, Indonesia and Malaysia. *Pacific Affairs, 81*(3), 339–359.

Nooteboom, B. (2009). *A cognitive theory of the firm: Learning, governance and dynamic capabilities.* Cheltenham: Edward Elgar Publishing.

Nordås, H. K., Vatne, E., & Heum, P. (2003). *The upstream petroleum industry and local industrial development: A comparative study.* SNF Report.

Nurkse, R. (1953). *Problems of Capital Formation in Underdeveloped Countries.* Oxford: Basil Blackwell.

O'Malley, E., Hewitt-Dundas, N., & Roper, S. (2008). High growth and innovation with low R&D: Ireland. In C. Edquist, & L. Hommen (Eds.), *Small country innovation systems: Globalization, change and policy in Asia and Europe,* Cheltenham: Edward Elgar Publishing, 156–193.

Ocampo, J. A. (Ed.) (2005). *Beyond reforms: Structural dynamics and macroeconomic stability.* Stanford: Stanford University Press for ECLAC.

OECD. (1996). *Reviews of national science and technology policy: Republic of Korea.* Paris: OECD.

OECD. (1997). National innovation systems. Paris: OECD.

OECD. (2017). *TiVA 2016 Indicators – Definitions*. Paris: OECD.

OECD. (2020). *Covid-19 in Africa: Regional socio-economic implications and policy priorities*, Paris: OECD.

Oh, C., & Joo, S. H. (2015). Is the technological capability gap between Hyundai and Mitsubishi converging or diverging? Findings from patent data analysis. *Asian Journal of Technology Innovation, 23*(sup1), 109–128.

Oikawa, H. (2016). Resource-based industrialization of the Malaysian palm oil industry. In Y. Sato, & H. Sato (Eds.), *Varieties and alternatives of catching-up*. London: Palgrave Macmillan, 247–276.

Pack, H. (1992). Learning and productivity change in developing countries. In G. K. Helleiner, *Trade policy, industrialization, and development: New perspectives*. Oxford: Clarendon Press, 20–45.

Pallares-Barbera, M., Suau-Sanchez, P., Le Heron, R., & Fromhold-Eisebith, M. (2012). Globalising economic spaces, uneven development and regional challenges: Introduction to the special issue. *Urbani izziv, 23*, S2–S10.

Park, J., & Lee, K. (2015). Do latecomer firms rely on 'recent' and 'scientific' knowledge more than incumbent firms do? Convergence or divergence in knowledge sourcing. *Asian Journal of Technology Innovation, 23*(sup1), 129–145.

Park, K. H., & Lee, K. (2006). Linking the technological regime to the technological catch-up: Analyzing Korea and Taiwan using the US patent data. *Industrial and Corporate Change, 15*(4), 715–753.

Park, S. (1996). Networks and embeddedness in the dynamic types of new industrial districts. *Progress in Human Geography, 20*(4): 476–493.

Park, S. O., & Markusen, A. (1995). Generalizing new industrial districts: A theoretical agenda and an application from a non-Western economy. *Environment and Planning A, 27*(1), 81–104.

Park, Y. C. (1990). Development lessons from Asia: The role of government in South Korea and Taiwan. *The American Economic Review, 80*(2), 118–121.

Penang Institute. (2015). *Penang economic indicators*. Issue 4.15.

Peng, M. W. (2000). Controlling the foreign agent: How governments deal with multinationals in a transition economy. *MIR: Management International Review, 40*(2) 141–165.

Penrose, E. T. (1959). *The theory of the growth of the firm*. Oxford: Basil Blackwell.

Perez, C. (2008). *A vision for Latin America: A resource-based strategy for technological dynamism and social inclusion*. Globelics Working Paper, No. WPG0804.

Pietrobelli, C. (1998). *Industry, competitiveness and technological capabilities in Chile: A new tiger from Latin America?* London: Palgrave Macmillan.

Porter, M. E. (1998). Clusters and the new economics of competition. *Harvard Business Review, 76*(6), 77–90.

Porto, T. C., Lee, K., & Mani, S. (2021). The US–Ireland–India in the catch-up cycles in IT services: MNCs, indigenous capabilities and the roles of macro-economic variables. *Eurasian Business Review, 11*, 59–82.

Potter, K., & Hatton, R. (2013). Data mining of US patents: Research trends of major technology companies. *SAS global forum, 101*, 1–11.

Qian, Y. (2003). How reform worked in China. In D. Rodrik (Ed.), *In search of prosperity: Analytic narratives on economic growth*, Princeton: Princeton University Press, 297–333.

Radosevic, S., Curaj, A., Gheorghiu, R., Andreescu, L., & Wade, I. (Eds.). (2017). *Advances in the theory and practice of smart specialization*. London: Academic Press.

Raj-Reichert, G. (2020). Global value chains, contract manufacturers, and the middle-income trap: The electronics industry in Malaysia. *The Journal of Development Studies, 56*(4), 698–716.

Ramanayake, S. S., & Lee, K. (2015). Does openness lead to sustained economic growth? Export growth versus other variables as determinants of economic growth. *Journal of the Asia Pacific Economy, 20*(3), 345–368.

Ramanayake, S. S., & Lee, K. (2018). Differential impacts of currency underval-uation on growth and exports in natural resource vs. manufacturing export-ing countries, In J. Niosi (Ed.), *Innovation policy, systems and management*. Cambridge: Cambridge University Press, 306–321.

Rao, P. M., & Balasubrahmanya, M. H. (2017). The rise of IT services clusters in India: A case of growth by replication. *Telecommunications Policy, 41*(2), 90–105.

Rasiah, R. (1988). The semiconductor industry in Penang: Implications for the new international division of labour theories. *Journal of Contemporary Asia, 18*(1), 24–46.

Rasiah, R. (2006). Electronics in Malaysia: Export expansion but slow technical change. In C. Vandana (Ed.), *Technology, adaptation, and exports*. Washington, D.C.: World Bank, 127–162.

Rasiah, R. (2017). The industrial policy experience of the electronics industry in Malaysia. In P. John & T. Finn (Eds.), *The practice of industrial policy*. Oxford: Oxford University Press, 123–144.

Rasiah, R., & Chandran, V. G. R. (2015). *Malaysia, science report*. United Nations Educational, Scientific and Cultural Organization. Paris: UNESCO, 700–715.

Rasiah, R., & Shahrin, A. (2006). *Development of palm oil and related products in Malaysia and Indonesia*. Kuala Lumpur: University of Malaya, 1–54.

Ravenhill, J. (2003). From national champions to global partners: Crisis, globalization, and the Korean auto industry. In W. W. Keller & R. J. Samuels (Eds.), *Crisis and innovation in Asian technology*. Cambridge: Cambridge University Press, 108–136.

Ravenhill, J. (2005). FDI in the Korean Auto Industry. *Les Études de l'Ifri, 3*, 1–26.

Rikap, C. (2022). Becoming an intellectual monopoly by relying on the national innovation system: The State Grid Corporation of China's experience. *Research Policy, 51*(4), 104472.

Rodríguez, J. C., Navarro-Chávez, C. L., & Gómez, M. (2014). Regional innovation systems in emerging economies: Evidence of system failures for innovation. *International Journal of Innovation and Regional Development, 5*(4–5), 384–404.

Rodrik, D. (2006). Goodbye Washington Consensus, hello Washington Confusion? A review of the World Bank's economic growth in the 1990s: Learning from a decade of reform. *Journal of Economic Literature, 44*(4), 973–987.

Rodrik, D. (2011). *The globalization paradox: Democracy and the future of the world economy*. New York: WW Norton & Company.

Rodrik, D., & Stantcheva, S. (2021). *A policy matrix for inclusive prosperity* (No. w28736). Cambridge, MA: National Bureau of Economic Research.

Rodrik, D., Subramanian, A., & Trebbi, F. (2004). Institutions rule: The primacy of institutions over geography and integration in economic development. *Journal of Economic Growth, 9*(2), 131–165.

Rokach, L. & Maimon, O. (2005). Clustering methods. In Maimon, O., & Rokach, L. (Eds.), *Data mining and knowledge discovery handbook*. New York: Springer, 321–352.

Ryu, H. (2002). An empirical study on secondary school expansion: Time Series Analysis 1952–1995. PhD Dissertation, Seoul National University.

Sachs, J. D., & Woo, W. T. (2001). Understanding China's economic performance. *The Journal of Policy Reform, 4*(1), 1–50.

Sakong, I. (1993). *Korea in the world economy*. Washington, D.C.: Institute for International Economics.

Sato, Y. (2016). Curse or opportunity? A model of industrial development for natural resource–rich countries on the basis of Southeast Asian experiences. In Y. Sato & H. Sato (Eds.), *Varieties and alternatives of catching-up*. London: Palgrave Macmillan, 211–246.

Saviotti, P. P., & Pyka, A. (2011). Generalized barriers to entry and economic development. *Journal of Evolutionary Economics, 21*, 29–52.

Schumpeter, J. A. (1934). *The theory of economic development*. Cambridge, MA: Harvard University Press.

Schumpeter, J. A. (1942). *Capitalism, socialism and democracy*. Abingdon: Routledge (Routledge Classic 2010 version).

Seabra, F., & Flach, L. (2005). Foreign direct investment and profit outflows: A causality analysis for the Brazilian economy. *Economics Bulletin*, 6(1), 1–15.

Sen, A. K. (1957). Some notes on the choice of capital-intensity in development planning. *The Quarterly Journal of Economics*, 71(4), 561–584.

Sharif, N., & Baark, E. (2008). From trade hub to innovation hub: Hong Kong. In C. Edquist & L. Hommen (Eds.), *Small country innovation systems: Globalization, change and policy in Asia and Europe*. London: Edward Elgar, 194–234.

Shim, K., & Seo, J. (2015). A study on the factors influencing new product development performance: Focusing on new product development with government conditional purchase option [in Korean]. *Research on Management Consulting*, 15(2): 75–89.

Shin, H. H, & Lee, K. (2012). Asymmetric trade protection leading not to productivity but to export share change: The Korean case from 1967 to 1993 1. *Economics of Transition*, 20(4), 745–785.

Shin, H. H, & Lee, K. (2019). Impact of financialization and financial development on inequality: Panel cointegration results using OECD data. *Asian Economic Papers*, 18(1), 69–90.

Shin, H. H., & Park, Y. S. (1999). Financing constraints and internal capital markets: Evidence from Korean chaebols. *Journal of Corporate Finance*, 5(2), 169–191.

Shin, K. (2016). The effect of government SMEs R&D supports for the outcome and cooperation between large enterprises and SMEs: Focused on new product development by the AMC (advance market commitment) program. MA Thesis, Graduate School of Industrial & Entrepreneurial Management, Chung-Ang University, Seoul Korea.

Soete, L. (2007). From industrial to innovation policy. *Journal of Industry, Competition and Trade*, 7, 273–284.

Song, S. (2002). Historical development of technological capabilities in Korean steel industry: Posco from the 1960s to the 1990s [in Korean]. PhD Thesis, Seoul National University.

Soskice, D. W. & Hall, P. A. (2001). *Varieties of capitalism: The institutional foundations of comparative advantage*. Oxford: Oxford University Press.

Steers, R., Shin, Y. K. & Ungson, G. (1989). *The Chaebol: Korea's new industrial might*. New York: Harper and Row.

Stiglitz, J. E. (2022, June 3). *Getting Deglobalization Right*. Project Syndicate. www.project-syndicate.org/commentary/deglobalization-and-its-discontents-by-joseph-e-stiglitz-2022-05?barrier=accesspaylog

Stiglitz, J. E., Lin, J. Y., & Patel, E. (2013). *The industrial policy revolution I: The role of government beyond ideology.* London: Palgrave Macmillan.

Storz, C., Amable, B., Casper, S., & Lechevalier, S. (2013). Bringing Asia into the comparative capitalism perspective. *Socio-Economic Review, 11*(2), 217–232.

Sturgeon, T., & Gereffi, G. (2012). Measuring success in the global economy: International trade, industrial upgrading, and business function outsourcing in global value chains. In C. Pietrobelli and R. Rasiah (Eds.), *Evidence-based development economics.* Kuala Lumpur: The University of Malaya Press, 249–280.

Sturgeon, T., & Lester, R. K. (2004). The new global supply base: New challenges for local suppliers in East Asia. In S. Yusuf, M. A. Altaf, & K. Nabeshima (Eds.) *Global production networking and technological change in East Asia.* Washington, D.C.: World Bank Publications, 35–87.

Sun, P., Mellahi, K., & Thun, E. (2010). The dynamic value of MNE political embeddedness: The case of the Chinese automobile industry. *Journal of International Business Studies, 41*(7), 1161–1182.

Sun, S. L. (2009). Internationalization strategy of MNEs from emerging economies: The case of Huawei. *Multinational Business Review, 17*(2), 129–156.

Szirmai, A., & Verspagen, B. (2015). Manufacturing and economic growth in developing countries, 1950–2005. *Structural Change and Economic Dynamics, 34,* 46–59.

Tai, W. P., & Ku, S. (2013). State and industrial policy: Comparative political economic analysis of automotive industrial policies in Malaysia and Thailand. *JAS (Journal of ASEAN Studies), 1*(1), 52–82.

Tendulkar, S. D., & Bhavani, T. A. (2005). *Understanding the post-1991 Indian economic policy reforms.* Paper presented and submitted to the GDN and its annual meeting. New Delhi: GDN.

Thun, E. (2004). Industrial policy, Chinese-style: FDI, regulation, and dreams of national champions in the auto sector. *Journal of East Asian Studies, 4*(3), 453–489.

Thun, E. (2006). *Changing lanes in China: Foreign direct investment, local governments, and auto sector development.* Cambridge: Cambridge University Press.

Thun, E. (2018). Innovation at the middle of the pyramid: State policy, market segmentation, and the Chinese automotive sector. *Technovation, 70,* 7–19.

Thuy, N. B. (2008). *Industrial policy as determinant of localization: The case of Vietnamese automobile industry.* In Vietnam Development Forum, VDF Working Paper Series (No. 810).

Tian, Z., Li, C., Yang, Q., Wang, H., Liu, L., Zhu, L., & Zhu, S. (2010). The business strategy of the weak entrants in China's automotive market: Based on case studies of Chinese cars such as Geely, Chery, Brilliance, Byd and Hafei [in Chinese]. *Management World, 8*, 139–152.

Tordo, S., & Anouti, Y. (2013). Local content in the oil and gas sector: Case studies. Washington, D.C.: World Bank.

Trajtenberg, M., Henderson, R., & Jaffe, A. B. (1997). University versus corporate patents: A window on the basicness of invention. *Economics of Innovation and New Technologies, 5*(1), 19–50.

UNDP. (2006). *Malaysia: International trade, growth, poverty reduction, and human development*. Kuala Lumpur: United Nations Development Programme.

Van Dijk, M., & Bell, M. (2007). Rapid growth with limited learning: Industrial policy and Indonesia's pulp and paper industry. *Oxford Development Studies, 35*(2), 149–169.

Vernon, R. (1966). International trade and international investment in the product cycle. *Quarterly Journal of Economics, 80*(2), 190–207.

Viner, J. (1958). Stability and progress: The poorer countries' problem. In F. Benham (Ed.), *Stability and progress in the world economy: The first congress of the international economic association*. London: Palgrave Macmillan, 41–65.

Wad, P. (2009). The automobile industry of Southeast Asia: Malaysia and Thailand. *Journal of the Asia Pacific Economy, 14*(2), 172–193.

Wad, P., & Govindaraju, V. C. (2011). Automotive industry in Malaysia: An assessment of its development. *International Journal of Automotive Technology and Management, 11*(2), 152–171.

Wade, R. (1990). *Governing the market: Economic theory and the role of government in East Asian industrialization*. Princeton: Princeton University Press.

Wan, W. P., & Hoskisson, R. E. (2003). Home country environments, corporate diversification strategies, and firm performance. *Academy of Management Journal, 46*(1), 27–45.

Wang, Y. (2007). China's independent brand promotion strategy. *Shanghai Automotive, 5*, 10–12.

Wang, Z., Wei, S. J., & Zhu, K. (2013). *Quantifying international production sharing at the bilateral and sector levels* (No. w19677). Cambridge, MA: National Bureau of Economic Research.

Wei, Y., Liu, X., Parker, D., & Vaidya, K. (1999). The regional distribution of foreign direct investment in China. *Regional Studies, 33*(9), 857–867.

Westphal, L., Kim, L., & Dahlman, C. (1985). Reflections on the Republic of Korea's acquisition of technological capability. In Rosenberg, N., & Frischtak, C. (Eds.), New York: Praeger, 162–221.

Williamson, J. (1990). What Washington means by policy reform. *Latin American Adjustment: How Much has Happened, 1,* 90–120.

Winter, S. G. (2006). Toward a neo-Schumpeterian theory of the firm. *Industrial and Corporate Change, 15*(1), 125–141.

Wong, C. Y., & Lee, K. (2018). Projecting the arena of inclusion: The case of South Korea in pursuing a phased inclusive growth process. *Review of Policy Research, 35*(4), 590–616.

Wong, C. Y., & Lee, K. (2021). Evolution of innovation systems of two industrial districts in East Asia: Transformation and upgrade from a peripheral system and the role of the core firms, Samsung and TSMC. *Journal of Evolutionary Economics, 32,* 955–990.

Wong, C. Y., Hu, M. C., & Shiu, J. W. (2015). Governing the economic transition: How Taiwan transformed its industrial system to attain virtuous cycle development. *Review of Policy Research, 32*(3), 365–387.

Wong, C. Y., Ng, B. K., Azizan, S. A., & Hasbullah, M. (2018). Knowledge structures of city innovation systems: Singapore and Hong Kong. *Journal of Urban Technology, 25*(1), 47–73.

Wong, C. Y., Wang, I. K., Sheu, J., & Hu, M. C. (2021, July). Resilient cities during times of upheaval. In a presentation at the 18th ISS conference held in Rome, July (pp. 8–10).

Wong, P. K., & Singh, A. (2008). From technology adopter to innovator: Singapore. In Edquist, C., & Hommen, L. (Eds.), *Small country innovation systems: Globalization, change and policy in Asia and Europe.* Cheltenham: Edward Elgar Publishing, 71–112.

World Bank. (2005). *Economic growth in the 1990s: Learning from a decade of reform.* Washington, D.C.: World Bank Publications.

World Bank. (2010). Exploring the middle-income-trap. *World Bank East Asia Pacific Economic Update: Robust Recovery, Rising Risks,* vol. 2, Washington, D.C.: World Bank.

World Bank. (2012). *China 2030: Building a modern, harmonious, and creative society.* Washington, D.C.: World Bank.

Xia, F., & Walker, G. (2015). How much does owner type matter for firm performance? Manufacturing firms in China 1998–2007. *Strategic Management Journal, 36*(4), 576–585.

Xin, S., & Lee, K. (2022). *The role of big businesses in entrepreneurship: A cross-country panel analysis using the GEM data.* Manila: Asia Development Bank.

Xin, X., & Wang, Y. (2000). *Kuayue Shikong: Zhongguo Tongxin Chanye Fazhan Qishilu* [Crossing time and space: Revelation from the development of telecommunication industry of China]. Beijing: Beijing Youdian daxue Chubanshe (Beijing University of Post and Telecommunication Press).

Xu, J., & Girling, R. H. (2004). *Huawei Technologies Co. Ltd*. Sonoma: Sonoma State University.

Yang, C. (2015). Government policy change and evolution of regional innovation systems in China: Evidence from strategic emerging industries in Shenzhen. *Environment and Planning C: Government and Policy, 33*(3), 661–682.

Yean, T. S. (2015). Diversification and industrial policies in Malaysia. In Felipe, J. (Ed.), *Development and modern industrial policy in practice*. Cheltenham: Edward Elgar Publishing, 320–345.

Yeung, H. W. C. (2016). *Strategic coupling: East Asian industrial transformation in the new global economy*. Ithaca, NY: Cornell University Press.

Yeung, H. W. C. (2021). Regional worlds: From related variety in regional diversification to strategic coupling in global production networks. *Regional Studies, 55*(6), 989–1010.

Yoon, H., Yun, S., Lee, J., & Phillips, F. (2015). Entrepreneurship in East Asian regional innovation systems: Role of social capital. *Technological Forecasting and Social Change, 100*, 83–95.

Yu, Z., Ming, N., & Hui, Z. (2008). Research on the development model of Chinese automobile enterprises in the global value chain [in Chinese]. *Research and Development Management, 4*, 1–7.

Yusuf, S., & Nabeshima, K. (2009). *Can Malaysia escape the middle-income trap? A strategy for Penang (June 1, 2009)*. World Bank Policy Research Working Paper Series (No.4971).

Zhao, X. (2013). Independent innovation of China's automotive industry: An analysis of the institutional roots of the failure of the "market for technology" strategy [in Chinese]. *Journal of Zhejiang University (Humanities and Social Sciences), 43*(3), 164–176.

Index

absorptive capacity, 173
Alibaba, 231
AMC (advance market commitment), 233
Anglo-American economic systems, 19
Anglo-American model, 21
Aramco, 230
Argentina, 28
Asian
    capitalism, 205
    economies, 29, 36
    tigers, 29, 32
Asian financial crisis, 177
asymmetric opening, 163
authoritarian regime, 149
authoritarianism, 164
automotive industry
    China, 86
    Korea, 80
    Malaysia, 84
    Thailand, 82

backward citation lag, 43
backward linkages, 11, 65, 83
Baidu, 231
balanced development, 134
Baldwin, 6
berries, 58, 68
big businesses, 4, 12, 47, 106, 146
bio-similar, 242
biotechnology, 199, 241
Brazil, 28, 198
    footwear sector in, 227
BRICS, 32
business groups, 176, 228
    top 30, 179, 187
BYD, 223

capability failures, 208
catching-up, 145
    balanced, 15
    economies, 26
    imbalanced, 48

    market, 116
    mode of, 216, 218
    paradox, 5, 22, 114, 203
    path-following, 226
    technological, 115, 136
CBUs (completely built units, namely fully
    assembled cars), 81, 82
Celtrion, 199, 242
chaebol, 183, 187
Chery, 77, 223
Chile, 9, 14, 67
Chile–California Program, 68
China, 12, 18, 29, 76
Chinese Industrial Enterprises
    Database, 122
ChiNext, 236
Chosun Dynasty, 148
CKD (complete knock down), 81, 82, 84, 90
climate change, 253
cluster analysis, 33
coefficient of variation, 39
coevolution, 7, 14, 18, 244
colonial rule, 148
comparative advantages, 22, 188, 243
concentration
    of economic power, 177
    of innovation, 47
    of NIS, 108, 187
Confucianism, 148
conglomerates, 180, 227
convergence, 19, 109, 140, 205
coordination failure, 208, 234
copper, 70
corporate innovation systems, 135
COVID-19, 1, 243, 246
creative destruction, 8, 192
Creative-Lab (C-Lab), 239
cycle time of technologies (CTT), 8, 27,
    118, 146
    of a firm, 136
    long, 8, 44, 198, 241
    short, 8, 21, 40, 44, 60, 118, 136, 192, 247

Daewoo, 80
decentralization, 8, 48
de-industrialization, 50
    pre-mature, 11, 65
democracy, 149, 203
development detour
    non-linear, 20
development pathways, 3
developmental state, 100
digital platforms, 183
digital switch, 112
digital TV, 213
discipline
    from global markets, 85, 105
    from markets, 163, 181
diversification
    diversification, 32
    technological, 8, 16, 27, 44, 133, 135
domestic value-added, 17, 20, 58
DRAM, 212
drugs, 16
dual price policy, 155

economic complexity, 5
electric and electronics (E&E), 71
Electronics and Telecommunications
        Research Institute, 43
emerging economies, 40, 92
enrollment in secondary education, 156
entrepreneurial states, 3
entry barriers, 5, 13, 44, 146, 211
entry control, 90, 161
Ericsson, 112
Ethiopian Air, 230
European
    economies, 30, 36
    Northern, 36
    peripheral, 49
    Southern, 32
excessive investments, 179
export
    competition, 10
    duty, 75
    growth, 166
    orientation, 17, 21, 182
    performance, 15, 56
    promotion, 146

fast follower, 100, 214
FDI, 3, 10, 64, 78, 181

financial control, 159
financial restraints, 160
firm values, 140
firms
    catching up, 135
    domestically owned, 216
    in emerging economies, 120
    indigenous, 89
    Korean, 135, 137
    mature, 143
    US, 136
flagship, 226
food shortages, 152
foreign value added (FVA), 83, 167
forestry, 69
Fortune Global 500, 230
France, 33
free-trade agreements, 20
Fundación Chile (FCh), 67, 220

Geely, 77, 85, 88
Germany, 33
getting prices wrong, 158
global financial crisis, 20, 151
Global Fortune 500, 12, 177
global governance, 252
global innovation systems, 10
Global South, 56
global value chains (GVCs), 6, 11, 20, 65, 83,
        211, 225
    disruption, 59
    foreign-dominated, 74
    indicators, 77
globalization paradox, 2
global–local interfaces, 3, 10, 23,
        146, 244
GM-Daewoo, 83
government intervention, 22
Greece, 30
growth money, 160
growth regressions, 42

Hangul, 148
Hecksher–Ohlin trade theory, 189
high end, 89
high-income economies, 28
Hong Kong, 50
hostile takeover, 74
Hsinchu, 19
Huawei, 102, 107, 112, 218

human capital, 164
Hyundai, 78, 85, 107, 111, 162, 201

imbalanced development, 62
IMF, 19, 150
imitation, 107
  to innovation, 89
imitative creation, 95
imitative innovation, 171
import substitution, 166
inclusive growth, 208
incumbents, 141
India, 15, 32, 39
indigenous development, 102
indigenous firms, 92
industrial district, 126
  Hub-and-Spoke, 126
  Marshallian, 126
industrial policy, 3, 11, 16, 43, 51, 70, 72,
    73, 78, 79, 161, 207
  in Korea, 158
  Korean style, 87, 222
Industrial Technology Research Institute
    (ITRI), 100, 128, 214
inequality, 204
Infosys, 54
innovation systems, 7, 208, 248
  corporate, 17, 19
  firm-level, 135
  corporate; regional, 106
in-out-in again, 11, 64, 167
institutions, 14, 18, 107, 118, 164
  inclusive or exclusive, 146
intellectual property rights, 5, 6, 22
  disputes, 244, 250
internationalization, 95
inter-regionalization, 96
intra-regionalization, 96
Ireland, 25, 30, 50
Israel, 30
IT cluster, 103
IT sector, 65
IT services, 9, 16, 50, 52, 247
Italy, 33
ITRI, 229

Japanese
  carmakers, 82
  investment, 81
  manufacturers, 81

JVs, 78, 80, 82
  foreign, 81, 83, 86
  strategy, 80

Kakao, 232, 238
knowledge
  base, 135
  codifiable, 172
  external, 131
  indigenous, 95
knowledge localization, 8, 27, 32, 44
knowledge spillover, 219
Korea, xi
  North, 164
  South, 21
Korea Development Bank, 160
Korea New Exchange (KONEX), 236
Korean model, 21, 146
  as a miracle, 205
KOSDAQ, 235

land reforms, 252
late entrants, 64
latecomer
  countries, 13
  country, 145
  disadvantages, 147, 158
  economies, 64
  firms, 18, 107, 110
  industrialization, 158
latent comparative advantages, 189
Latin America, 29, 47
leapfrogging, 5, 193, 241, 246, 251
learning-by-doing, 180
liberalization of trade and investment, 4
liberalization trap, 11, 65, 248
licensing
  know-how, 173
  technology, 172
local content requirements (LCRs), 77–79,
    85, 89, 224
local embeddedness, 91
local ownership, 70
localization of knowledge, 95, 131
London Stock Exchange, 74
long jumps, 193
low middle-income, 29
low-income
  stage, 22
Lundvall, 8, 26

M&A
    international, 88, 223
    of Volvo, 89
made in China, 83
Malaysia, 9, 14, 30, 216
manufacturing, 5, 51
    IT, 71
market competition, 79
market economies
    coordinated, 36
    mixed, 36
market failure, 13, 176, 208, 227, 233
market for technology, 86, 221
market forces, 73
market structure, 78, 182, 211
marketization index, 123
Mauritius, 28
Mazzucato, 3
Mexico, 28
middle class, 149
middle-income trap (MIT), 6, 9, 15, 25, 55,
        65, 71, 100, 151
    escaping, 65
mission-oriented innovation policy, 207
Mitsubishi, 80, 81, 111
MNCs, 93
more is better, 24
Motorola, 217
multiplicity, 6
mutual citations, 116

national brand, 77
national innovation systems, 7, 8, 26, 95
    balanced, 16, 47
    balanced mature, 33
    catching-up, 8, 30, 40
    imbalanced, 33
    in Korea, 198
    index, 27
    mixed, 39
    trapped, 7, 26, 30, 60
    types, 27
    varieties of, 39
nationalization, 70
Naver, 183, 238
Nelson, 135
Netherlands, 33
niche, 138
    strategy, 43
non-linearity, 6, 210, 247

OBM, 80
openness to trade, 166
original design manufacturer (ODM), 225
original equipment manufacturing (OEM),
        43, 80, 225
originality, 8, 27, 135
ownership, 78
    diverse, 107, 120
    domestic, 11, 16
    firm, 16, 18
    foreign, 80, 96, 201
    of innovation, 102
    knowledge, 95
    local, 64, 70, 200
    local firm, 98
    majority, 81
    of patents, 97

palm oil, 15, 55, 72
    processed, 58
Park Chung Hee, xi, 149, 229
patent rights, 6
patents
    citations, 110
    locally-owned, 97
    quality of, 110
    US, 94
    US-filed, 91
pathway
    alternative, 41, 106
    multipule, 23
    NIS, 62
    non-linear, 61
Penang, 16, 91, 216
Penang Development Centre (PDC), 217
Penang Skill Development Centre
        (PSDC), 217
Petronas, 73, 230
pharmaceuticals, 39, 54
plantation, 74
Plaza Accord, 81
Pony, 162
Portugal, 30
POSCO, 171, 228
privately-owned local enterprises (POLEs),
        18, 121
product life cycle, 195
product space, 190
productivity, 51
    labor, 122

Proton, 17, 77, 81, 84
pure-play
    foundry, 129

R&D, 59
    consortium, 100, 102, 168, 212, 219
    efforts, 75
    government-funded, 76
    incentives, 73
    in-house, 174, 214
    investment to GDP ratio, 165
    private, 215
    public-private, 214
    tax exemption for, 182
regional innovation systems (RIS), 90, 126
    catching-up, 134
    mature, 143
    measures of, 96
    of Hsinchu, 127
    peripheral, 94, 131
resiliency, 147
re-skilling, 216
resource-based sectors, 9, 56, 247
resource-based view of firm
        growth, 120
revealed comparative advantages
        (RCA), 56, 162
reversal of fortune, 165
reverse engineering, 112
Rodrik, 2
rubber, 15, 55, 72
    sector, 76
Russia, 32, 49

salmon, 15, 55, 67
Samsung, 107, 110, 212, 239
    memory chip, 180
Samsung Biologics, 199, 243
Schumpeter, 12
Schumpeterian, xii, 7, 26, 31, 90,
        176, 208
    theory of the firm, 119, 135
secondary stock market, 235
self-citations, 95, 113
    at the firm level, 136
semiconductor, 72, 128, 215
services, 51
Shanghai Auto Industry Corporation
        (SAIC), 221
Shanghai Bell, 102, 219

Shenzhen, 16, 66, 91, 112, 200, 218
Shenzhen Stock Exchange, 236
Singapore, 25, 50
SMEs, 12, 127, 183, 214
SMIC, 237
SOEs, 230
soft budget constraints, 160
Sony, 110
sophistication
    trade structure, 190
South Africa, 28
Spain, 25
special economic zones (SEZ), 92, 102
specialization, 15, 43, 47, 58
    smart, 146
spillover effect, 64
startups, 13, 125, 232, 240
State Grid Corporation, 230
state-owned enterprises (SOEs), 18, 107
structural transformation, 5, 188
sustainability, 253
sustainable development, 253
Sweden, 33
system failures, 208

Taipei, 16, 91
Taiwan, 11, 19
Taiwan Semiconductor Manufacturing
        Company (TSMC), 229
takeover, 230
tariffs, 75, 84, 213
    asymmetric, 163
    effectiveness of, 161
Tata, 54
technological capabilities, 10, 79,
        110, 170
technological development, 107
technological diversification, 16
technological independence, 116
technologies
    long cycle, 6, 16, 53, 134, 195
    recent or old, 114
    short cycle, 6, 19, 240
    similar or different, 18, 106
technology transfer, 250
telephone switch, 219
Tencent, 220
Thailand, 12, 29, 76
Time-Division Exchange (TDX), 168
Tobin's Q, 140

total factor productivity (TFP), 162
Toyota, 82
trade openness, 56
trade surplus, 56
trademarks, 6
trading market for technology, 102, 224
trajectory
    technological, 106
transaction cost economics, 176
trapped economies, 44
TSMC, 19, 108

UMC, 129
unicorns, 227
United Kingdom, 33
university-industry linkages, 131
upgrading, 104, 134

upper middle-income
    stages, 28
utility models, 6

varieties of capitalism (VoC), 27, 36
venture companies, 235
Volkswagen, 77

Washington Consensus, xii, 2, 4, 156
windows of opportunity, 242
wine, 15, 55, 67, 69
Wipro, 54
World Bank, 25
WTO, 66, 77, 85, 222, 224
    China entry, 88

ZTE, 102

For EU product safety concerns, contact us at Calle de José Abascal, 56–1°, 28003 Madrid, Spain or eugpsr@cambridge.org.

www.ingramcontent.com/pod-product-compliance
Ingram Content Group UK Ltd.
Pitfield, Milton Keynes, MK11 3LW, UK
UKHW020357140625
459647UK00020B/2529